Digitalization of Society and Socio-political Issues 2

Series Editor
Jean-Charles Pomerol

Digitalization of Society and Socio-political Issues 2

Digital, Information and Research

Edited by

Éric George

WILEY

First published 2020 in Great Britain and the United States by ISTE Ltd and John Wiley & Sons, Inc.

ISTE Ltd
27-37 St George's Road
London SW19 4EU
UK

www.iste.co.uk

John Wiley & Sons, Inc.
111 River Street
Hoboken, NJ 07030
USA

www.wiley.com

Library of Congress Control Number: 2019951005

British Library Cataloguing-in-Publication Data
A CIP record for this book is available from the British Library
ISBN 978-1-78630-498-8

Contents

Acknowledgments

First of all, it is important to thank the Social Sciences and Humanities Research Council of Canada (SSHRC) and the *Fonds de recherche du Québec – Société et Culture* (FRQSC) for their financial support, without which the collaborations developed in Quebec, Canada and internationally between several of the authors of this book and the conference that hosted the vast majority of them could not have taken place.

I would also like to express my sincere thanks to the people who contributed to the production of this book: Oumar Kane, Associate Professor at the Université du Québec à Montréal (UQAM), member of the Executive Committee of the *Centre de recherche interuniversitaire sur la communication, l'information et la société* (CRICIS); Michel Sénécal, Full Professor at the Université TÉLUQ, member of the Executive Committee of CRICIS; Lena Hübner, doctoral candidate in communication studies at UQAM in charge of CRICIS' scientific activities, who evaluated texts; Karelle Arsenault, doctoral candidate in communication studies at UQAM, who performed the systematic review of all texts and made the preparatory layout; Siavash Rokni, doctoral student in communication studies at UQAM, who proofread this book; and everyone who contributed to the production of this book.

Acknowledgments written by Éric GEORGE.

Introduction

About the Digitalization of Society

Not everything that can be counted counts...
and not everything that counts can be counted.

William Bruce Cameron

What does digital mean? The question was asked on May 2, 3 and 4, 2018, at an international Conference organized in Montreal by the *Centre de recherche interuniversitaire sur la communication, l'information et la société* (CRICIS). Under the title *"Numérisation généralisée de la société: acteurs, discours, pratiques et enjeux"* (Widespread digitalization of society: actors, discourses, practices and challenges), it brought together some 100 researchers who have devoted their reflections to the theme of digitalization of our societies, to discourses and social practices in this field, to mobilized actors and to communicational, informational and cultural issues. This two-volume publication is a follow-up to this event. However, these are not conference proceedings for three reasons. First, this publication brings together the texts of about a third of the people present during these three days. Second, a significant number of text proposals were rejected, and for the other selected texts, significant editorial work was carried out. Third, some of the texts in this publication are from people whose contributions to the Conference had been accepted but who were unable to attend. This opus is the result of this work.

The term *digital* is now present everywhere and applies to almost all the activities of our advanced capitalist societies (Bravo 2009; Cohen-Tanugi 1999;

Introduction written by Éric GEORGE.

Doukidis *et al.* 2004; Rushkoff 2012; Stiegler 2015). It is a question of digital technology about the economy (Illing and Peitz 2006; *Les Cahiers du numérique* 2010), security and surveillance (Mathias 2008; Lévy 2010; Kessous 2012), identity (*Les Cahiers du numérique* 2011), social relations (*Les Cahiers du numérique* 2017) and many other fields (divide, solidarity, friendship, innovation, etc.). Almost all the information circulates in the form of binary computer coding. Media, screens of all kinds (computers, televisions, tablets, video game consoles, multifunctional telephones and a whole range of so-called connected everyday objects) and networks (wired, satellite, microwave, etc.) are omnipresent in both the private and public spheres of our daily lives, two spheres whose boundaries tend to blur each other in part. Big Data circulates almost instantaneously and is processed by increasingly powerful computers and algorithms that bring to the fore the idea of artificial intelligence (AI), which has been regularly challenged since the 1950s when cybernetic thinking had contributed to its development. There is now a reference to "digital culture" (Doueihi 2011; Gere 2002; Greffe and Sonnac 2008) in reference to the uses of technologies that utilize digitalization and the use of these algorithms that require a minimum of interactivity (Denouël and Granjon 2011). Some even speak of the "digital age" or "digital revolution" (Collin and Verdier 2012; *Esprit* 2006). In short, digital technology is present both in a vast set of discourses and in countless practices. But what exactly does this term refer to? So who are the actors who talk about it, who put it into practice? And what economic, cultural, political, political, social and technical issues does it raise, particularly from the point of view of communication studies? Here are the questions to which the contributions in these two collective works attempt to provide answers.

However, we wanted to focus not only on digital technology as such, but also, and beyond, on the idea of digitalization of our societies. We have made the scientific choice to approach digitalization as a long and constant process in which all areas of societies' activity, from industry to leisure, from art to studies, from health to the environment, are concerned by this digitalization and reconfigured – and if so, to what extent – by it. To this end, the two volumes of this book put emphasis on analyses of communication, information and cultural phenomena and processes. That said, our ambition is also of a socio-political nature, because it is not only a question of analyzing and understanding, but also of contributing in a decisive way to changing the world, through the proposal of different critical perspectives that emphasize both several of the ways in which digital technology participates in power and domination relationships and can contribute to possible emancipatory practices. All these elements explain the title of the two books: *Digitalization of Society and Socio-political Issues.*

I.1. What does digital technology involve?

Speaking about digital involves putting it in numbers, to represent the world, society and individuals. For a researcher, a researcher in the human and social sciences, this operation immediately refers to the many debates that, in recent centuries, have dealt with epistemology about philosophy, the natural sciences and the human and social sciences, with oppositions that have, among other things, crystalized around the respective merits of quantitative methods, on the one hand, and qualitative methods, on the other hand, to better analyze the "real" (Pires 1997). Do the figures provide a more objective, representative view of reality than the participating observations and other life stories? Or is it not rather the way we look at the different data at our disposal that determines our positioning, positivist, neo-positivist, constructivist, realistic, critical or other? As we can see, the debate is not recent, but it has been updated in recent years with the production of a considerable amount of data, called *Big Data*. Would these mega data processed by algorithms provide us with a privileged mode of access to the world or is it a mode of representation of the world among others?

That said, not unrelated to the above, the word *digital* also leads us to another field of research, that of information and communication technologies (ICTs), sometimes preceded by a "d" for "digital", digital information and communication technologies (DICTs) . Perhaps it would be more relevant here to talk about socio-technical information and communication systems. The use of the word *device* would refer to the idea of addressing different interdependent tools, the whole forming an infrastructure, a system, a device therefore, which facilitates informational and communicational practices, at least some of them, because any device is both enabling and binding. The material dimension of the device, starting with the choices made in terms of socio-technical design, provides a framework for the related communication processes (Proulx 1999). Nevertheless, no terminology stabilization has been observed over the past five decades, as the terms used vary significantly over time. Thus, there has been alternating references to IT, then to ICT and now to DICT, as well as to "media technologies" and "new media" (George and Kane 2015). More recently, various syntagmas combining several of the words *media*, *networks*, *socionumeric*, *digital social* or *social* have emerged, such as "digital platforms".

Writing is therefore not stabilized on this subject. However, behind this variety of expressions lie notable choices that are often not very explicit. Thus, emphasizing the "media" underlines the fact that these devices constitute organized groups from the cultural, economic, aesthetic, political, social and technical points of view. They are characterized by their interface, their mode of financing, the provision of access to a production of formatted cultural content and the way in which they create links between the supply of goods and services, on the one hand, and demand, on the other hand. Most of the time, private companies are behind these media, and not small companies, since the most important of the digital social media, Facebook, is part of the prestigious "GAFAM" (Google, Apple, Facebook, Amazon and Microsoft). Moreover, this acronym is sometimes slightly modified, to GAFAN for example, when we want to highlight the role of Netflix. On the contrary, speaking of *networks* rather aims to highlight the reticulated technical dimension of the devices, which recalls the historical development of the Internet, as well as the older development of the telegraph, or even the railway, in an Innisian perspective (Innis 1950, 1951), its fundamentally decentralized nature and the fact that these networks largely rely on the participation of all parties, in order to produce the famous user-generated content (UGC).

That said, the only terminological issue is not the use of the words *media* or *network*. Thus, in some cases, we are talking about "social networks" or "social media". But doesn't such a task reveal a certain blindness, a new oblivion of history when it comes to ICTs? Indeed, the very expression "social networks" refers to analyses that do not necessarily concern digital technology and that predate its development. As for the expression "social media", it is also questionable, because all media are part of social processes. Unless, as mentioned above, reference is made to a "digital platform", which means that neither the term *media* nor the term *network* can be used. Such websites that aim to link supply and demand can cover transport and accommodation activities as well as cultural products and many other sectors of the economy. These new mechanisms have even spread so widely that there is now talk of a "platform" for the media and culture or even society (in different registers, Colin and Verdier 2012; Guibert *et al.* 2016; *tic&société*, forthcoming) order to highlight the idea that these mechanisms are at the heart of large-scale societal transformations, likely to concern jointly the forms of capitalism, democracy and sociability. We will also discuss these possible mutations in the chapters of these two volumes, and you will see that the analyses developed there are characterized above all by great finesse.

The term *digital* therefore has various meanings and, *de facto*, refers to objects and analyses that sometimes seem distant from each other. This is not surprising in a context where the scientific approach is increasingly oriented towards hyper-specialization, following the social division of labor that is characteristic of capitalist economies. However, if, to a certain extent, the development of disciplines and specializations brings new knowledge, it is possible to wonder, like Bernard Lahire (2012), whether this Balkanization does not lead to a loss "of the meaning of social totalities" (p. 322). However, while the terms "DICT", "digital platforms", "Big Data", "GAFAM" and others refer to analyses that are often separate from each other, they all reflect – and also participate in – more global changes that are underway, which can be presented in terms of the "digitalization of society".

We will therefore return to this in two stages, given that, by its scope, this publication is proposed in two volumes. The subtitle of the first volume is "Digital, Communication and Culture", and this second volume, whose subtitle is "Digital, Information and Research", is divided into three parts that focus on: (1) the transformations that affect information in the digital context, whether it concerns its characteristics, production methods and actors, journalists and other citizens; (2) the forms taken by socio-political mobilizations that are based on the appropriation of DICTs and the practices of information activism; (3) some issues that appeared particularly important to highlight and likely to be the subject of public debate. We will discuss, among other things, the renewed relationships between research and the digital.

I.2. The digital and information

The production of information is particularly affected by digital changes in many respects. **Valérie Croissant** and **Annelise Touboul** (Chapter 1) worked on the creation of new media formats, such as *Brut*, *Monkey*, *Konbini* and *Minute-Buzz*, which circulate via socio-digital networks in France and contribute to changing the way the media is constructed and the corresponding current discourse. This questioning is all the more important as these services tend to become new sources of information for young people. Croissant and Touboul note, among other things, that digital social networks present themselves and behave as media in their own right by building editorial space and time, controlling access to audiences, and establishing rules and publication formats, without producing anything. They also note that, unlike traditional media based on the permanence and archiving of information, digital social networks focus on the circulation of content. The media that provide this information readily accept the principles of transformation and appropriation of their content by these networks.

Pascal Ricaud (Chapter 2) also wondered about possible changes in the work of information and journalism. His research leads him to believe that, if there is anything new about this profession, it is, above all, the formation of a new, more participatory media contract with the audience. However, he concluded by stating that the public participation is that of a very specific group of citizens, especially students and graduates of journalism and communication fields. This is a far cry from the optimistic discourse that saw the relationship between journalism and digital media as one of new horizons in producing information that largely involves citizens, or even, beyond that, one that deepens the democratic nature of our political systems.

Fábio Henrique Pereira (Chapter 3) also discusses the relationships between the digital and journalism, but from another point of view, by analyzing the ways in which the ideological injunctions that use this term, particularly around the question of innovation, contribute to the development of the career projects of French and French-speaking Canadian journalists. From the comparison of the relationships between individual paths, national media systems and the transnational circulation of digital practices and discourses, it emerges in particular that, if certain discourses play a role in the trajectories, it is above all those dealing with journalistic innovation from the United States and Great Britain. It also appears that, while some journalists adopt enthusiastic positions towards digital technology, others maintain relationships characterized by mistrust, or even resistance, with regard to the introduction of technological innovations into their practices.

That said, digital technology is at the root of other major issues related to information, such as "fake news". Once again, it must be noted that the phenomenon is not entirely new. After all, this so-called information is characterized by its deliberately false dimension, with the aim of misleading the public, which reminds us of a much older term: *propaganda*. Nevertheless, in the digital age, the current situation presents certain specificities (Troude-Chasteney 2018). Digital social media is making a renewed contribution to the production of propaganda, so much so that we have begun to talk about a "post-truth" era. By their mode of operation, they facilitate the fastest possible circulation of a vast amount of unverified and (re)transmitted information in a completely anonymous manner. **Louis-Philippe Rondeau** (Chapter 4) considers the hypothesis that this trend could develop even further, with the anticipated convergence between digital social media and virtual reality platforms that could lead to an ever more altered conception of "reality". Fortunately, not all uses of socio-technical communication devices are intended to promote misinformation.

Alexis Clot (Chapter 5) focused on the uses of politically motivated content creators on YouTube. He noted that, on the one hand, the practices were traditionally part of the journalistic, communicational and activist registers, but that, on the other hand, there was a desire to be free of reproductions of the traditional codes of the media–political environment. These new media players are therefore not creating from scratch in the digital "world"; rather, they are inventing new practices that have some continuity with older ones. Another observation: contrary to what is sometimes written, the Web appears to be a space where there is not only clearly polarized discourse, but also nuanced discourses.

Finally, the relationships between the digital and information were addressed from the perspective of socio-political struggles. **Christelle Combe** (Chapter 6) worked on the practices of amateur Internet users who seize political information in France and popularize it in vlogs, thereby opening the way to an alternative, people's form of educational political journalism. She observes, among other things, that expression on the Web leads to other social practices, such as physical encounters during public debates, the dissemination of this information to a variety of media (newspapers, radio stations, YouTube channels) and even the writing of a book. In these ways, these Internet users, who can be described as "expert amateurs", seize political information and popularize it, paving the way for an alternative form of citizen-based daytime political educationalism, according to the author.

I.3. Digital and mobilizations

Digital technology can therefore be conducive to socio-political activities and, beyond that, to mobilization (Granjon *et al.* 2017). The case study carried out by **Philippe-Antoine Lupien** (Chapter 7) is exemplary in this respect. The latter discussed the modalities of using alternative media practices by the two million Catalans who participated, on October 1, 2017, in a referendum on the Spanish region's self-determination, even though it had been deemed illegal by the Madrid authorities. However, in a context where this was an illegal mobilization and likely to lead to prison, it was necessary to use some alternative tools, such as the IPFS protocol and the Telegram, Messenger and FireChat applications. Lupien also noted that the actions carried out by the independents drew more on a repertoire of conventional actions (information, posters, etc.) and, to a lesser extent, disruptive actions (coordination of public demonstrations, dissemination of opponents' abuses, etc.), but in no way on the side of violent actions, including on the part of Catalan hackers, who did not take any violent action against the sites and servers of the Spanish authorities, at least before the referendum.

Ghada Touir (Chapter 8), for his part, focused on emerging practices and even new trends in citizen engagement in environmental and eco-citizenship issues in Quebec, while digital social media (mainly Facebook) are increasingly mobilized. The analysis shows that the nature of the activities around which collectives organize themselves, whether in terms of monitoring, networking, mobilization or information-sharing, is not so different from the "pre-digital" era. In this respect, it leads to conclusions similar to those of Lupien. However, he also notes that greater emphasis is being placed on the flow and sharing of information.

In her own way, **Sklaerenn Le Gallo** (Chapter 9) also considers what we observe on the Web to be a digital extension of much older debates. She has thus studied the place of online anti-feminist discourse in France that comes, possibly surprisingly at first glance, from the republican left, more precisely from *la France insoumise*, Jean-Luc Mélenchon's political party. It should be noted, however, that if there is anything new in this area, it is still in terms of the flow of information. It may be recalled that the circulation of all discourses on the Internet – but perhaps we should rather speak here of data circulation, given that the value itself, in socio-political terms of information for example, matters little – is crucial to ensuring the dynamism of capitalism.

However, do all these citizen activities promote the construction of a global public media space? In order to provide some answers to this question, **Raymond Corriveau** and **France Aubin** (Chapter 10) "followed" a text on the Web to see if the digital social media promoted a freer circulation of speech. For them, it is important to be very careful before talking about democratizing communication. Indeed, the low circulation of the "control" text produced for their test showed that it was far from certain that the new media would ensure the visibility of its content within civil society. The idea of emancipation through digital technology therefore appears, once again, to be problematic.

Martin Bonnard (Chapter 11), meanwhile, draws our attention to the consequences of the citizen use of closed proprietary systems. It is impossible to approach the social relations mediations implemented by digital platforms without considering the roles of large capitalist companies, including GAFAM. The protocols are imposed by these giants, and the management of data traffic on the Web depends on the characteristics of the search and recommendation algorithms put in place, hence the importance of grasping the materiality of digital technology from a critical perspective. Such a materialistic approach to online culture can help capture the functioning of the digital universe itself and thereby improve the chances of observing new trends towards emancipation, just as it can reveal new trends towards alienation. This includes the relevance of a critical dialectical perspective.

I.4. The digital: some major issues to conclude

Through all the texts collected in this work, readers will note that we have addressed many themes related to digital technology and, as a result, highlighted different ways in which this term is used in communication research and, beyond that, in the humanities and social sciences. We have chosen to complete this second volume by returning to some of the issues that seem to us to be of major importance.

First, digital and related technologies are often associated with ideas of transparency and legitimate public interest. **Ndiaga Loum** (Chapter 12) wonders whether, in this context of the "all-digital", so-called information society, these concerns should always prevail over what is presented as security requirements and the necessary protection of state secrets. Can these latter notions resist the transparency imposed by the information society, while the Internet facilitates the circulation of information and its speed and makes censorship difficult? In any case, he sees it as a new area of confrontation between the political and media fields.

For her part, **Lisiane Lomazzi** (Chapter 13) addresses the theme of "commonalities", while the main digital actors – as discussed earlier in this text – are increasingly involved in the privatization and commodification of information and culture. Some may see the "commonplace" as an alternative to the omni-commodification of the world. However, it is important to keep in mind that emphasizing the commonplace does not necessarily mean questioning commodification. This is evidenced by the fact that in France, the State is trying to redress the tension between ways of conceiving the commonplace while pursuing a general policy favorable to the commodification of all human activities.

Dominique Carré (Chapter 14) returns to the "generalized digitalization of society" by considering it to reflect an already relatively old process, formerly addressed by the expression "social computerization". According to him, we would still be in the same dynamic, that of a deepening of the general process of social computerization that began in the 1960s and 1970s and has since included, among other things, a "technicization-rationalization" of the establishment of relationships. He sees the Internet as a concrete instrument for exchanges that encourages the production of an important relational state and incessant, if possible uninterrupted, requests in order to multiply the number of connections on the basis of the most varied applications and services. Finally, he proposes a new research orientation: an ecology of solicitation that aims to study the ecosystem of cross-relationships produced, via TNICs, by industrialists and users, as well as by users among themselves, while taking into account social, economic and environmental interactions.

It is then once again a question of the relationships between the digital and science in relation to the digital humanities. Research conducted under this term may be relevant when asking questions about the roles of computer technologies in research practices (Hirsch 2012) or about the value of adopting approaches that go beyond disciplines (Dacos 2011). But don't they also tend to reduce both the individual and the social to quantified data, adopting a positivist position that is questionable to say the least? It is therefore important to approach them from a critical perspective. This is what **Christophe Magis** does (Chapter 15) as he underlines that digital technology crosses – pierces? – not only more and more academic work, but also universities themselves. However, very often, proponents of the digital humanities adapt very well to the neoliberal shift in our societies. They contribute to the fact that humanities and social sciences are increasingly called upon to provide visible research results, as do the so-called exact or hard sciences. Then, he adds, one may wonder whether, through the term "digital humanities", it is not much more a question of digital than of humanity itself. Finally, Magis calls, contrary to what many digital humanities advocates propose, for us not to disconnect ourselves from human and social "experience" when we mobilize various methodologies.

Luiz C. Martino (Chapter 16) also addresses the theme of "digital humanities" from a critical, but different, point of view. Those who claim to be part of this trend, he writes, underline the merits of new methods of research and the organization of knowledge based on digital technology. They claim the emergence of a collaborative and sharing ethos and above all emphasize the relevance of "doing", to the point of supposing a revolution in knowledge. However, according to Martino, more than a new epistemology, it would be an intellectual movement whose ethos would go beyond digital technologies alone, the digital humanities basing their epistemology on current events. The boundaries between university and society, between scientific work, particularly in the field of conceptualization, and public opinion are reportedly becoming increasingly blurred, with the media playing an active role in this process of at least partial indifference to the different types of discursive productions.

Finally, and to conclude this second volume, **Michel Sénécal** (Conclusion) offers a last look at the process of digitalizing our societies. Drawing inspiration from Luc Moullet's documentary film, *Origins of a Meal* (1978), he revisits the need to develop, in the same way as the process of the narrative frames he chooses, a dialectical and totalizing approach to the digitalization process, while insisting on its genealogy and its long-term nature, as well as on the multiplicity of the actors and social issues involved. Above all, he sees it as a new version of an ever-increasing accumulation and an endless exploitation, which is more than ever the credo of globalized capitalist thinking, while raising the question of the role that we, as researchers, play in reproducing the system under examination here, as well as the conditions under which the results of the research carried out can be appropriated, particularly outside academic circles.

I.5. Concluding the introduction

As you will see from reading Volume 2, all the definitions of the digital that are mobilized throughout the chapters are inextricably linked to each other. Numbers, digitalization, quantification, Big Data, algorithms, digital social media and platforms – all these terms refer to changes at work today and to the process of generalizing the digitalization of society. However, it is impossible to decide whether these are developments or a revolution, continuities or ruptures, "simple" changes or major mutations. Many analyses invite us to see continuity in some respects, as well as elements in favor of certain breaks, unless it is above all a question of an acceleration of more or less recent trends. The answer to these questions also depends, of course, on the objects studied and the temporality of the observations. Only an analysis that gives due consideration to the long term will allow us to go further. Moreover, our objective consists, from a critical perspective (George 2006), of looking at the multiple dimensions that make the world what it is, the relationships of seeing and domination that exist, as well as the "possible" ones that could shape our world. These "possibilities" refer to emancipation, a central notion in any critical research, but one that is rarely explained. However, as Jean-Guy Lacroix (2009, p. 300) tells us:

> "Emancipation takes multiple forms. It concerns individuals, specific social groups (workers, peasants…), communities, societies, women, indigenous peoples, […] the human being, […] the being in general… It is defined as emancipation, a rational liberation from constraints, limitations, oppression, exploitation, poverty… It provides autonomy, freedom, equality… It necessarily also requires respect for the Other, for others, for the extended otherness. Finally, it 'participates' in states of civilization, in the action of civilizing".

It is this multiplicity of faces of emancipation that is also present in the chapters of these two volumes. Nevertheless, beyond the variety of cultural, informational and communicational objects, processes and phenomena studied, it is clear from these studies that it is essential to adopt an epistemology-methodology based on the practice of dialectical criticism rooted in the long term.

We hope you enjoy reading this book!

I.6. References

Bravo, A. (2009). *La société et l'économie à l'aune de la révolution numérique : enjeux et perspectives des prochaines décennies (2015–2025)*. La Documentation française, Paris.

Cohen-Tanugi, L. (1999). *Le nouvel ordre numérique*. Odile Jacob, Paris.

Colin, N. and Verdier, H. (2012). *L'âge de la multitude : entreprendre et gouverner après la révolution numérique*. Armand Colin, Paris.

Dacos, M. (2011). *Manifeste des Digital humanities*. THATCamp Paris [Online]. Available at: http://tcp.hypotheses.org/318.

Denouël, J. and Granjon, F. (eds) (2011). *Communiquer à l'ère numérique. Regards croisés sur la sociologie des usages*. Presses des Mines, Paris.

Doueihi, M. (2011). *Pour un humanisme numérique*. Le Seuil, Paris.

Doukidis, G., Mylonopoulos, N., and Pouloudi, N. (2004). *Social and Economic Transformation in the Digital Era*. Idea Group Pub, Hershey.

Esprit (2006). Que nous réserve le numérique ?. *Esprit*, 5.

Fluckiger, C. (2010). La culture numérique adolescente. *Les Cahiers de l'Orme*, 3 [Online]. Available at: https://hal.univ-lille3.fr/hal-01613667/document.

George, É. (2006). Perspectives critiques et études en communication. In *Perspectives critiques en communication 2*, Aubin, F., George, É., and Rueff, J. (eds). Presses de l'Université du Québec, Quebec.

George, É. and Kane, O. (2015). Les technologies numériques au prisme des approches critiques. Éléments pour l'ébauche d'une rencontre. *Canadian Journal of Communication*, 40(4), 727–735.

Gere, C. (2002). *Digital Culture*. Reaktion Books, London.

Granjon, F. (2017). *Mobilisations numériques : politiques du conflit et technologies médiatiques*. Presses des Mines, Paris.

Greffe, X. and Sonnac, N. (2008). *Culture Web : création, contenus, économie numérique*. Dalloz, Paris.

Guibert, G., Rebillard, F., and Rochelandet, F. (2016). *Médias, culture et numérique – approches socioéconomiques*. Armand Colin, Paris.

Hirsch, B.D. (ed.) (2012). *Digital Humanities Pedagogy. Practices, Principles and Politics*. OpenBook Publishers, Cambridge.

Illing, G. and Peitz, M. (2006). *Industrial Organization and the Digital Economy*. MIT Press, Cambridge.

Kessous, E. (ed.) (2012). *L'attention au monde : sociologie des données personnelles à l'ère numérique*. Armand Colin, Paris.

Lacroix, J.-G. (2009). Conclusion : pour une nouvelle éthique de l'émancipation. In *L'émancipation d'hier à aujourd'hui*, Tremblay, G. (ed.). Presses de l'Université du Québec, Quebec, 297–303.

Lahire, B. (2012). *Monde pluriel. Penser l'unité des sciences humaines et sociales*. Le Seuil, Paris.

Les Cahiers du numérique (2010). Piloter l'entreprise à l'ère du numérique. *Les Cahiers du numérique*, 6(4) [Online]. Available at: http://www.cairn.info/revue-les-cahiers-du-numerique-2010-4.htm.

Les Cahiers du numérique (2011). Identité numérique. *Les Cahiers du numérique*, 7(1) [Online]. Available at: http://www.cairn.info/revue-les-cahiers-du-numerique-2011-1.htm.

Les Cahiers du numérique (2017). Bénévolat, lien social et numérique. *Les Cahiers du numérique*, 13(2) [Online]. Available at: http://www.cairn.info/revue-les-cahiers-du-numerique-2017-2.htm.

Lévy, A. (2010). *Sur les traces de Big Brother : la vie privée à l'ère numérique*. L'Éditeur, Paris.

Mathias, P. (2008). *Des libertés numériques : notre liberté est-elle menacée par l'Internet ?* Presses universitaires de France, Paris.

Ollman, B. (2003). *Dance of the Dialectic: Steps in Marx's Method*. University of Illinois Press, Chicago.

Pires, A. (1997). De quelques enjeux épistémologiques d'une méthodologie générale pour les sciences sociales. In *La recherche qualitative. Enjeux épistémologiques et méthodologiques*, Poupart, J. (ed.). Gaëtan Morin, Montreal, 3–44.

Proulx, S. (1999). L'américanité serait-elle ancrée dans les dispositifs techniques ? In *Variations sur l'influence culturelle américaine*, Sauvageau, F. (ed.). Presses de l'Université Laval, Quebec, 209–230 [Online]. Available at: http://retro.erudit.org/livre/CEFAN/1999-1/000546co.pdf.

Rushkoff, D. (2012). *Les 10 commandements de l'ère numérique*. Fyp Éditions, Limoges.

Stiegler, B. (2015). *La société automatique 1 – l'avenir du travail*. Fayard, Paris.

Tic&société. (n.d.). Les industries culturelles à la conquête des plateformes ? *Tic&société*, 13(1–2).

Troude-Chastenet, P. (2018). Fake news et post-vérité. De l'extension de la propagande au Royaume-Uni, aux États-Unis et en France. *Quaderni* (96), 87–101 [Online]. Available at: http://journals.openedition.org/quaderni/1180.

The Digital and Information

Part I

The Digital and Interruption

1

New News Formats on/by Digital Social Networks

Over the past two years, new informational objects that choose short video format as their main form of content production have been emerging in France. They have been successful in reaching younger audiences through Digital Social Networks (DNS). They are produced by *Brut, Monkey, Konbini* and *Minute-Buzz*, and others are under development. Meanwhile, international Web companies such as Snapchat or Facebook have also developed applications dedicated to news. While their implementations are of varying quality and not always successful, some of them, diffused over our digital social networks, are gaining ground and, with them, a short information format combining video and text as they diffuse their content over DSN.

The objectives of these media[1], who share their content on DSN, are multiple. In particular, they offer new information formats – that they described as "powerful" and that are adapted to mobile phone use – to audiences between the ages of 15–35 years who use traditional media less frequently.

The work presented here is based on a reflection on media devices and their evolution. The confrontation with these new informational objects questions certain notions within the framework of media research, including that of device or even editorial enunciation. We wish to examine these media objects by questioning their methods of writing current events in a context that has been marked for more than 20 years by the diversification of information devices, actors and practices.

Chapter written by Valérie CROISSANT and Annelise TOUBOUL.
1 In this chapter, when we refer to "news media" we mean professional media organizations that produce journalistic content in order to distinguish them from platforms and DSNs that do not produce journalistic content.

The hesitation in the title of this chapter, "by/about DSNs", reflects the ambiguity of the link between these new media and DSNs: they tend to present themselves as mere content diffusers, while we try to show their role in co-construction of information.

Considering that information media on the Web initially sought to free themselves from the materiality of traditional media, a process often referred to as *dematerialization* or *digitalization*, would the contemporary period correspond to a "deformalization" of media? Not that media no longer has forms, but that it no longer has its own form, or models, only fragmented formats, partly imposed by the DSNs, who guarantee access to the public. That is the assumption behind this work. At the heart of our questioning is the type of relationships that are being built between news producing media and DSNs.

1.1. Framework for the exploratory analysis

Our approach is based on a twofold theoretical approach. The first is the socio-economics of media, which analyzes the relationship between media and Web industries (Smyrnaios 2017). These new media are editorial manifestations of the power relations that are established between traditional media, or *pure players*, and DSNs. The battle between content producers and those controlling access to audiences has been analyzed from the point of view of the cultural industries to be examined (Bouquillion *et al.* 2013).

Our second theoretical approach is the study of media devices, media narrative and editorial enunciation. The study works on two levels. At the macro level, it seeks to understand the diversity of editorial systems. They are not all equivalent and, if their common denominator lies in their mobilization of DSNs, their modalities vary: it is about beginning an attempt to distinguish them in a changing media landscape that is difficut to read.

At the micro level, we look at the particularities of the productions of three of these new media to identify the proposed information discourse, while considering their semiotic density. The implementation of meaning involves several combined languages (icon, sound, verbal, gestural, computer-based) in a limited space (often the screen of the mobile phone). To take into account the details of the articulation between the material and the symbolic in this discourse is to understand which editorial enunciation is at work.

These informational objects, particularly semiotics and discourse, are so resistant to analysis that they can be difficult to grasp. They are therefore characterized by a high degree of diversity in their production and distribution methods. We have selected three of them, based on their differences and their emblematic character. All three media are free of charge and are financed by, among other sources, paid publications and commercial partnerships.

– *Brut* is a recently established French media outlet, created in 2016 by personalities with experience in information, generally audiovisual, as well as Web-based information. It is enjoying rapid success and is currently developing versions abroad, particularly in the United States. It presents itself as "a new information medium, 100% video, 100% digital" and publishes videos (between 1 and 3 minutes in length) that are shared or diffused exclusively on DSNs. These are systematically subtitled. *Brut* has no website, and the content is produced for distribution on digital social networks[2]. Recently, thematic channels have been developed: *Brut Nature*, *Brut Sports*. Always looking for a profitable business model, this outlet broadcasts content that is displayed as "paid", i.e. videos are produced in partnership with a brand, institution or other media outlet and are therefore comparable to promotional content.

– *Konbini*, launched in 2009 by two advertising and Web entrepreneurs, is the oldest of the three media outlets selected for this study. Initially, *Konbini* did not produce informational content, but promoted itself as a branded content production company. The link with the journalistic world was therefore very weak. It is only recently that it has emerged as an *infotainment* medium, with pop culture-related content. The information shift took place in 2017 with two concurrent events: the creation of the *Konbini News* channel and the arrival of Hugo Clément, a journalist known for his participation in the television show *Le Petit Journal*[3]. *Konbini* highlights six thematic channels on its website, including a channel dedicated to information. Some are produced in permanent collaboration with a brand (Coca-Cola, Netflix). *Konbini* also distributes its content on its DSN, Facebook, Twitter and Snapchat accounts.

– *Le Monde* (on Snapchat), whose configuration is very different here as it is a known medium, publishes in its name via the Snapchat application, according to the rules laid down by the latter within a kiosk-type space called "Discover", which hosts some media (*L'Équipe, Vice, Paris Match, Konbini, Cosmopolitan, Vogue*, MTV, *Melty, L'Express*), as well as, more recently, publications by influential personalities

---

2 Building on its success, *Brut* signed an exclusive partnership with France Info in March 2017, which allows the television channel to broadcast a few *Brut* videos on the air in the 6 p.m.–8 p.m. period in *L'instant module*, a program that offers "an original treatment of current events through a selection of modules with a different tone and perspective" (France Info press release, March 2017).
3 French infotainment show broadcast on the Canal+ television channel from 2004 to 2017.

and brands. The form of *Le Monde*'s publications is very elaborate: still and animated images with folders, sometimes large, that you can choose to open to read (no buttons, everything is activated by sliding movements on the screen) according to the "map" model[4] and only visible for 24 hours by the users of the application.

Our observations took place over a week, from March 19 to 24, 2018. The informational productions were captured and cross-referenced from several DSNs. We looked at both the devices and the content produced, while trying to measure their degree of "informational sociability", i.e. the way in which information is mobilized to generate commitment from users (Nicolas 2018). This is also a question of understanding the internal mechanics of each of these media, their editorial policy and also the editorialization methods that are developed there, because we are not dealing with a simple aggregation of content, but rather with editorialized information (Vitali-Rosetti 2016). This work summarizes some of the transversal points that characterize these media, while remaining at a fairly general level, because a detailed analysis would require too much space for each of them; they are neither identical nor even equivalent.

The first salient point that characterizes the information discourse is the relationship with time, which is central to any current discourse. The second point that will be addressed, known, a little broadly, as "media territories", refers to the way in which each media structures its symbolic space. The nature and modalities of the circulation of publications by DSNs will be discussed.

1.2. Media temporalities

The question of media temporalities is at the root of the very definition of news and journalistic practices. Following an initial exploration, two points should be noted: the way in which these media signify time and the relationship with the media agenda.

1.2.1. *Signifying time*

The first feature characterizing the consumption of this information is the difficulty in identifying traditional time benchmarks; not that time benchmarks are non-existent, but rather their identification is unclear or is not central to the device. Each of the three media develops a different relationship to temporality in the context of its information production, which is not always easy to assess given the opaque nature of the information production and dissemination processes.

---

4 Also known as "snaps", maps are vertical visual formats, designed for the mobile phone screen, containing photographs, videos, computer graphics or texts that are scrolled by tapping or sliding your fingers on the screen.

What we call the "time marking of information" corresponds to the signs that allow the user to situate himself or herself in relation to the time of the event and the time the information is produced. It is the elements of meaning that make it possible to answer the questions: when did this happen? How old is this information? When was it distributed or diffused?

The publications appear on several social networks (on *Konbini's* website as well), with a time indication located in relation not to the calendar (date) but to the present time of the consultation: *one hour ago, two days ago, 13 hours ago*. This is certainly very uncomfortable for the researcher who is trying to reconstruct a publication chronology, but it is very consistent with the way in which digital social networks manage a timeline based on the individual time of use.

It can be seen that time marking is defined primarily by the DSN, especially with regard to Facebook. It is the latter that materializes the space and time of information from the moment of consultation, and not from the moment of dissemination. The reader/user – from whom the time stamping of publications by the social media takes place – is the center of the system, the bona fide place of media practice.

The media time that governs the other information media (daily, weekly or even continuous information) is none other than that of the present moment of consultation, a perpetual present, the time of the user in the context of his or her social network use, an individual time. According to Jean-François Tétu (2018), this news discourse aims to make the "feeling of everyday life" (p. 90) tangible, a temporality common to the information and the reader: from the present to the presence.

Another way for the media/DSN[5] to build its temporality is to distance itself from the media agenda, which corresponds to a social, collective time, built by the classical media and their resonances.

1.2.2. *The media agenda*

The notion of flow did not appear with the Internet since it already characterized the production of information on radio and television. In the context of this research, it is singular because it is a flow that shifts in relation to a social time (that of the news, of the calendar). This is visible at several levels and, in particular, in the choice of subjects, which is intended, on a voluntary basis, as counterprogramming to other media.

---

5 This term, *media/DSN*, tends to refer to the media narrative analyzed by taking into account the technical and semiotic interweaving of the media (e.g. *Brut*) to the DSN (e.g. Facebook).

The news coverage of these three media is quite different. As far as *Brut* is concerned, its editorial line is singular because it prides itself on not sticking to the news "dictated" by other media. In this respect, it claims a position that is far removed from traditional media, both from the point of view of the agenda and of the processing of information. Most of its publications correspond to contemporary social topics, treated from a personal perspective, a testimony, but which is not systematically in the news of the last few days. It also increases their lifespan, the possibilities of exchanges and circulation on DSNs. This counterprogramming sometimes leads it to adopt a meta posture, as shown in this publication, which had some success in January 2017 (Figure 1.1). *Brut* claims to be a decoding medium, distancing itself from traditional media, which is strategically considered unattractive for young audiences.

Figure 1.1. *Publication of Brut from January 2017 about the slap received by Manuel Valls. The juxtaposition of media titles in itself builds Brut's position*

The "fresh" news is not totally excluded from the content, it is present through live broadcasts, interviews, carried out by a single journalist (Rémy Buisine) who, on long formats (one hour on average), reports on events at the time they take place.

For *Konbini*, given the origin of this medium and its mode of financing through so-called "native" advertising[6], the news is mainly based on that of cultural industries, such as film releases. *Konbini* is not a general information medium, with its origins and editorial line being more oriented towards content marketing. Nevertheless, the arrival of Hugo Clément in autumn 2017[7] and the launch of the *Konbini News* channel at the end of January 2018 have committed it to a more traditional news approach, i.e. professional and distinct from other content. The channel offers two types of topics: hot social and political news, as well as many social topics that concern basic issues, different from the media agenda.

We also find these two temporalities of informational content on the daily editions of the newspaper *Le Monde* on Snapchat. The editorial team[8] works on current topics, in a very didactic and pedagogical way, according to the very young audience of Snapchat users (e.g. "All about the strike of 28 March 2018"). Each edition also proposes specific topics to a precise target group. For example, the "love break-up seen by science", or "those fitness applications that don't only want good things". All this is interrupted with games, quizzes or other surveys and advertisements. This is a clear indication of the editorial tension between subjects that fall within the political and general information medium of *Le Monde*, and subjects adapted to Snapchat's audience.

For the three media, we see the construction of a news period that combines, in a minority way, subjects on the media agenda with subjects that distance themselves from them using themes and formats closer to those of the magazine press. In any case, whether the media are native to the Web or from traditional media, they distance themselves from the referent media agenda, which is consistent with the economic model and the search for original subjects capable of capturing the attention of "mobile users". All are free and their funding depends on the audience for their publications.

For the user, consulting information via the platforms does not allow him or her to be in a media time; the one that has been built on the periodicity for the written press or the program schedule for audiovisual media, which is nevertheless based on

---

6 "Native" advertising is sponsored online content with an editorial appearance that integrates it into the form of the medium by addressing themes similar to those covered by the informative text.

7 A young journalist known for the television show *Quotidien*.

8 On a daily basis, *Le Monde* has a team of seven people dedicated to producing content for Snapchat.

social time: working hours, family hours, the calendar, a time linked to the collective dimension of social activities. Another focus reinforces the hypothesis that these media are asynchronous to social and media time, which is embodied here in the modalities of production and circulation of articles.

1.3. Media territories

The second point of attention concerns the difficulty of identifying a media territory, as it is so logical in terms of fragment and fragmentation. We are then prevented from defining the physical and symbolic limits of the medium, identifying its editorial line or understanding the ways in which its information is produced and circulated. The media, with no clear boundaries, is defined by its publications and their distribution methods, which, for at least two of the three media analyzed, can be considered circular. It is not easy to identify the methods of distribution and circulation of publications on the different DSNs, but from what we have observed, what strikes us are the phenomena of loops.

1.3.1. Broadcasting tactics on Konbini

Observation of the publication activity over a week shows that *Konbini* has information loops that can be broken down into several stages. In a first step, the different channels produce themed content whose nature and size vary according to the subject. *Konbini News* generates video reports, interviews and articles. In a second step and first loop, the homepage of the website acts as a curator, insofar as, through these three sections ("Latest News", "What's Trending" and "The Big Stories"), it makes a double selection: the presence on the homepage, then a distribution in one of the three sections. Finally, there is a third stage and second loop where some of the thematic information, most of it on the *Konbini* website home page, is published on DSN, namely Twitter and Facebook: in short (hyperlink) on Twitter or long (video, title text and subtitle) on Facebook.

Another type of loop that should be note is the way information circulates several times on DSNs after a period of time ranging from one to several days.

As a result, during our observation week, we observed that some "flagship" subjects were repeated several times on DSNs: this is the case of subjects from *Konbini News* on hunting (repeated five times in one week on Facebook and at least three times on Twitter) or on an attack on a homosexual couple in a supermarket (three times on Facebook and once on Twitter). The topics are discussed once at the beginning of the week, then again a few days later, with the same catchphrase or sometimes with a different title. Information on *Konbini* is therefore relatively redundant, even though the traffic strategies spread over the week give the impression of rich and varied content. The user's impression of an informational richness is based above all on a form of artifice, initially based on repetitiveness. *Konbini* is not the only alone in doing this. However, this characteristic must be looked at as a strong modality of production and, primarily, of the dissemination of information. It should be recalled that it is impossible, from the point of view of the reader/user, as well as the researcher, to attribute these re-postings to one of the actors in particular: the media or platform that distributes their productions.

1.3.2. *Tactics and dependencies for Brut and Le Monde*

As *Brut* does not have a website, all publications are accessible via its DSN feed (Facebook, YouTube, Twitter, Snapchat, Instagram). There are between five and eight new publications daily, but the user sees more than a dozen of them circulating in the feed of their DSNs. This difference is partly due to the principle of re-posting mentioned above. We have identified two types of re-posting. On the one hand, some (old) posts return several times to our news feed, but there is no sign that they are indeed old posts, only the feeling of having already seen them guides the user. On the other hand, some posts appear at different times, such as re-posts between thematic channels: between *Brut, Brut Nature* and *Brut Sport*. Here, on the contrary, the origin of the channel is mentioned.

Without having been able to verify it technically, we assume that the first type of re-post is the responsibility of the DSN (in particular to provide somewhat sparse news feeds), whereas re-postings between channels would be the responsibility of the media outlet itself in order to make its, to make its productions profitable by extending their lifespan and increasing the possibilities of being read.

As far as Snapchat is concerned, the situation is different, as this DSN relies on identified media that it integrates into its "Discover" kiosk. *Le Monde* publishes 12 maps every day of the week at around 5:30 pm, which constitute its daily edition. The Snapchat application is presented as a closed application, which therefore maintains, for *Le Monde* in any case, an identifiable daily publication frequency. *Le Monde* therefore uses the traditional practices of the written press. There is no loop, but a daily edition that is original, ephemeral and vaguely interactive.

These looping phenomena cannot be reduced here to the notion of the circular circulation of information (Bourdieu 1996), since these loops actually reflect complex ways of making content visible on DSNs. They act as powerful filters on media publications, which then develop tactics to try to get around them. The presence of these media on several DSNs allows them, for example, not to be totally dependent on a single broadcasting platform for which they do not control the filtering conditions, and even less the possible modifications of the algorithm.

1.4. Conclusion

As this work is only in the exploratory phase, it is not a question of setting out conclusive elements, but rather of setting out a few questions or even milestones.

Our first observations from the study question the very notion of *editorial enunciation*, as the role of DSNs is so important in the ways in which stories are told, visibility is raised and information is shared. The notion of editorial enunciation, developed in particular by Souchier (1998), is regularly used and questioned as forms of publication, particularly writing on screens, evolve. The question that might arise is: "Who are the media?" Asking the question is an attempt to uncover the technological, organizational, editorial and economic intertwining between companies producing information and the DSNs that control the dissemination, reading and interaction mechanisms. As such, DSNs feel and behave like media by building editorial space and time, controlling access to audiences, and establishing publication rules and formats without producing any content.

The second point concerns our approach to the intellectual tools for the analysis of these media forms. The notion of the triviality of cultural beings proposed by Yves Jeanneret (2014) seems quite appropriate here, because it emphasizes not only the circulation of objects and representations, but also the power of mediation mechanisms. The notion allows us to link the semiotic dimension of media forms to the socio-economic dimension of power games and social practices.

For two of the three media/DSNs analyzed, the principle of the triviality of circulating information being transformed according to the whims of traffic and exchanges constitutes the editorial project itself. They produce information units designed not only to inform, read and understand, but also, and above all, to meet their audience on the basis of the rules for content circulation established by DSNs. The media providers accept the principles of the transformation and appropriation of content, which, moreover, are produced for this destination. In this respect, we can see the difference with the so-called "classical" or "historical" media, which build media stories through permanence, the column, the signature or the archive.

1.5. References

Bouquillion, P., Miège, B., and Moeglin, P. (2013). *L'industrialisation des biens symboliques. Les industries créatives en regard des industries culturelles.* Presses universitaires de Grenoble, Grenoble.

Jeanneret, Y. (2014). *Critique de la trivialité. Les médiations de la communication, enjeu de pouvoir.* Éditions Non Standard, Paris.

Nicolas, J. (2018). De Brut à BFM, la chute de l'engagement Facebook n'épargne aucun média. *Le Journal du Net* [Online]. Available at: https://www.journaldunet.com/media/publishers/1209006-taux-engagement-facebook-medias/.

Smyrnaios, N. (2017). *Les GAFAM contre l'Internet, une économie politique du numérique.* INA, Paris.

Souchier, E. (1998). L'image du texte : pour une théorie de l'énonciation éditoriale. *Les cahiers de médiologie*, 6(2), 137–145.

Tétu, J.-F. (2018). *Le récit médiatique et le temps. Accélérations, formes, ruptures.* L'Harmattan, Paris.

Vitali-Rosati, M. (2016). Qu'est-ce que l'éditorialisation? *Sens Public* [Online]. Available at: http://www.sens-public.org/article1184.html.

New Information Practices and Audiences in the Digital Age

This chapter is part of a research project on Radio-Canada that continues to follow the work initiated with my colleague Nozha Smati (2015 and 2017, concerning RFI) and more broadly with the editorial team of Radio Morphoses magazine. It focuses on the changes (real or more or less fantasized) caused by the digitalization of the media on the (re)definition of the place of the audience and the practices of information professionals. Here, we focus on the first aspect. We will discuss a digital transition rather than a turning point, and even less so a revolution. The period is still very largely experimental, as most public media managers confirm: "We are all with our flashlights," says one Radio-Canada executive director, when another talks about a "large-scale laboratory"[1].

2.1. Understanding the reality of media change in a context of digital transition

Beyond the reality of the concrete gains – in terms of flexibility and working time – made on a daily basis from a technical point of view (recording, editing), digital technology raises many questions. These questions – at least the way I try to deal with them – are part of a dual socio-technical and socio-constructivist framework. Journalism today is a constantly changing professional environment, requiring the acquisition of new knowledge and the development of new skills (the

Chapter written by Pascal RICAUD.
1 Ginette Viens (Senior Director, Journalistic Deployment, July 3, 2018) and Jonathan Trudel (Editor-in-Chief, Digital Editor, June 18, 2018).

process can be individual, but it is most often intersubjective, learning from others)[2]. Technology is understood in terms of appropriation (or even re-appropriation) and in its social dimension (each one adapting it to their needs, the vision they has of their profession or mission, as well as according to the representations they have has developed around the technology). The analysis is therefore necessarily socio-technical in order to capture the complexity of how journalists reinvent themselves today considering that they are caught in a dual movement of injunction to participation and a form of transparency, on the part of information departments or multimedia managers, and also facing ever-increasing demands from the public regarding the clarity, quality and veracity of information. More precisely, these requirements are expressed by Internet audiences in the public sphere, as well as, increasingly, in the private sphere of journalists.

Our approach is qualitative and based on "comprehensive" interviews whose spirit and even intention can be described as ethnographic (Kaufmann 2007). One could simply speak of a "qualitative" interview (Poupart 2012), even though any interview other than qualitative is more based on a survey than on an interview itself, whose primary meaning ("to be maintained" in 12th-Century French) means "to support each other". We are therefore in a balanced meeting and relationship. When we do interviews, we first try to *understand*, as Bourdieu said in *The Weight of the World* (1993). It is a question of describing, as well as of being able to explain social realities. And who can reflect on their own social realities better than the social actors themselves? It is also through the confrontation of different experiences that we can draw some answers as to what really affects and changes their practices. To this end, a few group interviews have also been scheduled.

We therefore seek to analyze the meaning that journalists give to their practices. In a more interactionist approach, it is even a question of co-constructing, with the actors, the meaning they give to their work. This implies that we must not settle only on open ended interviews where topics for reflection are launched and follow-up is carried out. This is where the difficulty is located. To achieve this, a thorough knowledge of the field studied is necessary (of the issues at stake, the logic of the actors, the speeches produced internally by the departments, etc.). The interviews must be placed not only in context, but also in time, in a history of the media.

---

2 Interesting initiatives have been carried out at Radio-Canada that allow for mutual learning and sharing of experiences between a young journalist (Web or multimedia) and a more experienced journalist linked to the "old media" (TV or radio reporter). The first pairing of its kind brought Michel (radio reporter, interview of March 6, 2018) and Pasquale (from RAD [Radio-Canada's journalism laboratory], totally dedicated to digital information) together for a series of reports and papers on the border between the United States and Mexico.

The speeches of journalists or editors interviewed at Radio Canada, and previously at RFI, therefore, reveal some similarities as well as dissonances concerning their representations of their profession and practices in the digital age. Digital technology does not cause the journalists interviewed to be eclipsed or frightened, but often leads to a rich reflection on how it influences not only their ways of doing things, but also their priorities (or a rediscovery of what is essential for them and gives meaning to their work).

2.2. A new media contract

To the Internet audience, the journalist no longer enjoys the same prestige or, at least, no longer enjoys the same symbolic status. He/she is considered with more or less respect, mistrust or even indifference. With digital technology, we have to do more and more with the public, and with its presence, participation and demands. Indeed, Internet users are increasingly selective and actively react – or at least a minority of them – to the content they read or listen to, especially since they now have the means to do so (comment systems, digital social networks). All journalists must always be closer to the public. Conversing with the public, and even collaborating with them, has become an obligation (Rieffel 2014). However, our observations and interviews show that they do not transform themselves into community managers for their media. If they develop privileged relationships with some of their followers, it is largely on their own digital social networks, based on their personal accounts.

Nevertheless, there are always more and more interactions, and the journalist is led to be more transparent – sometimes playing the game of explanation – by revealing elements related to the conditions or context of a report, as experienced, for example, by Étienne, a specialized journalist with Radio-Canada[3]. One may wonder to what extent this evolution serves or undermines the journalist's work, whether or not it enhances his or her credibility. For example, the "evidence" provided of his or her professionalism, or the application of ethical rules. Those in the production process must increasingly comply with this game of transparency which, without disclosing all of the process, allows recipients to better understand the conditions of production of information, or even to participate in it.

We see the emergence of a new media contract, less unbalanced than before, with a production authority dominating a reception authority (understood as a vague set of knowledge and beliefs), and considered above all in terms of "target audience" (Charaudeau 2000). It is the question of the reciprocal influence between radio (the media in general) and its audience that is being asked:

---

3 Étienne, journalist specializing in the environment (interview of March 28, 2018).

"In the age of the Internet and social networks, and of journalism that is increasingly collaborative and participatory, can we consider ourselves to no longer be confronted with a 'transaction without exchanges' (Baudrillard 1970), but, on the contrary, with more balanced, equitable and ethical exchanges between those who make the information and those who receive it?" (Ricaud 2016, p. 183).

In its communication about a vision of its channels and stations by 2020, Radio-Canada's management, giving predominant if not almost exclusive place to the digital, uses two words for its target: individuals and communities. On the one hand, the response to individuals' expectations, translated into the most personalized offer possible, is not without reminding us of the principle of SMD (smallest marginal difference) theorized almost 40 years ago (Baudrillard, 1970). We could see the end of the process of segmentation of audiences, this time being properly fragmented. On the other hand, there is a redistribution of cards, with content around which existing communities (gender-based, cultural, immigrant) and others that are sometimes emerging and online (mainly young people constituting niche audiences) will be structured and for which specific and adapted marketing responses have already begun to be found.

These niche audiences are now captured through digital social networks and dedicated online applications, which allow for greater proximity and personalization not only of product content (updated newsletters, alert systems, personal accounts), but also of relationships between certain journalists and Internet users, as in the case of Radio-Canada's RAD (journalism laboratory), which is entirely oriented towards digital content (website, digital social networks). However, in the speeches of several representatives of Radio-Canada's management, echoing those of journalists expressing their attachment to a public service mission or the desire to be part of a public journalism audience (Tétu 2008), the idea of first addressing citizens to whom we provide insights, a real analysis and contextualization of information, coupled today with a public invitation and the opportunity to participate. Throughout the discourses of Radio-Canada's managers, there is a clear will to not mention the "2020" project, whose marketing dimension is certainly not addressed or barely appreciated.

2.2.1. *Redefining the problematic figure of an audience*

In this new digital context, the aim is to explore radio journalists' new relationships with the increasingly difficult to grasp "being" that is the audience "endowed [more than ever] with the capacities for self-government, deliberation or participation or media and cultural reception skills[4]" (Cefaï and Pasquier 2003, pp. 13–14). Each citizen would become a potential contributor, or better, a capable journalist, whose presence can be felt as threatening by the professional. Yet none of the journalists interviewed (about 20 in all), among those of RFI or Radio-Canada today, said that they felt threatened or embarrassed in any way by this new status granted to the public. Their attitude, which is also reflected in a number of practices on digital social networks where journalists are in contact with their audiences, is at best benevolent and at worst indifferent. This should nevertheless lead us to question this vision of the audience that is widely accepted and disseminated by a number of researchers – particularly in Information and Communication Science (ICS) – who suggest that they would use a participative approach, which the field compellingly contradicts.

This discourse is based in particular on an immoderate and already old belief in the potentialities of Web 2.0. It is nourished by an ideology of networks of Saint-Simonian essence, as well as a cult of the rational and autonomous individual. Inherited from cybernetics and taken up by the ins and outs of "counter-culture", it is leading a figure of an Internet user who is necessarily competent and creative (Rebillard, 2007). This is not to deny that such an individual can exist, but to recognize that there is little opportunity to exist in an online environment that, even today, as 15 years ago (Ricaud 2004), offers few "truly" participatory or deliberative spaces.

Moreover, speaking of "audiences" in the plural seems more necessary than ever, given the diversity of practices linked to the same media and the fact that they concern different individuals. It is now increasingly accepted that Internet users – Web newspaper readers, online listeners, commentators, people active on online pages or accounts of media on social networks – are not (or only slightly) the same as those who listen to radio or watch live television. The latter remain the most numerous, except for the fact that the potential and actual audience or popularity of online information is not easy to measure. Yet, the idea of a new informational world – participatory and even collaborative – is emerging as a dominant model, considering that information is consumed and passes first through digital social networks today, effectively excluding all those who are still in the majority and who consume information in a traditional way on radio, television and in the press (including online). As a result, the audience for radio – a medium that is already highly participatory at the grassroots level[5] – remains very high in France with

---

4 More broadly, we are simply renewing and updating the figure of a rational and competent public, as John Dewey theorized a long time ago (1927).

5 Hertzian radio, without even mentioning the experiences of free broadcasting, traditionally offers programs that rely heavily on the contributions of listeners. We can mention *Le téléphone sonne* on France Inter or *L'After* on RMC, which give a lot of importance to questions and exchanges with listeners.

79.3% of daily listeners in 2018 compared to 81.6% in 2008. This shows a strong stability given that the cumulative audience for digital media barely exceeds 12%[6].

The idea that the audience is plural and that at its core it is composed primarily of autonomous individuals with unique practices did not emerge with the digitalization of society. For John Dewey, "an audience is composed of plural audiences and each audience includes individuals whose roles, functions, status or places are unique. This diversity is evident in the first moments of an audience's appearance" (quoted in Zask, 2008). If we consider that this audience is built around a more or less shared knowledge and practices – assuming that they are more or less mastered – then we can consider this audience to be as diverse as there are individuals.

2.2.2. *What is the real place and involvement of the audience?*

Most interviews show that journalists are not particularly sensitive or even attentive to comments left on their Web newspapers. In addition, Web papers related to a program such as *Désautels le dimanche* (Radio-Canada) are not generally the subject of much comment. The papers themselves represent very few views compared to the audiences of public affairs programs, which are also not among the most listened to.

In the rare cases where the journalist is personally targeted on subjects that may be of a sensitive nature – and in particular those related to immigration or community issues in a tense national context in a country that has also experienced attacks – the information professional does not emerge unscathed. The journalist is tested in his or her convictions as a journalist, as well as a citizen especially when he or she feels that he or she has done useful work without really falling into. But is this journalist aware that it is not so much his or her person who is targeted as the subject that is being treated?

In the case of comment systems, we may wonder whether this does not renew the long-standing observation that the audience is as much there to see as to be seen. "Any audience refers to another audience watching it," according to Daniel Dayan (2000, p. 430). The rest of his remarks may give us a better understanding of what is happening in discursive digital arenas today. To be an audience is to perform. "This performance may be consensual or controversial, but it cannot be invisible" (p. 431). In addition to a quantitative, statistical vision of the audience – always useful to the media for performance indicators measured in the form of cumulative audiences,

6 Source: Médiamétrie, Radio Panel 2017–2018, period: September 2017–June 2018.

trust indices or satisfaction – there is also an approach that characterizes the digital age of the media: personalizing the relationship with viewers and Internet users by offering spaces for expression.

It should also be noted that the few contributors to "official" or public publications in traditional media, such as the Web papers linked to the RFI Media Workshop, have a particular profile that does not make them *ordinary* citizens in terms of their capacity to process and format information. They are the basis of communication professionals or, more broadly, middle managers, students (especially in journalism), for some of the bloggers with a certain audience. Their cultural and intellectual capital and their appetite for and knowledge of current events are above average. They have experiences and skills that are comparable or even similar to those of journalists. They function a little like peers, even in a more or less symbolic way. On this subject, our analysis corroborates the results of other studies (Aubert 2008; Rebillard 2011).

2.3. The new intermediate figures of information (the partition of participation)

Semi-professional information, amateur contributor, auxiliary information and so on. This new reality – although very relative since it concerns an online elite – cannot be ignored, even if it is nourished by many fantasies and is ideologically marked. Even tough participatory culture has become increasingly mainstream (Jenkins *et al.*, 2017) and yesterday's bloggers, news influencers and amateur contributors have become symbolizing, participatory journalism remains a relatively rare category, attached rather to citizen media along the lines of AgoraVox.

One may even wonder whether this "participatory journalism" is in some respects a myth in progress, asking many questions about the modalities of participation, the real and recognized status of contributors, the recognition and enhancement of their production (including the question of copyright[7]) or their motivations and real intentions. This is while one of the challenges is to preserve the public space as a place to share (able to free itself, at least to accommodate as much as possible, from economic imperatives) (Mathien 2010; Ricaud and Smati 2017). In the continuity of a journalism mythology, notably analyzed by Denis Ruellan (1992, 2007), it is also a question of questioning the structuring role – undoubtedly

---

7 Several studies raise the question of the rare but existing cases of information sites (more often *pure players* such as *Rue 89*) where there are direct, semi-professional contributors who acquire full author status (implied by their direct participation in the media's information spaces). Obviously, the borderline between trained journalists and neo-journalists – occasional or regular contributors – is becoming difficult to define and justifies equal treatment of each other's productions.

essential – played by the symbolic (and historical) representations of a profession confronted with new representations (those of social-digital networks and the Internet in general) linked to the figure of an autonomous and active user with regard to information. In this new social and ideological context (essentially neoliberal), the primary role of the journalist in the dissemination of knowledge and the very existence of an audience in the traditional sense of the term can be profoundly challenged. Moreover, and finally, the contributing citizen does not exist independently of the professional journalist and is also defined in relation to him or her, in relation to a frame of reference, conventions and ways of doing things. Journalists, can still be considered as reference among each other.

Nathalie Pignard-Cheynel and Arnaud Noblet (2008) hypothesized that online information sites (with a professional vocation) developed around two poles. First of all, "a participation juxtaposed with journalistic content which, in fact, offers little porosity between the two contributions" (p. 2) and which is more or less true for many online media outlets. There is also the other pole mentioned by the two authors, namely that of a co-production of the editorial offer. However, the latter appears, to date, as an ideal standard of participatory journalism 2.0 that would validate the idea of the existence of a new integrated journalistic world (lack of distinction between journalistic and participatory spaces or dedicated to Internet users). To date, we have not met with the latter, while the observation advanced for *Rue 89* by Pignard-Cheynel and Noblet overlapped with our conclusions for RFI's Media Workshop: "If participation can therefore be quantitatively very present on these sites, it is in its lack of valorization and in its low journalistic exploitation that the editorial interest of the editorial staff for this type of contribution manifests itself" (Pignard-Cheynel and Noblet 2008, p. 3). Based on an analysis of the websites of the French dailies *Libération* and *Le Monde*, Annelise Touboul (2006) also finds that "the editorial offices want to keep control, to remain at the origin of the information" (p. 288).

In addition, interactions and collaborations between journalists and some of their readers/listeners, which also reveal intermediate figures described as "information auxiliaries" or "amateur contributors" or "semi-professionals" (notably Flichy 2010), most often take place "elsewhere", in particular on journalists' personal Facebook or Twitter accounts. This assumes an adherence by and a closer proximity to these subscribers or followers, the ways of doing things and understanding a profession, and a certain journalistic culture based in particular on ethics and professional principles. The contribution of amateurs – which is not to be reduced to an ideal-typical figure (Ferron *et al.* 2015) sometimes bordering on caricature – obviously raises the question of task-sharing in the production of information (who does what?) and according to which conventions (Becker, 1999). This is true even though we have observed not only that practices are far from uniform and stable, but also that the time or energy savings achieved are also counterbalanced. Therefore, in addition to the time and quality of production (recording, editing, broadcasting) saved by digital technology, the additional time of multi-production, task diversification and hyper-connection must be contrasted.

2.4. Conclusion

Rather than focusing on the amateur contributor, it may be more appropriate to seek to create the conditions for greater public autonomy in the individual ability to decipher, understand and critically analyze information (through training younger people in critical media evaluation methods[8]), the trade-off for this is to give priority to content that is at the center of interest for the online public, to the detriment of certain content or editorial choices that are traditionally proposed by journalists. The meeting between journalists and members of the online community can take place elsewhere or in other manners. It can take shape through the collection of topics or themes that the media can help to address and enlighten. It can also function the other way around where the media can use the skills and knowledge produced by the online community without it being reduced to digital labor. We must consider these hybrid spaces, which already exist on an *ad hoc* or more systematic basis, as in the case of Radio-Canada's RAD, which allow the circulation and sharing of information and knowledge between the media and its audiences. Experiments in this direction could also be developed in the context of "public affairs", a "place" that seems more appropriate to me, in particular, in relation to social issues of interest to the greatest number of people.

The media contract would therefore be redefined within the framework of a renewed public space, in the sense that the co-production of content and knowledge by journalists and the public would then make it possible to consider giving substance to a communicative action that can flourish in deliberation and enlightened citizen action.

2.5. References

Aubert, A. (2008). Rue89 : un modèle horizontal de la production d'information ? *Médiamorphoses*, (24), 99–104.

Baudrillard, J. (1970). *La société de consommation : ses mythes, ses structures*. Denoël/Folio, Paris.

---

8 In this field of media education, more than ever necessary in a message saturated environment, there is a need for the acquisition of methods and skills for source assessment and, more broadly, for a critical analysis of online media (see Sahut 2017).

Becker, H.S. (1999). *Propos sur l'art*. L'Harmattan, Paris.

Bourdieu, P. (ed.) (1993). *La misère du monde*. Le Seuil, Paris.

Cefaï, D. and Pasquier, D. (2003). *Les sens du public. Publics politiques, publics médiatiques.* Presses universitaires de France, Paris [Online]. Available at: https://halshs.archives-ouvertes.fr/halshs-00805315/file/Cefai_Pasquier_Les_sens_du_public_PUF2003.pdf.

Charaudeau, P. (2000). L'événement dans le contrat médiatique. *Dossiers de l'audiovisuel*, 91 [Online]. Available at: http://www.patrick-charaudeau.com/L-evenement-dans-le-contrat.html.

Dayan, D. (2000). Télévision, le presque public, *Réseaux*, 100, 427–456.

Ferron, B., Harvey, N., and Tredan, O. (eds) (2015). *Des amateurs dans les médias. Légitimités, autonomie, attachements*. Presses des Mines, Paris.

Flichy, P. (2010). *Le sacre de l'amateur. Sociologie des passions ordinaires à l'ère numérique.* Le Seuil, Paris.

Jenkins, H., Ito, M., and Boyd, D. (2017). *Culture participative (Une conversation sur la jeunesse, l'éducation et l'action dans un monde connecté)*. C&F Éditions, Caen.

Kaufmann, J.-C. (2007). *L'entretien compréhensif*. Armand Colin, Paris.

Mathien, M. (2010). "Tous journalistes" ! Les professionnels de l'information face à un mythe des nouvelles technologies. *Quaderni*, 72, 113–125.

Pignard-Cheynel, N. and Noblet, A. (2008). L'encadrement des contributions "amateurs" au sein des sites d'information : Entre impératif participatif et exigences journalistiques. *Web Participatif – Usages 2.0 : Mutation de la communication ? Symposium* [Online]. Available at: https://archivesic.ccsd.cnrs.fr/sic_00427124/document.

Poupart, J. (2012). L'entretien de type qualitatif. Réflexions de Jean Poupart sur cette méthode. À partir des propos recueillis et rassemblés par Nadège Broustau et Florence Le Cam. *Sur le journalisme*, 1(1), 60–71.

Rebillard, F. (2007). *Le Web 2.0 en perspective*. L'Harmattan, Paris.

Rebillard, F. (2011). Création, contribution, recommandation : les strates du journalisme participatif. *Les cahiers du journalisme*, 22–23, 29–41.

Ricaud, P. (2004). Vers de nouvelles situations délibératives via Internet : espaces publics partiels ou micro-espaces publics ?. In *La situation délibérative dans le débat public 2*, Castagna, B. *et al.* (eds). Presses universitaires de France, Tours, 87–103.

Ricaud, P. (2016). Analyser la radio en termes d'effets. In *Analyser la radio : concepts, objets et méthodes*, Antoine, F. (ed.). De Boeck Supérieur, Brussels, 176–184.

Ricaud, P. and Smati, N. (2017). Numérisation de la radio : effets sur les pratiques des professionnels de l'information et la participation des publics. *Les Enjeux de l'Information et de la Communication*, 18, 33–46 [Online]. Available at: https://lesenjeux.univ-grenoble-alpes.fr/2017-dossier/03-Smati-Ricaud/.

Rieffel, R. (2014). *Révolution numérique, révolution culturelle ?* Gallimard, Paris.

Ruellan, D. (1992). Le professionnalisme du flou. *Réseaux*, 10(51), 25–37.

Ruellan, D. (2007). *Le professionnalisme du flou.* Presses universitaires de Grenoble, Grenoble.

Sahut, G. (2017). L'enseignement de l'évaluation critique de l'information numérique. *tic&société*, 11(1).

Smati, N. and Ricaud, P. (2015). Les nouveaux modes de relation des journalistes à leurs publics. Les usages numériques chez les journalistes de RFI. *Revue française des sciences de l'information et de la communication*, 7.

Tétu, J.-F. (2008). Du "public journalism" au "journalisme citoyen". *Questions de communication*, 13, 71–88.

Touboul, A. (2006). Interactivité des sites de presse : relégation et exploitation de la parole profane. In *Document numérique et société. Actes de la conférence DocSoc – 2006 : semaine du document numérique*, Chartron, G. and Broudoux, E. (eds). ADBS, Paris, 279–289.

Zask, J. (2008). Le public chez Dewey : une union sociale plurielle. *Tracés – Revue de sciences humaines*, 15, 169–189 [Online]. Available at: http://journals.openedition.org/traces/75.

3

The Effects of Innovation on the Careers of Journalists

In this contribution, I would like to discuss how ideological injunctions around digital technology – particularly the question of innovation – are part of the career project of French and French-speaking Canadian journalists. The research is based on 20 in-depth biographical interviews. It is part of a broader comparative research program on the careers of online journalists in Argentina, Belgium, Brazil, Canada, France and Portugal. It seeks to compare the relationships between individual paths, national media systems and the transnational circulation of digital practices and discourses.

This chapter begins with a presentation of the theoretical framework, followed by a review of the studies that address the research questions. The methodology used in this study will then be discussed. The analysis will focus on the interviewees' representation of digital innovation, followed by a discussion of how they integrate these ideological injunctions into their career plans. Finally, the chapter will propose possibilities for comparison between these two bodies of French-speaking journalists.

3.1. Theoretical framework

3.1.1. *Profession and segments*

This research is based on the interactionist tradition in sociology, particularly the concept of a *career*, defined as a "sequence of movements

---

Chapter written by Fábio Henrique PEREIRA.

from one position to another in an organizational system" (Becker 2009, p. 35). This concept makes it possible to link individual paths, motivations and choices to a collective order (the professional group, the labor market). In this case, speaking of a career consists of working on a more or less "controlled" evolution of identity within an occupation system (Strauss 1992), which results in individual and collective mechanisms for anticipating possible paths, even though they are always adapted and renegotiated according to the contexts of choice.

The career concept integrates the professional sociology program of Bucher and Strauss (1961), who propose thinking of a profession in terms of "segments": "We shall develop the idea of professions as loose amalgamations of segments pursuing different objectives in different manners and more or less delicately held together under a common name at a particular period in history" (p. 326). Talking about segments makes it possible to escape the normative definition of functionalist sociology and reveal the heterogeneity of journalism insofar as each segment refers to various interests, values, ideologies, careers, etc. In this case, we are talking about journalistic *careers* (in the plural), the different ways of becoming and being a journalist.

In a previous work on the careers of journalists in Brazil, I discussed precisely how investment in certain segments (e.g. becoming an executive in an online newsroom) was linked to the construction of specific career paths: career projects that promote management tasks, the internalization of a specific set of conventions related rather to the worlds of management and human resources. In addition, people who have followed a career in these segments will share another ideological base, sometimes closer to the company's interests than to that of the employers. One could say that within a specialty, such as digital journalists, it would be possible to find a diversity of segments that will conceive careers differently, have distinct expectations regarding the place of the Web in journalism, etc.

3.1.2. A transnational identity for online journalists?

In previous studies, we have observed strong similarities in the way Web journalists in different countries represent their identity and practices. This hypothesis around a transnational identity for online journalists was first proposed by Florence Le Cam in 2012 in a study on the socialization of Web journalists in France and Quebec[1]. In his work, Le Cam (2012) identified common identity traits

1 The hypothesis around a transnational identity for online journalists resonates with other approaches that seek to find traces of a universal professional culture (Hanitzsch 2007) or journalistic ideology (Deuze 2005). In the same vein, Nelson Traquina (2005) refers to the journalist as a member of a transnational interpretative community. Although I note important

about three salient aspects of online newsrooms: dispersion at work, the relationship to the temporality of information dissemination and the meaning of collective work. "We may then see how certain American models [...] then spread to other national spaces, leading to, on some aspects of identity, a certain form of homogenization of the online journalistic being" (Le Cam 2012, p. 84).

This hypothesis has been taken up and reworked in a more ambitious work in which I participate with Le Cam on a comparative socio-history of online journalism (2001–2016). The aim is to compare the results of interviews and observations in Belgian, Brazilian, French and Quebec newsrooms with the digital discourses broadcast by two international organizations: on the one hand, the *World Association of Newspapers and News Publishers* and, on the other hand, the *Pew Research Center*. In this study, we have identified what is called "rhetoric of change" that will provoke ideological injunctions to innovation in terms of practices, tools, relationships with audiences, management models, etc. These discourses will then be found in the words of online journalists, following the logic of appropriation, adaptation or resistance to these injunctions (Pereira and Le Cam 2017).

In this chapter, I use these findings to analyze the career project for online journalists. I assume that these injunctions to innovation would not only have an impact on the professional ideology of the different segments of digital journalism, but also on the motivations that partially explain the career choices of these journalists. These transnational discourses will therefore cross the macro (labor market, national media systems) and micro (individual paths) dimensions of the practice of French and Canadian "francophone" online journalists.

In short, three research questions emerge from this approach:

– How are these discourses about the digital appropriated by French and French-Canadian journalists for discussing the profession, the labor market and careers?

    How do these discourses end up in the different career projects of online journalists?

– How do these discourses contribute, as professional ideology, to the process of segmentation within the practice of digital journalism?

Finally, the research also includes a fourth level: that of comparison. Initially, the idea was to study the similarities and differences between the ideological discourses

theoretical differences between these works, it seems to me that a research avenue could be exploited by researchers who want to work on the professional identities of journalists.

and the career plans of online journalists placed in two different national contexts, but who share the same language. However, we do not yet have any empirical evidence to advance this dimension of the analysis.

3.2. Methodology

The methodology is based on in-depth biographical interviews with 20 journalists, including eight French-speaking Canadians and 12 French nationals. The first round of interviews was conducted in three cities across Canada (Ottawa, Quebec City and Montreal) in August 2017. In February 2018, journalists from five French cities (Lyon, Morlaix, Paris, Rennes and Tours) were interviewed. The field was built using a "snow bubble" strategy based on the indication of journalists and teachers residing in Canada and France (one has to consider that I am a foreigner in these two countries). This strategy allowed me to construct a non-probability sample, but one that was more or less representative of the professional environment (Deslauriers and Kérisit 2008) in terms of gender, age, geographical distribution and position held at the time of the interview (Tables 3.1 and 3.2).

Journalist	Gender	Age*	Position
C1	M	28	Head of Digital Information
C2	M	–	Director of Digital Information
C3	F	29	Digital editor
C4	M	50	Digital publisher
C5	F	–	Editor-in-Chief
C6	M	24	Web journalist
C7	M	27	Head of Digital News
C8	F	28	Blog Manager
* Some journalists did not reveal their age.			

Table 3.1. *Francophone Canadian journalists interviewed[2]*

---

2 The city where these journalists work is not mentioned to preserve their anonymity.

Journalist	Gender	Age*	Position
F1	M	43	Web journalist (data journalist)
F2	F	40	Journalist in the Magazine Department
F3	M	42	Responsible for the development of the digital contents
F4	M	–	Reporter, seconded to the multimedia department
F5	M	31	Publishing Director
F6	M	25	Journalist in the Sports Department
F7	F	27	Digital journalist
F8	M	33	Editor-in-Chief
F9	F	36	Journalist
F10	F	31	Multimedia writer
F11	M	31	Assistant Editor-in-Chief
F12	M	36	Manager of the digital hub
* Some journalists did not reveal their age.			

Table 3.2. *French journalists interviewed*

The interviews focused on the life stories of these journalists: their choice of profession, period of training, entry into the labor market, job changes, promotions and aspects of their personal life. For each of these motives, journalists were encouraged to describe and explain their choice. In this process, digital discourse has emerged as one of the structuring elements of these journalists' career plans. That is what I am going to use in the results.

3.3. Results

3.3.1. *Ideological Injunctions to Innovation*

The statements of online journalists reveal that innovation is a very present category in the way interviewees conceive their practices, the labor market and even the "future" of journalism. "We must innovate". This idea appears to be a kind of mantra for a considerable proportion of the journalists interviewed, even though the meaning given to the term *innovation* varies considerably. In an inductive reading of the interviews, three main themes emerge. The first refers to a kind of naturalization of innovation, as if it were an inevitable consequence of the technological development of society. The second seeks to attribute coherence to these innovations, placing it in a history of tools that have been made available to newsrooms since the late 1990s. The third, finally, associates the adoption of digital technology as the only way for the media to survive in a context of "crisis", with a declining audience, loss of advertising investment, etc.

3.3.1.1. *Innovation as an inevitable consequence of technological development in society*

Five journalists (C2, C7, F2, F10 and F12) expressed the idea of innovation as an inevitable consequence of a society increasingly structured around digital technology. This techno-determinist vision reveals a naturalization of innovation, while denying the economic and power issues involved in the development of these tools. Journalists feel uncomfortable with this context when it comes to their careers. Without knowing how or why things are changing, they can no longer anticipate developments in journalism:

> "[My former boss] told me, 'You know, in the digital world, 1 year is like 10.' I have trouble seeing myself in a job for more than a decade, unless the project changes" (C7).

> "[…] it changes every 2 years. One day we'll tell you that you have to write like that for reference, the next day the other way around, then you have to post on Facebook or not… It changes, so you have to like this permanent danger" (F12).

3.3.1.2. *A logic of digital innovation*

For respondents C1, C2, C5, C7, F1, F3 and F11, journalism remains a practice that is still being renewed. On the contrary, it would have a certain coherence in the development of tools that must be known and mastered by journalists:

> "There is a maturation dimension to the use of social networks. Users go through several phases […]. We were already experiencing the end of the era of blogs and the arrival of microblogs" (F10).

Some journalists are able to trace the history of the evolution of digital technology from their own experience:

> "We were also doing Minitel at the time, it was 2000. I managed the texts, whether it was the choice of the 'next' button or things like that" (F1).

"At the time, there was no continuous news yet, so we were taking up articles published in the morning paper, there was no own content yet, that came in 2002" (F1).

"And in 2006, we did the first Web news. We created a studio in the editorial department, a blog platform too, I had become a multimedia journalist" (F3).

This *subjectification* of digital development refers to a strategy of controlling a certain uncertainty that emerges with this rhetoric of change (Pereira and Le Cam 2017). However, it also expresses the willingness of journalists to position themselves as protagonists in this process (the idea that "I have also been part of this story"):

"Over the past 4 or 5 years, I have realized that Web journalism is not static and that it is up to us to reinvent it every time. So I saw things a little differently and that's why I started giving basic Web courses" (F10).

This logic will have significant impacts in the construction of the career plans of some journalists, as we will see later.

3.3.1.3. *The digital shift, the only way for media to survive*

Finally, for some interviewees, innovation remains the only way for media to survive in an environment marked by the crisis in the financing model for journalism companies (C1, C3, C7, C8, F3 and F12) and by competition with players in the technology sector, such as Google and Facebook (F3, F4, F7 and F9). These discourses reproduce the idea of adapting to digital technology as a major challenge for journalism and society:

"Everyone knows that the Web is the future, that tomorrow there will be no more TV, that my daughters will grow up with a phone" (F9).

"It is becoming more and more obvious for employers to realize that digital technology is an asset to bring to management. I have counterparts, like the one in Toronto, who came from digital media at a very young age and who see the importance that digital media people are beginning to take on" (C7).

And in this case, investing in Web formats is a strategy for attracting a new, younger audience:

> "It is the Web that is the gateway for readers, at least with the younger generation" (C7).

This strategy involves highlighting content that is better adapted to the consumption logic of this new audience:

> "For me, we should have more time for social media, it's better at getting them in. We have good content but it stays hidden. We have to make readers discover it" (C4).

On the contrary, some journalists know that income from the Web is not enough to finance the media:

> "The Internet remained secondary at the time [in 2000], we focused on print, even if today, it remains the print that keeps us alive" (F4).

3.3.2. *Innovation discourses found in careers*

The relationship with innovation and digital technology is also used to explain certain career choices. Three discourses emerged in the interviews: the commitment to innovation; the choice of the digital as a way of anticipating future labor market conditions; and the "random" entry into online journalism.

3.3.2.1. *Commitment to innovation*

The passion – in the sense described by Antoine Hennion (2004) – for experimentation and developing new digital formats was mentioned by a dozen journalists to justify their career projects. The commitment to innovation is expressed in two ways in the careers of French and French-speaking Canadian journalists. The first refers to the development of what are referred to here as "innovative careers". This is the case for some journalists (C7, C9, F1, F3, F9 and F11), who have oriented their career choices by constantly monitoring the practices and functions at the frontier of digital innovation. This situation can be well illustrated by the F1 journalist's career path. With a degree in literature, he began working as a guided tour manager in a regional daily newspaper. In 1998, at the beginning of the Web, he was hired in this medium to put the newspaper online. In 2001, he became news editor and, three years later, he obtained his press card in the wake of a movement to recognize this status in France. In 2012, disappointed by the site's management work, he proposed the creation of a community management department on a daily basis, for which he would be in charge. Then, in 2016, he decided to become a data journalist. His career therefore expresses a duality. On the one hand, he expresses his desire to explore new digital trends:

"It is a space of freedom because there were many things to invent with very flexible model constraints. And, like any new field, there isn't too much pressure from the hierarchy [...] there was a lot of autonomy, which I wouldn't have had elsewhere" (F1).

On the other hand, his career reproduces the international challenges of developing Web tools, the logic of digital innovation described in the previous section, which, in a way, is beyond the control of the F1 journalist.

Other respondents (C2, C3, C6, C8, C8, F7 and F12) did not claim to develop an innovative career, but acquired a taste for innovation throughout their journey as a result of their socialization process with digital practice. This is the case of F7, who initially wanted to pursue a career in the written press, but which found herself, at the time of our interview, in a regional site:

"Then I got a little involved in this, because the editor-in-chief [needed] someone but I liked it. I don't write all the time, we make videos, etc. In fact, it's the variety of formats that I like. And we are encouraged to propose our ideas if we want to make a video, computer graphics, etc." (F7).

3.3.2.2. *The labor market*

Some journalists have chosen the Web as a way to anticipate future conditions for accessing the labor market. However, in both countries, the data show a context of precariousness, in an environment characterized by a reduction in the number of journalists employed. In Canada, Statistics Canada figures show that in 2001, there were 12,965 journalists employed; this number then increased to 13,320 in 2006, 13,280 in 2011 and finally declined to 12,050 in 2016 (Skelton 2018). The curve is similar in France: 34,690 in 2001, 37,111 in 2006, 36,942 in 2011 and 35,294 in 2016 (*Observatoire des métiers de la presse* 2018). Under these conditions, pursuing a career as an online journalist becomes a strategy to remain active in a labor market marked by a logic of hyper-competition (Charron and De Bonville 2004).

In this context, two strategies emerge from the comments of journalists. For some respondents (C3, C7, F5 and F11) having a position in digital journalism is explained by the recognition of a set of skills that have contributed to relative success in the labor market:

"For me, there is work on the Web, I can make a good living with it. I don't see myself leaving it right away. Knowing that the Web needs specialists and that it is a reporting ground. You also need curiosity and a good trainer will not teach you how to be a good Web journalist; it is up to you to learn, to be curious" (F11).

These interviewees very frequently mention the idea of self-learning to justify their success, presenting themselves as "resourceful" (F11). That is what C7 tells us:

"So gradually, I acquired knowledge about, for example, HTML code, how to integrate maps, etc. I also developed knowledge about other platforms, we developed software, with our developers, to make our own maps, to make our videos, etc." (C7).

Another strategy observed in the interviews was to describe labor market conditions, particularly precariousness and media "crisis", to justify the decision to become an online journalist. This is the case for C1, C2, C5, F2 and F5:

"So I thought either a newspaper [to make my career], but I knew that at that time we were working extremely hard to make this shift to digital [...] We were hearing rumors that they [the owners of a media in Montreal] were going to stop writing. So, for me, it was clear that my career was probably not going to be on paper, but on a website" (C1).

"After a year, I decided to go back to Paris and looked for work on the Web because people in the industry said that the written press was dead, that there was no more money, etc." (F10).

3.3.2.3. *Become an online journalist by chance*

Finally, I identified three French journalists (F4, F8, F9) for whom the Web has never been part of their career plans. They did not express a passion for the Web. On the contrary, some of them preferred the written press. They have not gone digital as a survival strategy in the labor market. Online journalism is the only work they saw as a possibility:

"When you're a young journalist, you're going to knock on every door. When you are already recognized, you can choose your media, but a young journalist? No, he has to try everything" (F9).

In short, we see how the contingency/control ratio is materialized in this diversity of careers, which constitute different segments of online journalism.

3.3.3. *An international circulation of discourses on innovation?*

The fact that no significant differences were found in the speeches of French and French-speaking Canadian journalists suggests the existence of an international circulation of discourses on innovation, which is in line with the results of my research with Florence Le Cam (Pereira and Le Cam 2017). In the interviews, the same poles of dissemination of practices considered innovative were mentioned: *The New York Times*, *The Guardian*, some bloggers, possibly the discussions proposed by the *Online News Association*.

In a way, journalists are aware that they are reproducing, with a certain delay and fewer resources, something that has been designed elsewhere:

> "We had an eye on what was happening in the United States, Japan, *The Guardian*, *The New York Times*, etc. Even for the design we were inspired. But we always had a quest for legitimacy, people didn't have to say 'yeah, it's the Web'. Today, I still monitor it; for example, I keep an eye on *The New York Times,* which made a video using the suggestions people sent it on Facebook and I found that it was a perfect narrative mode. I would do the same if I still had a site" (F5).

> "I have the impression that we are late, that we are having trouble, that there are obstacles in people's lives. The editor often goes to other media, *The New York Times*, but we're late. Besides, we're not a national, we have to get people interested. There are economic constraints" (F7).

Finally, this finding suggests that the modalities for the circulation of innovation discourse come from English-speaking countries, particularly the United States, to different national contexts (here, France and Canada) without necessarily going through other mediation bodies – for example, a circulation within the same linguistic community as I had initially assumed.

3.4. Conclusion

In this study, I analyzed the extent to which digital discourse has been reflected in the stories that French and French-speaking Canadian journalists tell about their careers. Based on in-depth interviews with journalists, I sought to discuss how the ideology around digital innovation circulates among respondents. Finally, I noted a variation in the profiles of journalists.

Some respondents adopted enthusiastic positions towards digital technology, and others stated mistrust, or even resistance, with regard to the introduction of innovations in journalistic practices. From the point of view of professional sociology, the status of "digital journalism" itself therefore refers to very diverse professional segments, which also present significant variations in ideologies, practices and career plans.

In the current state of this research, it is still very difficult to find significant differences in the way journalists in the two national contexts studied appropriate digital discourse. The similarities found from this research seem to be more related to the innovation discourses produced from the United States and Great Britain than to a logic of circulation within a linguistic media space, which here would be a "francophone" one. This research must therefore continue by carrying out more specific work contextualizing the careers studied and the use of other empirical data, which will allow progress in the construction of a methodological design closer to a transnational comparison program.

3.5. References

Becker, H.S. (2009). *Outsiders. Estudos de Sociologia do Desvio*. Zahar, Rio de Janeiro.

Bucher, R. and Strauss, A. (1961). Professions in process. *American Journal of Sociology*, 66(4), 325–334.

Charron, J. and De Bonville, J. (2004). Le journalisme et le marché : de la concurrence à l'hyperconcurrence. In *Nature et Transformation du Journalisme. Théorie et Recherches Empiriques*, Brin, C., Charron, J., and De Bonville, J. (eds). Les Presses de l'Université Laval, Quebec, 273–316.

Deslauriers, J.-P. and Kérisit, M. (2008). O delineamento de pesquisa qualitativa. In *A pesquisa qualitativa: enfoques epistemológicos e metodológicos*. Poupart, J., Deslauriers, J.-P., Mayer, R., and Pires, A.P. (eds). Vozes, Petrópolis, 127–153.

Deuze, M. (2005). What is journalism? Professional identity and ideology of journalists reconsidered. *Journalism*, 6(4), 442–464.

Hanitzsch, T. (2007). Deconstructing journalism culture: Toward a universal theory. *Communication Theory*, 17(4), 367–385.

Hennion, A. (2004). Une sociologie des attachements. D'une sociologie de la culture à une pragmatique de l'amateur. *Sociétés*, 85(3), 9–24.

Le Cam, F. (2012). Une identité transnationale des journalistes en ligne ? In *Journalisme en ligne. Pratiques et recherches*, Degand, A. and Grevisse, B. (eds). De Boeck, Brussels, 61–86.

Observatoire des métiers de la presse (2018). *L'espace data* [Online]. Available at: https://data.metiers-presse.org/.

Pereira, F.H. and Le Cam, F. (2017). Rhetoric of Changes: The International Circulation of Discourse about Online Journalism. In *IAMCR Conference 2017*. IAMCR, Cartagena, Colombia.

Skelton, C. (2018). There are fewer journalists in Canada than 15 years ago – but not as few as you might think. *J-Source – The Canadian Journalism Project* [Online]. Available at: http://j-source.ca/article/canadian-journalists-statistics/.

Strauss, A.L. (1992). *Miroirs et masques : une introduction à l'interactionnisme*. Métailié, Paris.

Traquina, N. (2005). *Teorias do Jornalismo: A tribo jornalística – uma comunidade interpretativa transnacional*, 2. Insular, Florianópolis.

4

Virtual Reality and Alternative Facts: The Subjective Realities of Digital Communities

In 2014, an unusual event occurred in the high-tech world: the Facebook Corporation acquired Oculus VR, which is the flagship of the emerging domestic virtual reality industry. The question on everyone's lips was the following: "What interest could a digital social media company have in virtual reality headsets?"

By dissecting this unusual marriage, I will attempt to bring together two phenomena at the forefront of communication studies: the democratization of virtual reality technologies – which offer a subjective, interactive, immersive and explicitly fictitious experience – and the acknowledgment of the significant influence fake content exerts on society via digital social media.

In making this comparison, the following question arises: how does the anticipated convergence of digital social media with virtual reality platforms have the potential to undermine the credibility of content in the digital social space, specifically in a context of proliferating misinformation?

4.1. Social media and alternative facts

First, it is necessary to look at the role of digital social media. It has been shown that a significant share of the population receives most of its information from this type of media. A 2016 study by Gottfried and Shearer put the figure at 62% of American adults (cited in Allcott and Gentzkow 2017). Although there is a

---

Chapter written by Louis-Philippe RONDEAU.

temptation to discredit the newsfeed as a mere source of entertainment, it might nevertheless play an important role: digital social media may be the reification of an orality that is marginalized in a digital world, an orality that is "the base of all human experience" (Lance Strate, cited in Wright 2007).

Our reliance on digital social media is not without consequence. Like any technology, these platforms are not neutral, quite the contrary: thanks to algorithms, they highlight some publications and hide others – a process known as *curating* (Van Buskirk 2010). Although often translated in French as *conservation*, curation differs from aggregation in that it involves an active role in the selection and promotion of content (Van Buskirk 2010). In doing so, content challenging the reader's pre-existing ideologies does not penetrate this filter, and the network gradually becomes homophilous, i.e. it forms a self-realizing system, where normative thinking is encouraged while discouraging dissenting ideas (Mihailidis and Viotty 2017). However, the shortcomings of these algorithms have been ostensibly revealed since the spread of "fake news" during the last American presidential elections. The repercussions of these events are still being felt, as is illustrated by the Cambridge Analytica case. The public's tendency to reject any information that violates their preconceptions has been crystallized in the now famous "alternative facts" phrase, coined by Kellyanne Conway, advisor to President Trump. This "echo chamber" phenomenon not only erodes public confidence in traditional media, but also exposes the lack of judgment exercised by users in regard to content conveyed on the Web (Allcott and Gentzkow 2017).

4.2. VR: a surrogate reality

In parallel, we are currently witnessing the advent of virtual reality (VR) devices on the domestic market. These devices generally consist of a headset worn by the user, often connected to a computer by cables. Stereoscopic images are displayed according to the orientation of the user's head and ideally its position. The device is equipped with headphones for spatialized sound. More advanced platforms also include hand controllers to manipulate objects and provide an interface with the content.

When new media emerges, so-called "prophetic" discourses tend to accompany technical developments: benefits are readily bestowed upon these technologies. In the case of VR, these include the treatment of psychological afflictions (such as phobias) (Carlin *et al.* 1997), analgesia (virtual reality is used to divert patients' attention during dressing changes) (van Twillert, Bremmer and Faber 2007) and the alleviation of post-traumatic stress (veterans are virtually exposed to stressful situations to help them better manage them) (Robertson and Zelenko 2014).

According to its "evangelists", while posturing as a replacement for reality, virtual reality has the potential to simulate any human experience in a logic of *transparency* of mediation, i.e. where the medium seeks to eclipse itself. Interestingly, however, the two objects that stir our interest (the Facebook platform and virtual reality) are at opposite ends of the mediation spectrum. In their book *Remediation*, Bolter and Grusin (2000) contrast what they call *hypermediacy* with *transparent immediacy*.

On the hypermedia side, mediation is ostentatious; the medium openly displays what it is composed of: "Its raw ingredients are images, sound, text, animation and video, which can be brought together in any combination" (Bolter and Grusin 2000, p. 31). The interface invites the user to interact with the content. The Facebook platform fits strongly into this camp. On the side of transparent immediacy, the traces of mediation fade, content merges with reality, and the temporal discordance with the medium disappears in the present moment:

> "The user will move through the space, interacting with the objects 'naturally,' as she does in the physical world. [...] In this sense, a transparent interface would be one that erases itself, so that the user is no longer aware of confronting a medium, but instead stands in an immediate relationship with the contents of that medium" (pp. 23–24).

In the latter case, all traces of interface are hidden from the eyes of the interactor: it is an interface without interfaces.

When researching immersive devices, the term *sense of presence* is put forth, which, according to Lombard and Ditton (1997), is an "illusion that a mediated experience is not mediated".

The efforts surrounding virtual reality have gravitated around this *modus operandi*, as VR has once again aroused the fantasy of conquering our senses with an imperceptible technology. However, this type of discourse stirs up strong reactions, firstly because of the disconnectedness between the enthusiasm of this claim and the current state of technology: requiring users to wear a bulky device and hand prostheses is anything but transparent. Secondly, virtual reality is disturbing because it evokes the menace of alienation and perversion: as life is full of pitfalls and doubts, wouldn't it be comforting to take refuge in a complacent reality, however illusory it may be? A superficial glance at the way in which virtual reality is presented in works of fiction immediately reveals these recurring concerns[1].

---

1 From William Gibson's *Neuromancer* (1984) to Ernest Cline's *Ready Player One* (2011), to Brett Leonard's *The Lawnmower Man* (1992), virtual reality is often portrayed in an alarmist way in popular fictional media. Alienation and depravity are recurring themes.

Among the so-called "apocalyptic" discourses accompanying this technology, there is the issue of perversion: one might fear that individuals might appropriate this technology for perverse purposes, such as pornography. However, let us not delude ourselves, virtual pornography already exists, as it does in all media[2]. Paradoxically, what might prevail in a VR sexual experience is a sense of co-presence and intimacy, not the voyeurism generally prevalent in the genre (Rubin 2015). Could we hope that virtual reality will succeed in humanizing this domain?

In addition to the pitfalls of alienation and perversion, there are also challenges of a completely different kind: the perception that virtual reality has the potential to subordinate, or even render obsolete, all other media. By pretending to substitute itself for reality, it thereby emulates our experience of interacting with these media, at least from a phenomenological point of view. If we adhere to the McLuhanian notion that "the content of a medium is always another medium" (McLuhan 1964, p. 23), the re-emergence of virtual reality would be the quintessential example of media cannibalization, the "new" medium monopolizing and obscuring previous media to the point of making them obsolete. However, this type of thinking is reductive, as existing media do not cease to exist when a new one emerges. This logic of cannibalization would be best described by a process of *remediation*, a phenomenon in which traditional media are constantly being taken over and transformed by new ones – in an ostentatious or transparent manner[3] – which is according to Bolter and Grusin (2000) "a defining characteristic of the new digital media"[4] (p. 45).

The idea of a totalizing meta-medium that would encompass all others has already been brought up: this is the *"Black Box Fallacy"*, which assumes that the *terminus ad quem* of media devices is a convergence towards a single omnipotent device, the aforementioned black box[5] (Jenkins 2008). This type of reflection is simplistic: it instrumentalizes the processes of convergence, postulates that

---

2 The saying goes: pornography determines the viability of a medium. Peter Johnson (1996) argues further: "Throughout the history of new media, from vernacular speech to movable type, to photography, to paperback books to videotape to cable and pay-TV to '900' phone lines to the French Minitel, to the Internet to CD-ROMs and laser discs, pornography has shown technology the way" (p. 217).

3 Virtual movie theater simulators already exist. This is an example of what Bolter and Grusin (2000) call "visible remediation", since the assemblage of new and old media is perceptible: "The work becomes a mosaic in which we are simultaneously aware of the individual pieces and their new, inappropriate setting" (p. 47).

4 There are already virtual cinema simulators available. This is an example of what Bolter and Grusin (2000) call "visible remediation", since the assembly between the new and old media is perceptible: "The work becomes a mosaic in which we are simultaneously aware of the individual pieces and their new, inappropriate setting" (p. 47).

5 Whether it is with smart TV, smart phones or virtual reality, this type of discourse tends to resurface when new media technologies arise.

technology prevails over culture and demonstrates technical determinism. Quite the contrary, the current trend is moving towards multiple screens and platforms. We are, however, witnessing a convergence in terms of *content*.

In addition to these recurring concerns, the one that I find most unsettling is the potential for the emergence of a hegemonic medium, where both the platform and the conveyed content would be controlled by a technological elite. Indeed, if virtual reality were to reach the status of a mass medium while realizing its potential to falsify reality, those who hold the reins of content would once again have the power to determine what the user perceives to be *his or her* reality. Through curation, the corporations holding these platforms would be able to *prescribe* a reality, even though it is patently fake.

In this most fantastical implementation, virtual reality would constitute the ultimate example of what Baudrillard (1976) calls a "third order simulacrum", i.e. a device where what is represented no longer has any basis in reality, a total mirage in itself[6]. In 1936, concerned about the issues of his time, Walter Benjamin (2009) warned us of the influence of mass media, which had previously pushed people to extremes such as fascism. By merging a mass medium with a simulacrum conveyed through a totalizing sensory device, one would then have immense propaganda power.

4.3. Convergence of social and virtual realities

These hypothetical issues took a concrete step forward in 2014, when Facebook acquired Oculus VR, a small company that instigated the contemporary interest for virtual reality, mentioned above. When it was introduced, its headset – called *Oculus Rift* – conjured the dream of a democratic and accessible virtual reality. However, the return to reality was painful: the founding myth suddenly collapsed, carried away by the realities of the market. At the time of this acquisition, a certain skepticism was expressed within the community: what motivations could justify such a convergence?

If we refer to the writings of game studies professor Edward Castronova (2005), this kind of merger is not absurd. On the contrary, online meeting places can indeed constitute a contemporary form of virtual reality. However, these are not *sensory* realities, but rather *communitarian* ones. Castronova bases this observation on

---

6 The three orders of Jean Baudrillard's simulacrum (1976) are as follows: the first order, where the image represented is a faithful copy of the original; the second order is a perverse or manipulated copy of its referent; and the third order is no longer a reproduction. The image is synthesized from scratch, i.e. the link with its referent is broken.

multiplayer online games which, in the eyes of their users, form in effect a reality: "Community does not generate the illusion of a reality, it confirms a reality that is actually there" (p. 292). In a logic of transparency, blurring the interface of a hypermedia device would make it possible to amplify the feeling of presence and belonging to the community. This convergence between social and affect is also part of a trend towards the *gamification* of the social universe, a practice in which gaming processes are transferred to non-game contexts to encourage user engagement and make an experience rewarding (Deterding *et al.* 2011). It has even been argued that beyond a virtual community, digital social networks such as Facebook and Twitter are actually online multiplayer games, where the goal is to acquire as many "likes" or followers as possible (Brooker 2013).

As for determining whether or not it is absurd to abandon oneself in "realities" detached from the real, one can look at the writings of William James (1950), who does not seem overly concerned: "Reality simply means relation to our emotional and active life [...] whatever excites and stimulates our interest is real" (p. 295); the only reality that matters is the one that currently piques our attention, regardless of whether it is "inherited or synthetic", to quote Castronova (2005, p. 294).

4.4. Virtual reality as a vector of empathy

While digital social media confines us to homophilous content, many have, on the contrary, highlighted the potential of virtual reality as a catalyst for empathy, since it has the ability to immerse us in the universe of another. For example, in the 360-degree documentary *Clouds Over Sidra* (Gabo Arora and Chris Milk 2015), we are immersed in the daily life of Sidra, a 12-year-old girl who describes life in her daily environment: the Za'atri refugee camp in Jordan. In a series of crossfades, we are teleported across her universe. Unpretentious, this work brings to life in a few minutes – and in a much more immediate way – what prose would take several pages to evoke.

In parallel, installations designed specifically for virtual reality offer the possibility of letting oneself be taken by sensations unexplored by other media. Foremost, there is the feeling of otherness, an impression of living someone else's subjective experience, of putting yourself in their skin. In their interactive work *The Machine to Be Another*, the BeAnotherLab collective proposes to experience the opposite sex. In an installation context, a man and a woman are each equipped with a virtual reality headset adorned with a camera, and the image from one's point of view is presented to the other. The result is a performative and collaborative work, where both participants commit to moving in a synchronized and consensual way, negotiating each movement with the tacit agreement of the other (BeAnotherLab 2014).

In order to denounce the inhumanity of prison isolation imposed on 100,000 American prisoners, the British newspaper *The Guardian* created *6 x 9: A Virtual Experience of Solitary Confinement*, where people are virtually subjected to the anxiety of being sequestered in a cell. The experiment attempts to simulate the nightmare of the prolonged absence of stimuli through an increase in visual and auditory torment and – according to its authors – points towards a new form of militant journalism (*The Guardian* 2016).

These works take advantage of the intrinsic affinities of virtual reality, i.e. its ability to substitute our subjective experience with an altered version of it or even a completely synthetic reality. In doing so, it confronts us with ourselves and our relationship to reality. Whether through feelings of presence (where we share the world of the other), of agency (where we act on the world of the other) or of otherness (where we take the body of the other), virtual reality allows us to be witnesses by proxy in a subjective and holistic way.

4.5. Conclusion

What about Facebook's VR efforts since the acquisition of Oculus VR? In 2017, the company introduced a new beta application called *Facebook Spaces*, which partly distills Facebook's experience within virtual reality. It is a three-dimensional environment where you can join your friends (by invitation only) – or rather avatars representing your friends. We find a subset of the tools already present on the platform: virtual panels that float in space featuring messaging, videos and photos, which can be manipulated. In addition, a marker allows you to make doodles (and attach them to other avatars); you can even use a virtual selfie stick to capture the moment (Rubin 2017). The impression one gets from the current implementation of social virtual reality is that it is singularly *benign*. However, we could not have predicted the extent of the current fake news crisis based on Facebook's initial implementation. It would be wise to reassess the situation once a less innocuous product is released to the general public.

As to whether we should be wary of the convergence between social and immersive media, the question remains open. On the one hand, I have tried to demonstrate that establishing a real/virtual dichotomy is superfluous. From the user's point of view, the perceived facticity of this reality is not a relevant issue. On the other hand, the fake news phenomenon is not exclusive to digital social media, although social media – because of its absence of safeguards – facilitates its propagation and can even create a contagion effect, thanks to curation algorithms. In order to avoid excesses, governing bodies' temptation might be to institute censorship from the outset. However, to nip it in the bud, a medium that offers significantly different emotional experiences from its predecessors would be counterproductive. A solution that would be more beneficial in the long term would be to educate users in media literacy, by promoting coexistence with a shared objective of mutual wellbeing[7], potentially facilitated by the unique sense of presence that virtual reality provides.

4.6. References

Allcott, H. and Gentzkow, M. (2017). Social media and fake news in the 2016 election. *Journal of Economic Perspectives*, 31(2), 211–236.

Baudrillard, J. (1976). *L'échange symbolique et la mort.* Gallimard, Paris.

BeAnotherLab (2014). The machine to be another: Art investigation using embodiment and performances. *BeAnotherLab* [Online]. Available at: http://www.themachinetobeanother. org/.

Benjamin, W. (2009). *L'œuvre d'art à l'époque de sa reproductibilité technique.* Folio, Paris.

Bolter, J.D. and Grusin, D. (2000). *Remediation: Understanding New Media.* MIT Press, Cambridge.

Brooker, C. and Campbell, A. (2013). *How Videogames Changed the World* [video recording]. Endemol UK, London.

Carlin, A.S., Hoffman, H.G., and Weghorst, S. (1997). Virtual reality and tactile augmentation in the treatment of spider phobia: A case report. *Behaviour Research and Therapy*, 35(2), 153–158.

Castronova, E. (2005). *Synthetic Worlds: The Business and Culture of Online Games.* The University of Chicago Press, Chicago.

Deterding *et al.* (2011). From game design elements to gamefulness: Defining "gamification". In *Proceedings of the 15th International Academic MindTrek Conference: Envisioning Future Media Environments.* Association for Computing Machinery, Tampere, 9–15.

James, W. (1950). *The Principles of Psychology: In Two Volumes,* 2. Dover Publications, New York.

Jenkins, H. (2008). *Convergence Culture: Where Old and New Media Collide.* New York University Press, New York.

Johnson, P. (1996). Pornography drives technology: Why not to censor the Internet. *Federal Communications Law Journal*, 49(1), 217–226.

---

7 Mihailidis and Viotty (2017) offer a few suggestions: going beyond fostering critical thinking with regard to media, they propose cultivating rational discourses within a spirit of civic-mindedness.

Lombard, M. and Ditton, T. (1997). At the heart of it all: The concept of presence. *Journal of Computer-Mediated Communication*, 3(2) [Online]. Available at: https://academic.oup. com/jcmc/article/3/2/JCMC321/4080403.

McLuhan, M. (1964). *Understanding Media: The Extensions of Man*. McGraw-Hill, New York.

Mihailidis, P. and Viotty, S. (2017). Spreadable spectacle in digital culture: Civic expression, fake news, and the role of media literacies in "post-fact" society. *American Behavioral Scientist*, 61(4), 441–454.

Robertson, A. and Zelenko, M. (2014). Voices from a virtual past: An oral history of a technology whose time has come again. *The Verge* [Online]. Available at: http://www. theverge.com/a/virtual-reality/oral_history.

Rubin, P. (2015). Pornocopia: The immersive future of virtual sex. *Wired*, 23(3), 90–93.

Rubin, P. (2017). Facebook's bizarre VR App is exactly why Zuck bought Oculus. *Wired* [Online]. Available at: https://www.wired.com/2017/04/facebook-spaces-vr-for-your-friends/.

The Guardian (2016). 6x9: A virtual experience of solitary confinement. *theguardian. com* [Online]. Available at: https://www.theguardian.com/world/ng-interactive/2016/apr/ 27/6x9-a-virtual-experience-of-solitary-confinement.

Van Buskirk, E. (2010). Overwhelmed? Welcome the age of curation. *Wired* [Online]. Available at: https://www.wired.com/2010/05/feeling-overwhelmed-welcome-the-age-of-curation/.

Van Twillert, B., Bremmer, M., and Faber, A.W. (2007). Computer-generated virtual reality to control pain and anxiety in pediatric and adult burn patients during wound dressing changes. *Journal of Burn Care & Research*, 28(5), 694–702.

Wright, A. (2007). Friending, ancient or otherwise. *The New York Times* [Online]. Available at: http://www.nytimes.com/2007/12/02/weekinreview/02wright.html.

5

Professional Structuring of Political Content Creators on YouTube

In studies on so-called "traditional" media, such as radio and television, the structuring of speech and production spaces is no longer really called into question. This media structure obviously requires access to the media. Speech is precious, and one must be able to make a career within this field (Bourdieu 1996) to hope to express oneself. The individuals who develop in this field are professionals who respond to structured logics. With the arrival of the Web, the discourses that placed this new medium in opposition to traditional media structures began multiplying. The Internet was becoming a space of freedom, without constraint, a new Eden, more democratic, more creative and not governed by economic returns. These discourses have been disseminated since the very creation of the Internet, and then on the various social networks and other platforms (Cardon 2010). The most extreme political discourses have also found a space on the Internet where people can express themselves more freely. These Web players have become increasingly structured in their environment, but have also continued to develop economically and professionally. Articles and symposia then began to emerge on the subject of the effects of these new practices on the media and political fields, focusing on how newspapers and politicians adapt to these new tools (Anduiza *et al.* 2010; Dias da Silva 2015; Eyries 2018). Other approaches, notably through the prism of amateurs, or "ordinary" creators (Babeau 2014), provide interesting points of view that help us understand the changes in this environment. However, the scientific literature on new professional activists is rare, due to the novelty of this phenomenon and the difficulty for the researcher to access this particularly closed field. The observation of the Web therefore seems to be carried out by analyzing, in particular, the content rather than the creators themselves (Devars 2017).

Chapter written by Alexis CLOT.

The purpose of this chapter is to show that the emergence of these new digital players can be analyzed by focusing on the trajectories of the players, by concentrating on economic models and, more broadly, by looking at different strategies of capital accumulation. Behind the political content published every day are individuals who are subjected to logics that structure their activities. By reaching out to those who produce political speeches online, we can try to show that the Web is a structured space where new professional groups are born and evolve through the re-appropriation of the codes of the digital age, as well as the codes of more traditional fields of information, communication and politics.

This chapter also aims to highlight participant observation as a relevant approach for analyzing groups whose main activity is carried out on the Web, since this allows the possibility of gathering valuable information while moving away from the discourses that are produced by these groups, and in a way, naturalized. A field approach does not exclude content analysis, but, just as in media research, it seems necessary to include Web content in logic of production and moments of work. However, we were able to share these moments with French video activists as part of filming a documentary[1]. The video activists who we studied are linked not only by the themes they defend – ecology, solidarity and social progress – but also by the concrete existence of an organized group of meetings and exchanges among these committed individuals. Each person we met provided us with a contact to meet a new person. The choice of interviews was therefore made as we entered the field. However, among the videographers we met, there is a low representation of women and visible minorities, which testifies above all to the re-production of the gendered patterns that can exist when talking about politics on the Internet.

Through this field analysis, the goal is to perceive how video activists define themselves by creating a hybrid professional group. Here, "hybrid" is used in the sense of borrowing from different environments and different practices. This question constitutes the main purpose of this research, which has the objective of going beyond the cannibalistic vision that imagines the arrival of the Internet as a new uniform actor that crushes the old media, or, on the contrary, a mere technological adaptation of what was done before. In this chapter, we will therefore address several points that seem useful to address through the information obtained from a participatory observation.

First, we will see how these video activists deal with their relationship to politics and how they act politically. Second, we will deal with the complex mistrust and interdependence link that they maintain with the media, the same field with which they manage to define themselves as a professional collective.

---

1 Documentary on committed Web actors.

5.1. Being political on the Internet

It is not easy to characterize the political role these individuals play in the political arena. They operate in this field as "politically active agents" (Weber 1995), but are not political representatives. We will mainly see how videographers try to define themselves while remaining cautious about their identification as activists. Nor should they be conceived solely as such, but rather as being at the crossroads between activists and political representatives. Their position as relayers of opinions, as well as their economic model, put them in a position that goes beyond that of the activist. It is this ambiguity that we will explore further by looking at how one should be political and how to "do politics" on the Internet.

5.1.1. Algorithms and buzz

The political issue on the Internet has been studied extensively, particularly with regard to the expression of extreme positions and abuses of popular forums. Such cases have fascinated the media and interested researchers (Badouard 2017). The extreme right therefore very quickly found itself ahead on the Internet, on blogs and then on YouTube, with the figure of Alain Soral[2] being the perfect representation of this phenomenon. This is also due to the rapid arrival of alternative environments to freer speech, to the "counter-cultural spirit" (Cardon 2010) of the Web. Moreover, by analyzing the commercial logics that drive the Web and digital social networks, we can see that algorithms have tended to favor the content that generates enthusiasm, reactions and therefore, by extension, divisions. As a result, we may have been led to think that this way of doing online politics is inherent to the Web and that it is one of its characteristics. However, we propose to add further nuances to this vision in order to complete it. Of course, there are certain ways to make more people click on your content, by working with short incisive formats and creating content made to provoke a reaction, a *buzz*. Among the videographers we met, some of them follow this "barometer" logic and, even though the viewers do not agree with the proposed content, the traffic is still good because "it still makes for a flow on the channel" (Interview 1, 2018).

5.1.2. Moderation and openness

However, it seems wrong to say that video activists radicalize their discourse and make it more extreme to attract more people. The counter-hegemonic

---

2 Alain Soral is a well-known figure on the French far right. A former member of the National Front team, close to the comedian Dieudonné, he was particularly active on YouTube.

strategy does exist, but it is also accompanied by a logic of openness. It exists by opposing what exists – in this case, "old politics" party politics – as well as by regrouping as many themes as possible, hybridizing practices and seeking audiences, even if it leads to self-censorship. The places they frequently visit, such as the Huma festival and the Alternatiba villages, are political places. They talk about politics, they act politically, and they are radical in the sense of the total continuity of the idea toward action. Online, this radicality, this tone of freedom, cannot always be maintained. Content is often written by several people, with cooperation between three categories of professionals: producers, writers and journalists. Then follows a period of shooting and, finally, a moment of editing where the YouTube format and the humorous impact are just as important as the message. This process can then lead to a selection that causes self-censorship effects. This process is ultimately similar to a much more traditional political communication exercise, where radicalness is above all the result of a reflection in terms of impact. Since videos are also a moment of communication around one's own "brand", by highlighting the codes of the channel or the character, there are choices to be made that are not always based on political will.

Nevertheless, in more private moments outside the cameras and viewers, the speeches refer to more concrete and easily identifiable activist imaginations. To illustrate this, we can take several examples from our respondents. The vegan issue is a good illustration. One of our respondents is vegan and does not hesitate to show this during meetings. He speaks freely about it, and does so with a clear activist perspective. Although he made a video on the topic of animals, the videographer in question hesitated and finally decided to not add the slogan "go vegan" at the end of the video in order not to block the audience and to reach as many people as possible. Another example is that we selected a moment during the 2017 French presidential campaign. The issue here revolves around whether or not to say publicly who to vote for during the presidential election, whether or not to give a voting instruction to one's community. We then found videographers who have done so openly on their channel. In several conversations, without necessarily addressing the theme, several videographers told us about this voting instruction. In general, this approach is considered to be significantly risky, as it may not appeal to spectators who do not vote for the same candidate. Offline, this modesty is much less present and there is no risk of talking openly about the political game. Finally, we can also mention the fact that several respondents told us about different video topics being "niches to reach" to help their community grow, because the challenge around these practices is also to increase the communities, the number of subscribers and the number of "likes".

We therefore find ourselves with a political practice aimed at increasing visibility, by showing ourselves with guests, by working on several fronts and several themes and by trying as much as possible to open up. We could then make a comparison with different typologies of political parties. Without necessarily going towards the logic of a "catch-all party" entirely (Krichheimer 1996), we can still distinguish a logic of openness and of community growth despite, sometimes, purely activist logics. If the most extreme videographers are successful, it is because their discourse adapts well to the logic of the Web and their audience and unable to fit into similar discourses elsewhere, have ended up online. Yet, we see that political discourse can also be moderated to retain an audience from diverse backgrounds and to build a larger and less politicized community.

5.1.3. *To take on or not to take on politics*

In these videos, pedagogy is an essential element and is particularly pursued. During the interviews, there were numerous references to non-politicized television extensions. They therefore compare themselves to the far left "Fred and Jamy"[3] (Interviews 1 and 2, 2018). This genre mixing clearly shows the special relationship that these activist videographers have with politics. Their aim is to transmit knowledge and have an educational role, while talking about politics. Their relationship to policy may therefore not be presented as such. The result is a hybridization between the political and educational worlds, where the goal is to "make people laugh and think" (Interview 3, 2018): "the most important thing is to awaken people" (Interview 4, 2018), "if they ask themselves questions, then it is successful" (Interview 5, 2018).

During Frames festival, which brings Web creators (notably videographers), together every year in Avignon in the south of France, the idea of the teacher emerges. Political themes become a pretext for education. If this logic is reflected in each of our respondents, we should not imagine that all these individuals share the same relationship to politics. What we can see is that there is a real continuity between their offline political socialization and their online content and formats. The results of our study show that the more traditional the profile of an activist is, the less refined the format will be, with very little editing and visual work, and will resemble political speeches. On the contrary, video activists who come from a more artistic background, for example, will take on this political dimension much less and prefer to use different forms by mixing politics with humor, art, special characters and personal development.

---

3 Fred and Jamy are the presenters of a popular science TV show, *C'est pas sorcier* (meaning roughly "It's not rocket science"), broadcast on the French public service between 1993 and 2014.

During our interviews and meetings, we were able to see conflicts within the same group of videographers about whether or not to accept the term *activism* to talk about their program. Sometimes, there has even been an aversion to the use of these terms by explaining that "it's not committed, it's just normal, y'know, it's what we think" (Interview 6, 2018). We have also observed mistrust of the political world as it is and against which they define themselves in oppositional terms. For some, the reasons for such content production are obviously political – "to oppose Alain Soral" (Interview 1, 2018), "having a transformative impact" (Interview 6, 2018) – while for less politicized videographers, the reason is more personal and refers to the non-political part of their profession: they want above all "to laugh stupidly at my rushes"[4] (Interview 6, 2018), in other words, the most important is the personal pleasure that watching the videos brings. This way of making engaging content without really taking responsibility for it as such also refers to a central point of how video activists can define their own profession: they challenge it in opposition to and in relation to existing logics.

5.2. New grammars and old practices

These video activists seek to reinvent old practices, making the new with the old. They show, in the way that they remain suspicious of politics, a desire to get rid of the current codes in the political field so that they can impose their own politics. It is not a question of denying everything and starting from scratch, but rather of creating hybrid content with blurred boundaries. Here, we are interested in the continuity of media practices in the professional experience of these new actors. The aim is to show how video activists do not break with older media and political practices, but, on the contrary, how they use them to be part of a direct connection to better develop the environment from the inside.

5.2.1. *Doing politics differently (Interview 7, 2018)*

Each video activist approaches politics through a mix of genres and none necessarily claims the label "political", except in the case of videographers who have a more traditional relationship with activism. Here, politics is cultural, informational and humorous. The opinion leaders on these channels are also comedians, actors, writers or directors.

Politics is then mocked, caricatured. Politics is pointed out as an emanation of "them", while solutions come from "us", the people. Here, videographers differ from politicians physically and in their approach. In their videos, they are dressed in everyday clothes when they play their own roles. On the contrary, if they play another role, and particularly that of a politician or a powerful person, they will

---

4 Rushes are the raw, unedited footage shot whilst filming a video.

dress themselves up and carry external signs of wealth. They play politics and make a fool of them. Their vocabulary also differs with that of the political world. They all have distinctive elements that highlight the fact they do not come from the political world. This can therefore involve a mix of themes and formats, physical representation and discourse. Vincent, for example, always wears a cap in his videos to break with the image of politics. Ludo speaks with the language of the street. Professor Feuillage mixes ecology and cartoonish porn humor[5]. Usul also disguised himself as an editorial writer and then became "the man with the scarf", "the man with the pipe". He is now even trying to appear as a pornographic actor with his girlfriend[6], which in itself is a mixture of genres that totally supports the deconstruction of the myth of politics. Marion sums up this hybrid practice well during our interview, by explaining the strategic interest of this choice of a different political practice: "It was pointless to be an angry activist, it is much more useful to be an activist by making jokes" (Interview 7, 2018). This logic of modifying the practices of the political field by ridiculing the dominant codes is in a way found in the media field.

5.2.2. Journalists and videographers: "rival partners"?

This section borrows the same title as Legavre (2011) to show that while there is a very strong interdependence between the media and videographers, this relationship is not necessarily cordial. As with politics, videographers will also deconstruct and criticize the profession to define themselves as augmented journalists. This time, however, videographers and journalists are working together. The two worlds cooperate.

Many videographers have a professional relationship with the media. Their videos are produced by the media, purchased and broadcast. At the same time, video activists work on media, work with journalists or are intermittent editorialists.

5.2.2.1. A capital management system

The relationship between videographers and the media can be analyzed through the prism of a capital exchange. Videographers allow the media to renew their audience and, in this way, videographers act as the second stage of a two-tier communication (Katz and Lazarsfeld 1955). In the interest of videographers, there is, in cooperation with certain alternative media with similar ideological positioning, the possibility of attracting capital held by these same media.

---

5 Example of a video: "Professeur Feuillage. ARAL, TA MER EST TELLEMENT SÈCHE QU'ELLE MOUILLE DU SABLE", published on January 31, 2018 (https://www.youtube.com/watch?v=uajOhmmxYuc). The title translates as: "Aral, your sea is so dry, it wets the sand". This is a play on words. "mer" (sea) is a homonym of "mère" (mother).
6 See: Girard, Q. (2018). Olly Plum et Usul, jouir en ligne. *Libération.fr* [Online]. Available at: https://www.liberation.fr/france/2018/02/25/olly-plum-et-usul-jouir-en-ligne_1632239.

This capital is of various natures, but it is obviously economic capital in a large portion of the cases. The activity of videographers being very precarious, the financial support of media structures to produce content, as well as to have a salary, is not negligible.

By working with recognized institutions, videographers also reclaim symbolic capital that they lack as videographers. They do not yet have a recognized professional culture, unlike the media field, which has very strong representations. The videographers therefore constantly reminded us during the meetings that they work by cross-checking sources, like journalists, and that they collaborate with journalists. On the Tipeee funding platform, it is interesting to note that videographers are grouped into the "journalism" or "vlogging" categories, as the "political" category does not exist on the site. We see then that videographers do not have any mistrust towards the media as a matter of principle; on the contrary, they can be points of contact. However, one of the themes they address is very often media criticism.

5.2.2.2. *Collectively define standards*

By criticizing the media as they do, they are criticizing a certain vision of journalism, a corrupt journalism, dependent on economic and political powers. "A good journalist is an independent journalist" would be a bit like the adage they convey in their content, and also in their daily lives. On some Facebook groups of videographers, there are tips on whether or not to work with this or that media outlet and, if so, in exchange for what. The media they collaborate with most often have a strong political orientation, such as *Mediapart, Mr Mondialisation* or *Le Média*, all of which are independent French-language news sites. But even in these cases, negotiation and reflection are done collectively, and not without problems. On Facebook, in a private group designed to network videographers, members of associations and independent journalists, questions such as the following were asked[7]: "We are invited to be broadcast on *** (non-exclusive), on their 8 o'clock show, at least once a month (500 euros per video broadcast). We're hesitating: what do you think?". The answers were numerous and the testimonials leant towards negotiation: "if you are free and it can give you something, then go for it", "see what they want, but even the founders have left, *** can tell you better than I can, he left too", "despite their young age, they are part of the media elephants that will sink... Don't sink with them!".

This Facebook group also exists offline, with meetings every two months to create joint projects and facilitate professional projects. We therefore observe individuals who define themselves collectively and try to find professional solutions to their problems, but who, to do so, set the standards for what a good media professional should be. We find ourselves in a situation similar to what the *Syndicat*

---

7 The question and comments have been anonymized.

national du journalisme (the National syndicate for journalism) in France experienced, divided between a moral order and a union at the time of the structuring of the journalism profession (Dupuy 2014). This time, the profession of the communicator is also added to the discussions, which makes it possible to maintain one's own brand of new actors straddling activism and information.

The existence of such a collective, allowing, among other things, professional decision-making, is a sign of the emergence of a new group, an emergence in the sense that, until recently, they were only individuals working individually on a common platform. Recently, videographers have found themselves in physical places, getting to know each other better and better, creating interpersonal links, bonds of friendship and work. Until now, they existed and were defined by comparing themselves with the two fields closest to them, the journalistic field and the political field. Now it seems that they are beginning to think of themselves differently, creating common spaces, common stories and collective imaginations. We must now observe whether or not the field of media will eventually encompass this new activity by giving it the freedom to define itself and exist.

5.3. Conclusion

The lessons of this research lead us to emphasize the relevance of reflecting on challenges related to digital technology, while not forgetting to look at the structures that govern society, independently of digital technology. What we see with video activists is reflected in the broader history of the media. The group studied here is certainly a specific example, but shows that the Web is not only a space where every discourse must be hyper-polarized and that the new media actors do not create everything from scratch in the digital "world", but that they nevertheless invent new practices that have a certain continuity with the old ones. We can therefore succeed in making our idea of the Web professions a little more complex and take it beyond what is called "digital".

5.4. References

Anduiza, E., Gallego, A., and Cantijoch, M. (2010). WITP online political participation in Spain: The impact of traditional and internet resources. *Journal of Information Technology & Politics*, 7, 356–368.

Babeau, F. (2014). La participation politique des citoyens "ordinaires" sur l'Internet. La plateforme YouTube comme lieu d'observation. *Politiques de Communication*, 3, 125–150.

Badouard, R. (2017). *Le désenchantement de l'Internet : désinformation, rumeur et propagande*. FYP Éditions, Limoges.

Bourdieu, P. (1996). *Sur la télévision*. Raisons d'agir, Paris.

Cardon, D. (2010). *La démocratie internet*. Le Seuil, Paris.

Devars, T. (2017). Quand les youtubeurs investissent le champ politique. *Global, La Revue des industries créatives et des médias* [Online]. Available at: http://www.inaglobal.fr/numerique/article/quand-les-youtubeurs-investissent-le-champ-politique-9494.

Dias da Silva, P. (2015). La vidéo en ligne comme outil de communication politique en Europe. *Communication & Langages*, 183, 59–81.

Dupuy, C. (2014). Ordre ou syndicat ? Le Syndicat national des journalistes entre régulation corporatiste et défense du salariat. *Terrains & travaux*, 25(2), 113–129.

Eyries, A. (2018). La twitt-politique : l'élection présidentielle française de 2017 sur les réseaux socionumériques. *Pouvoirs*, 164(1), 87–97.

Katz, E. and Lazarsfeld, P. (1955). *Influence Personnelle*. Armand Colin, Paris.

Kirchheimer, O. (1996). The Transformation of the Western European Party System. In *Political Parties and Political Development*, La Palombara, J. and Weiner, M. (eds). Princeton University Press, Princeton, 177–200.

Legavre, J.-B. (2011). Entre conflit et coopération. Les journalistes et les communicants comme "associés rivaux". *Communication & langages*, 169, 105–23.

Weber, M. (1995). *Économie et société*. Plon, Paris.

6

When Vlogging Educates in Politics: The French Case of "Osons Causer"

At the dawn of the 21st Century, digital technology has become, according to some, a civilization (Doueihi 2011) and, according to others (Serres 2012), a civilizational mutation at least as important as the inventions of writing and printing. It changes the way we socialize, consume, engage in politics, teach, learn, love, honor the memory of our departed loved ones and, above all, communicate. Multimodal interactive platforms that allow the user to communicate in different modes (text, audio, video, graphics, etc.) are booming (Herring 2015), and new social practices combined with increased technical possibilities allow new forms of writing and publishing to emerge. YouTube, created in 2005, is one of the first multimodal interactive platforms. Today, more than 1.9 billion users connect each month and more than a billion hours of video are viewed daily[1]. In an initial analysis of different vlogs and an attempt to define them (Combe Celik 2014), I have observed that the title and framing of the video play an essential role in the overall staging, the opening and closing rituals have an important socio-affective role and serve to forge links with the recipients in order to encourage subscription to the channel, and, finally, I have seen the creation of a community of fans around the vlogger, and the theme he develops and deploys within the comments.

In this chapter, I am interested in a particular genre of vlog that deciphers politics. Indeed, on YouTube, Internet users grab political information and popularize it, thus paving the way for an alternative citizen form of political

Chapter written by Christelle COMBE.
1 Source: https://www.youtube.com/intl/fr/yt/about/press/.

educational journalism. My research objective is therefore twofold: on the one hand, I am looking to characterize the techno genre of "vlogging" as discourse, based on the theoretical framework developed by Paveau in 2017 for particularly analyzing digital discourse and to see, on the other hand, to what extent vlogging, in this particular case, makes a reconfiguration of political education and citizen debate possible between Internet users. After having presented the theoretical basis of this research as well as the methodological approach, I will present the analyses carried out.

6.1. Theoretical anchoring

The theoretical foundation of this research is in language sciences in the field of multimodal computer-mediated communication and the more recent field of digital discourse analysis.

6.1.1. Computer-mediated multimodal communication and digital discourse analysis

In language sciences, the filed of computer-mediated communication (CMO) has developed at the end of the 20th Century. The field has evolved in recent years with the advent of Web 2.0^2 towards what Herring (2015) calls "computer-mediated multimodal communication", which includes all online interactions, from video games to telepresence robots, and includes the object that interests me more particularly, namely multimodal interactive platforms. In order to study these platforms, I rely on recent insights from analysis of digital discourse, which studies the composite nature of techno-linguistic production in a connected digital ecosystem (Paveau 2017).

Discourse analysis traditionally gives "a key role to the types of discourses, which are not considered as types of texts from a taxonomic prospective, but as communication devices that are social and linguistic in nature" (Maingueneau 1995, p. 4). Among the defining constraints of a genre, the medium and modes of distribution play a fundamental role in its emergence and stabilization of and digital technology – and in particular Web 2.0 – promotes the emergence of new discursive genres (Barton and Lee 2013). Paveau (2017) refers to "techno-genre discourse" to designate discourses native to the Web "with a composite dimension, resulting from a co-constitution of the language and technology" (p. 300). In the case of the

---

2 By "Web 2.0" I mean the Web popularized in the early 2000s, which allows users to contribute content and interact more easily.

YouTube digital ecosystem, and more specifically the "vlogging" digital genre (Combe Celik 2014), it is a "prescribed techno-genre", still according to Paveau's typology (2017, p. 301). Therefore, i.e. it is strongly constrained by technological devices (the platform conditions online writing through the format it imposes) and it does not exist offline (vlogging is a genre native to the Web).

6.1.2. *Multimodal interactive platforms and participatory culture*

Multimodal interactive platforms are characterized by a convergence of communication modes (with text, graphics, audio, video, etc.) (Herring 2015) and a more accessible technology to users without computer skills. In particular, they make it easier to create content and also offer the possibility of sharing it more widely and instantly. On these platforms, a "participatory culture" is developing (Jenkins 2006), which can be defined as follows:

> "For the moment, let's define participatory culture as one: 1) with relatively low barriers to artistic expression and civic engagement; 2) with strong support for creating and sharing one's creations with others; 3) with some type of informal mentorship whereby that known by the most experienced is passed along to novices; 4) where members believe that their contributions matter; 5) where members feel some degree of social connection with one another (at the least they care what other people think about what they have created)" (Jenkins *et al.* 2006, p. 7).

On these sites reign amateurs whose practices revolutionize the way knowledge is produced, information is disseminated, works are created and activism is promoted. "Pro-am" (professionals–amateurs) are self-taught experts, citizen actors and creators in their own right (Flichy 2014). YouTube is one of the first multimodal interactive platforms, and it is also typically a site of participatory culture (Burgess and Green 2009). It should be noted that YouTube's operation rests on providing value to its parent company, Google, with all that it may imply. However, I will not make this my point in this article of the platform and that its owner is Google, with all that implies, but I will not make this my point. Rather, we will observe in this study, from a techno-semio-discursive point of view, how amateur Internet users grab political information and popularize it in vlogs with their audience, opening the way to the beginnings of an alternative citizen form of political educational journalism.

6.2. Purpose of the research and methodological approach

6.2.1. *The vlog "Osons Causer"*

The object of my research is the French YouTube channel "Osons Causer[3]" (roughly translated as "let's dare to speak"), enriched by the various media and other social networks that accompany it – namely a site[4], a Facebook page[5], a Twitter account[6] and a Tipee account[7]. Active since June 15, 2015, the channel "Osons Causer" defines its videos as "intellectual self-defense to understand the news, politics and the world". Hosted by three friends, the channel has 93 videos and more than 203,000 subscribers as of the day I write this chapter, probably more when it is read. Videos sometimes belong to headings, which are numbered by a hashtag: "blabla", "hot", "media chronicle" or "go further". Their duration varies from 1 minute 47 seconds to 38 minutes 6 seconds, and currently 62 videos are less than 10 minutes long. Their theme touches on major current political issues, generally French or European, such as "Macron candidate for finance?", "Privatized dams: the EU imposes them, only France submits", "Palm oil diesel, a disaster for the climate", etc.

6.2.2. *The methodological approach*

Studying native online discourse, "i.e. in a connected digital ecosystem" (Paveau 2015, p. 3), implies rejecting digital dualism and considering digital life to be part of our reality that requires a particular research posture. The data I studied are not strictly speaking "collected". On the contrary, they are observed *in situ*, a little like an ethnographer of the Web. Moreover, since these data are both massive and subject to rapid change, (Develotte 2012) in a qualitative, descriptive and comprehensive approach, I did not seek to be exhaustive, but rather to study a corpus, a sample, that I considered representative of the digital genre that I propose to characterize. It is therefore mainly the observation of the characteristic features of these new individual and social techno-semio-discursive forms that are emerging and spreading, or even becoming generalized, that I am interested in. My approach is qualitative, descriptive and comprehensive. For more details on the methodological approach to analyzing a multimodal interactive platform like YouTube, I refer the reader to Combe (2016).

---

3 https://www.youtube.com/channel/UCVeMw72tepFl1Zt5fvf9QKQ.
4 http://www.osonscauser.com.
5 http://www.facebook.com/osonscauser.
6 https://twitter.com/osonscauser.
7 http://bit.ly/tipeeeosonscauser.

6.3. Analyses

6.3.1. *Digital writing and building an ethos*

First of all, I focused on digital writing and the construction of ethos, in the sense that Amossy (2015) understands it, in a multimodal space. The writer is subject to the platform's architect (Jeanneret and Souchier 2005), and the multimodal staging is partly configured by the techno-genre discourse. Indeed, a videoblog is first characterized by a home page (Figure 6.1) that hosts a banner (1), the name of the channel (2) and a video tag (3), and then followed by the other videos. The "About" tab is a form of introduction, description of the string.

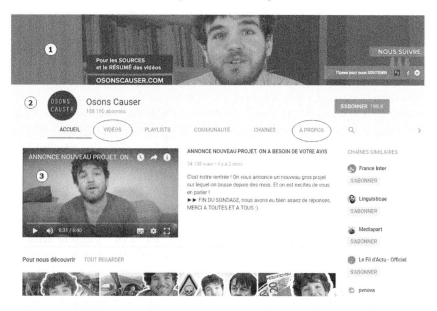

Figure 6.1. *Digital discourse on the home page of the "Osons Causer" blog*

It is through this staging, partly configured by the techno-semio-discursive device, that we observe the construction of the multimodal discursive ethos.

6.3.1.1. *From pseudonym to brand image*

One of the first elements of a YouTube channel is the pseudonym chosen by the author(s). *Pseudonymity* is the choice by an individual of a name other than his or her own and, on the Internet, it is *a priori* a matter of masking his or her official identity. However, pseudonyms are part of digital identity and perform two important functions of sociability in the digital context: identity and identification.

"Osons Causer" is the nickname of a team of three young men, Ludo, Xavier and Stéphane, students in human and social sciences (philosophy, sociology, psychology). Graphical and morphological features such as the imperative first-person form of the plural of "Osons Causer" mark a group and engaging authorship for the audience, associated with an injunction to speak out. We are faced here with a collective ethos that wants to constitute itself as a unified and active entity. The pseudonym that has become a slogan and logo – the graphic charter is the same for all digital spaces – is ultimately a form of self-registered trademark that is part of a self-promotion claimant. However, one speaker is predominant, Ludo (shown in Figure 6.1), who is the channel's real spokesperson, particularly within videos, which remain the central element of a YouTube channel.

6.3.1.2. Set design and ethos of a pro-am

The scenography of the video element is worked out with simplicity, the setting is always the same or almost the same: it is the intimacy of an apartment shared by the three young students, an informal space. As the videos progress, we observe the construction of a young ethos, between the student and the young person who is not yet completely active, with a relaxed, a familiar attitude and tone that gives a feeling of closeness to the audience that is *a priori* composite and with whom we must deal (they also propose two video formats, short and longer ones that explore certain issues). The choice is therefore made to build an ethos that is literally the opposite of what has become, in a way, the traditional media journalist.

The opening ritual is always the same: "Wesh wesh les amis", a formula derived from the young talk about the cities and which Ludo explains in video 24[8] "[FAQ #1] Osons Causer: un moment avec l'équipe – février 2016", video to answer his questions from the audience. That is how he greeted his family when he returned home, he says, and it is his way of getting into his listeners' homes. The closing ritual is also familiar: translated as "Hello, friends", "Goodbye, friends". The lexicon is chosen to be understandable, uncomplicated, and often Ludo expresses himself in a familiar register. The speech is therefore peppered with slang, but it is also well-documented. The texts are written, the videos are worked on and not improvised. The ethos that emerges is therefore that of simplicity mixed with competence, the ethos of the pro-am (professional–amateur) (Leadbeater and Miller 2004) who has succeeded in re-appropriating the spheres of social activity traditionally devoted to professionals, here politics, and who adresses an undefined audience, but which is intended to be as broad as possible: "It is essential to write for everyone, and this imperative requires both the choice of subjects and the way to treat them. When we write, we try to put ourselves in the shoes of those disgusted with politics, the disappointed of the left and the right, the border enthusiasts and the Europhiles", they say on their website.

---

8 https://youtu.be/ARtmmwrAH-c.

6.3.2. *Educating for politics: digital rhetoric and elements of didacticity*

As defined by Moirand (2002), *didacticity* is mobilized "to designate the didactic coloring of discourse whose social vocation is not fundamentally to transmit knowledge, and which is produced in situations that do not necessarily fall within the remit of social training and educational institutions" (p. 181). If we take the example of video 87 on the suspicions of cheating in Sarkozy's[9] election, we observe elements of didacticity at several levels (Figure 6.2).

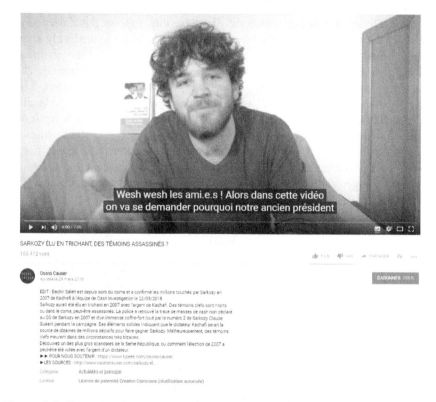

Figure 6.2. *Example of indirect questioning of the opening of the speech (video 87)*

First, the introduction of the carefully produced video, a real "hat" in journalistic terms, sets the subject of the video and serves as to catch the eye in the same way as the back cover of a thriller novel. The use of the conditional "Sarkozy would have been elected", and also the lexical field of the police type "money, key witnesses, dead or in a coma, murdered, police, trace, undeclared cash, HQ, huge safe, die, very

---

9 https://youtu.be/frPoD1717es.

strange circumstances", the questioning of the title "Sarkozy elected by cheating, murdered witnesses?" and the moments of suspense at the end of the introduction are all elements that encourage the audience to watch the video. A real *captatio benevolentiae* (capturing the good will of the audience at the beginning of a speech) is being set up.

There is also a staging with Arfi and Laske's book, *Avec les compliments du guide*, published in October 2017, on the secret history of Gaddafi and Sarkozy, the only element of the setting that appears discreetly in the background and helps to set the scene. Different elements within the discourse then support this didactic effect. The general question that is the subject of the video is asked immediately after the opening ritual: "In this video, we will ask ourselves why..." Like an informal teaching course, the speaker recalls the purpose of the upcoming speech. This is followed by many rhetorical questions, such as "Why is it said that touching Libyan money is a democratic scandal...", which are themselves followed by explanations. The speech is structured in several points that the speaker systematically reminds us: "So in this case, there are two important points: the first...". These discursive elements are highlighted and illustrated by numerous covert and iconic gestures (Cosnier and Develotte 2011) and Ludo can be attributed as being a true pedagogical actor in mimogestuality, in terms of how he can communicate through facial expressions and gestures (Figure 6.3) (Tellier 2016).

Figure 6.3. *Example of a co-verbal gesture to punctuate the speech (video 87)*

We note the work of pedagogical popularization through the use of a lexicon adapted to non-specialists in politics and media decoding, humorous elements "Fais pas bon être Monsieur Tune en Libye", "Don't be a good man, Mr. Money in Libya" hyperboles and repetitions. Finally, iconic and graphic elements are added, which illustrate, reinforce and support the explanation, as shown in Figure 6.4.

Figure 6.4. *Iconographic inlay indicating the source of the information (video 87)*

In particular, we observe here a form of intermediation, where the capture of a headline from a Swiss daily newspaper, *Le Matin*, is included in the video, accrediting the vlogger's statement by specifying the source.

Finally, didacticity is somehow claimed not only in the appropriateness of the channel, where it is a question of "explaining our world" or "understanding our societies", but also in the parent site which dedicates a whole page to the project "Pourquoi Osons Causer?" in a kind of committed and engaging manifesto:

"Osons Causer, it's a video blog that wants to reconcile us with politics.

Osons Causer is a video blog that seeks to put the public interest back at the center of political debates.

Osons Causer is a vlog with two types of current videos to reconcile us with politics by talking about the public interest.

Osons Causer is a benevolent and understanding vlog that wants to think like friends.

Osons Causer is a video blog that allows everyone to dare to talk, to dare to think and, finally, to dare to speak."[10]

---

10 http://osonscauser.com/le-projet/.

6.3.3. *Relationality of native digital discourse*

Linking with other Web discourse is one of the structural features of native digital speeches, particularly because of the hypertextual structure of the Web.

The networking of the discourse is mainly done through the different sites and parent networks with clickable buttons. The initial chain is associated with four other sites that the audience is strongly urged to follow: a Facebook page, a project explanation site, a Twitter account and a Tipee page for participatory financing (see Footnotes 1–5 and Figure 6.1).

Relationality is also intrinsic to the vlog, especially in the relationships that the vlogger maintains through the "like" or "dislike" buttons, or the comments with his or her audience.

Video number and title	Date	Duration	Like/Dislike	Comments
1. Pourquoi les arabes [*sic*] sont des voleurs (Why Arabs [*sic*] are thieves)	15-June-15	7:12	5 K/1 K	1 799
8. Médias : Pourquoi 10 milliardaires contrôlent notre information? (Media: Why do 10 billionaires control our information?)	17-Sept-15	27:58	12 K/629	2 103
15. Attentats de Paris : quel est le piège que nous tend Daesh? (Paris attacks: what is Daesh's trap for us?)	18-Nov-15	17:20	6 K/211	1 351
28. Nuit debout : analyse à chaud, décryptage et perspectives (The night standing: hot analysis, decoding and perspectives)	15-Apr-16	15:25	1 K/172	1 009
41. 10 faits qui montrent comment les multinationales achètent la politique européenne (10 facts that show how multinationals buy European policy)	29-Oct-16	23:55	7,1 K/195	1 151
43. Programme de Fillon : qui veut travailler plus pour gagner moins? (Fillon Program: who wants to work more to earn less?)	29-Nov-16	3:35	3,7 K/365	1 125
53. Emploi fictif : pourquoi cette affaire peut tuer Fillon? (Fictitious employment: why can this case kill Fillon?)	26-Jan-17	8:16	8,3 K/460	1 328

54. Fillon, nouvelles révélations : sa défense s'écroule, il doit partir ! (Fillon, new revelations: his defense is falling apart, he must leave!)	31-Jan-17	4:32	8,5 K/518	1 426
61. Hamon va-t-il faire gagner Macron? (Will Hamon make Macron win?)	30-March-17	5:18	5,1 K/430	1 034
65. Qui veut vraiment lutter contre l'évasion fiscale? (Who really wants to fight tax evasion?)	12-Apr-17	6:08	6,3 K/855	1 332
66. Si vous hésitez à voter Macron, regardez ça (If you're not sure about voting Macron, take a look at this)	16-Apr-17	5:06	23 K/5.2K	4 678
67. Que faire dimanche? Notre avis (What to do on Sunday? Our opinion)	21-Apr-17	5:59	15 K/4.8K	4 748
68. À ceux qui hésitent entre Mélenchon et Hamon (To those who are hesitating between Mélenchon and Hamon)	21-Apr-17	13:49	10 K/3.1K	3 036
69. 3 intox sur Mélenchon : Alba, Poutine, Europe (3 intox on Mélenchon: Alba, Poutine, Europe)	22-Apr-17	6:31	4.7 K/1.5 K	1 517
71. Réforme des impôts : Macron président des ultra [sic] riches (Tax reform: Macron president of the ultra-rich)	19-Jul-17	8:24	9.9 K/1K	1 523
78. Révélation climat : Macron a menti. Hulot doit choisir (Climate revelation: Macron lied. Hulot has to choose)	07-Oct-17	5:27	11 K/586	1 080
87. Sarkozy élu en trichant, des témoins assassinés? (Sarkozy elected by cheating, murdered witnesses?)	29-March-18	7:06	8,4 K/473	1 161

Table 6.1. *Videos with the highest number of "likes" and comments. An English translation of the video title has been provided*

In Table 6.1, which summarizes, at a specific point in time, the data from certain videos – data that will have changed as a result of reading this article – there is a significant number of "likes", from 1,000 to 23,000, as well as a significant number of comments, up to over 4,000. This willingness to communicate with peers is not only made possible by the interactive platform, but is also clearly stated by the "Osons Causer" team:

> "Finally, to break the asymmetry of the device, we try to make it as horizontal as possible, to give a lot and to build a relationship with our audience. We respond to comments in the most constructive way possible. And let's organize (soon) regular joyful debate meetings [*sic*] with our audience and radio broadcasts."

The weaving of this relationship occurs through the addresses and thanks to their audience in the videos, the written answers of "Osons Causer" in the comments thread of each video or on their Facebook page, but especially in the FAQ videos, in which the three vloggers work together and answer a panel of questions asked by Internet users, as shown in Figure 6.5.

Figure 6.5. *Question asked on social networks and video answer (video 91 "Osons Causer FAQ 3 years + channels we love")*

Darth 42 Il y a 7 mois
Ok sans doute que tout est vrai, mais dans ce cas je me pose plein de questions: Pourquoi Kadhafi aurait autant financé la campagne de Sarkozy ?
Est-ce le seul président français à avoir eue ce genre de financement?
Pourquoi on n'en a rien su avant et surtout pendant son mandat et sa candidature en 2012?
Y-a-t-il d'autre dictateur ou homme influent qui ont pu financés des élection française?

70   REPONDRE
Masquer les réponses ^

Osons Causer Il y a 7 mois
Très bonnes questions. Qques réponses rapides - y en a qui méritent des bouquins.

Kadhafi a financé Sarko, d'après ce qu'on sait, pour 3 raisons principales. 1) gagner de la respectabilité internationale. Rappelle toi Kadhafi avec ses tentes dans les palais parisiens.
D'ailleurs, Sarko a aussi accueilli en grande pompe Bachar Al Assad à un défilé du 14 juillet. 2) Sarko a signé av la Libye, peu de temps après son élection, un accord sur du nucléaire
Lire la suite

94   REPONDRE

Ady Tech Il y a 7 mois
Bonne reponse "Osons Causer"

3   REPONDRE

Alpagaa Il y a 7 mois
Osons Causer Merci pour cette question ainsi que cette réponse, ça m'a permis déclarer ma compréhension de la situation.

2   REPONDRE

zenox1000 Il y a 7 mois (modifiée)
y a chirac aussi qui était un bon gros zoum
http://www.lejdd.fr/Politique/Actualite/L-avocat-Robert-Bourgi-raconte-comment-il-a-convoye-jusqu-a-l-Elysee-les-millions-des-chefs-d-Etat-africains-interview-387001

@ludo si je me permettre une remarque, ça me tue de vous entendre utiliser le terme "démocratique", alors qu'on a aucun réel pouvoir politique et que tous les politiques susceptibles
d'avoir un pouvoir important sont connompus. la france est une république (de type aristocratique pour reprendre montesquieu), si on finissait par l'admettre et l'assumer y aurait peut-
être moyen d'envisager de réels changements.
d'ailleurs vu le niveau de pourriture qu'on ne peut plus nier depuis des années, et vu que malgré ça rien ne change, il serait peut-être temps de se demander s'il ne serait pas préférable de
les chasser nous-mêmes du pouvoir, comme l'ont fait nos ancêtres, pour le bien du pays et de notre avenir à tous...
Moins

9   REPONDRE

Figure 6.6a. *Excerpt from a polylog with 47 answers, including one from "Osons Causer" (video 87)*

0xB4DC0FF33 il y a 7 mois

zenox1000 malheureusement, c'est juste, on vit dans une démocratie représentative, et même si elle n'a de démocratie que le nom, ça reste une démocratie... C'est triste de voir à quel point on perd le contrôle des mots et, a fortiori, des idées qui sont derrière

👍 1 👎 REPONDRE

Tobiraco il y a 7 mois

Question 1 : La lybie avait été mise au banc de l'humanité après des attentats qu'elle avait perpétré contre des ressortissants étrangers. Elle a été directement incriminée dans l'explosion d'un avion. Du coup l'état se trouvais sur la liste noir des pays non fréquentables, avec les conséquences économiques que ça engendre. Apparaître auprès d'une "grande démocratie", c'était une manière de se réinsérer dans la diplomatie et l'économie mondiale.

Lire la suite

👍 2 👎 REPONDRE

Bamabe51Reims il y a 7 mois (modifié)

Darth 42 : "Pourquoi on n'en a rien su avant et surtout pendant son mandat et sa candidature en 2012 "
L'info est bien plus ancienne, je l'avais déjà lue en 2008, mais les médias couvrent les puissants.
Quand un président emmène le gratin de l'industrie Française en voyage officiel, des contrats de plusieurs millions sont signés, j'imagine qu'indirectement certains hauts fonctionnaires touchent leur part du gâteau. On peut aussi imaginer que certains dictateurs offrent des pots de vin pour avoir accès à ces contrats

👍 1 👎 REPONDRE

public enemy il y a 7 mois

Osons Causer salut et merci pour la réponse que tu lui a donné . Mais juste je voudrais savoir pourquoi dit tu que kadahfi à acheter du matériel de surveillance qu il a utilisé contre son peuple ????la je ne comprends pas kadhafi n à jamais été contre son peuple et bien au contraire la Libye de kadahfi était le pays le plus moderne et très sociable presque tt était gratuit en Libye !!!!! Il allait même donner gratuitement le téléphone à ttes l Afrique Kadhafi a toujours aimé le peuple avant tt ce n' était certainement pas le sale type que nos médias nous on dépeint !!!!! Je rêve d un président ici en France comme kadahfi il a été assassiné par Sarko qui c est salie les mains pour tout le monde surtout pour les usa. Non oublier pas que kadahfi
Lire la suite

👍 2 👎 REPONDRE

Figure 6.6b. Excerpt from a polylog with 47 answers, including one from "Osons Causer" (video 87)

Moreover, to use the example of video 87 on the election of Sarkozy and Libyan financing, we can observe, for example, more than 8,400 likes and 1,161 comments. And while there are many isolated or trolling comments, there are 88 comments that themselves generate a dialog or a polylog (up to 18, 37, 47 or 52 responses) and whose content is an exchange around the questions raised in the video and which lead Internet users to ask themselves other questions. Figure 6.6 shows this type of exchange, where we see "Osons Causer" responding, and also Internet users responding to each other.

Vlogging can therefore be a space for exchanges about politics not only with vloggers, but also between Internet users.

6.4. Conclusion

During this analysis, we have observed that the characteristic elements of the "vlog" techno-genre discourse (such as an initial self-starring video, *pseudonymity* in the context of a YouTube channel, inter-network relationality or between Internet users) allow the construction of a multimodal and intermediate discursive ethos of a pro-am who wants to be competent, accessible and engaging and that they are used here to try to reconfigure political education and citizen debate between Internet users. Based on a multimodal digital discourse adapted to a composite audience, we note that, on this new stage, several discourses intersect, discourses strongly imbued with *didacticity* in the explanatory introduction, as well as videos from vloggers that leave room for debate in the comments between Internet users and vloggers.

From a friendly mini-collective of three young students emerges a collective pseudonym that becomes an incentive to action, and then the brand image of a broader, committed collective. The intrinsic relationality of digital discourse allows discourse to spread not only between Internet users, but also between networks, thus extending the audience and developing the original project, with each network playing its part in reaching as many people as possible and defending the initial idea: exhibition on the site, distribution on Facebook and Twitter, and financing on Tipee. In addition to relationality, there is also intermediality: the Web is the starting point for other actions, such as physical information during public debates, broadcasting in other media, or even in newspapers, on the radio, on other YouTube channels and even through a book project. Breaking with the traditional media system, these expert amateur Internet users are taking political information and disseminating it to the general public, paving the way for an alternative form of citizen journalism in political education.

Whereas in the 18th Century, Beaumarchais made Figaro his spokesman on a theater stage to awaken his fellow citizens to a form of political consciousness, in the 21st Century, a vlog could play a similar role and serve as a new stage for political education. The engagement with climate of a collective of youtubers[11] with the #IlEstEncoreTemps (there is still time) initiative and around ecological challenges with the #onestpret (we are ready) initiative are very recent French examples.

6.5. References

Amossy, R. (2015). *La présentation de soi. Ethos et identité verbale*. Presses universitaires de France, Paris.

Barton, D. and Lee, C. (2013). *Language Online: Investigating Digital Texts and Practices*. Routledge, London.

Burgess, J. and Green, J. (2013). *YouTube: Online Video and Participatory Culture*. Polity, Cambridge.

Combe, C. (2016). Questions méthodologiques autour de l'étude de deux plateformes interactives multimodales : de la communauté de contenu à l'application intimiste. *Línguas e Instrumentos Linguítiscos*, 37 [Online]. Available at: http://www.revistalinguas. com/edicao37/artigo9.pdf.

Combe Celik, C. (2014). Vlogues sur YouTube : un nouveau genre d'interactions multimodales. In *Actes du colloque Interactions multimodales par ECrans 2014, Lyon 2 au 4 July 2014*, Colon De Carjaval, I. and Ollagnier-Beldame, M. (eds) [Online]. Available at: https://impec.sciencesconf.org/conference/impec/pages/Impec2014_Combe_ Celik.pdf.

Cosnier, J. and Develotte, C. (2011). Le face à face en ligne, approche éthologique. In *Décrire la conversation en ligne*, Develotte, C., Kern, R., and Lamy, M.-N. (eds). ENS Éditions, Lyon, 27–50.

Develotte, C. (2012). L'analyse des corpus multimodaux en ligne : état des lieux et perspectives. *SHS Web of Conferences*, 1, 509–525 [Online]. Available at: http://dx.doi. org/10.1051/shsconf/20120100213.

Doueihi, M. (2011). *Pour un humanisme numérique*. Le Seuil, Paris.

Flichy, P. (2014). *Le sacre de l'amateur. Sociologie des passions ordinaires à l'ère numérique*. Le Seuil, Paris.

---

11 Osons Causer (2018). [Vidéo 92] *IL EST ENCORE TEMPS – COMMENT AGIR POUR LE CLIMAT (MAXI COLLAB)* [Online]. Available at: https://youtu.be/XKgKsjnHarw. The title of the video translates as: "It's that time again - How to take action for the climate".

Herring, S.C. (2015). New frontiers in interactive multimodal communication. In *The Routledge Handbook of Language and Digital Communication*, Georgakopoulou, A. and Spilioti, T. (eds). Routledge, New York, 398–402.

Jeanneret, Y. and Souchier, E. (2005). L'énonciation éditoriale dans les écrits d'écran. *Communication & Langages*, 145(1), 3–15.

Jenkins, H. (2006). *Convergence Culture: Where Old and New Media Collide*. New York University Press, New York.

Jenkins, H., Clinton, K., Purushotma, R., Robison, A.J., and Weigel, M. (2006). *Confronting the Challenges of Participatory Culture: Media Education for the 21st Century. An Occasional Paper on Digital Media and Learning*. The John D. and Catherine T. MacArthur Foundation, Chicago [Online]. Available at: https://files.eric.ed.gov/fulltext/ED536086.pdf.

Leadbeater, C. and Miller, P. (2004). *The Pro-Am Revolution*. Demos, London.

Maingueneau, D. (1995). Présentation. *Langages*, 117, 5–11.

Moirand, S. (2002). Didacticité. In *Dictionnaire d'analyse du discours*, Charaudeau, P. and Maingueneau, D. (eds). Le Seuil, Paris, 181–184.

Paveau, M.A. (2017). *L'analyse du discours numérique. Dictionnaire des formes et des pratiques*. Hermann Éditeurs, Paris.

Serres, M. (2015). *Petite poucette*. Le Pommier, Paris.

Tellier, M. (2016). Prendre son cours à bras le corps. De l'articulation des modalités kinésiques avec la parole. *Recherches en didactique des langues et des cultures*, 13(1).

PART 2

Digital and Mobilizations

7

El dia de la mùsica: The Digital Organization of the 2017 Catalan Referendum

On September 29, 2017, two days before a referendum on Catalonia's independence was to be held, Catalan independence organizations held a large rally in front of the *Font Màgica de Montjuïc* to mark International Music Day in advance, *El dia de la mùsica*. Although this international day was initiated to highlight the importance of music in peaceful relations between peoples[1] and to promote democracy, in a way, it was of course not the music that the Catalans had come to celebrate two days before the referendum.

On September 7, 2017, the Spanish Constitutional Court suspended the referendum law adopted the day before by the Catalan Parliament. On the same day, the Constitutional Court informed the 948 municipalities responsible for organizing elections in Catalonia that they *could not* participate in the organization of the referendum. The State Prosecutor accused the members of the government and other elected independence supporters sitting in the Catalan Parliament of disobedience, fraud and embezzlement of public funds in order to prevent them from holding the referendum. By deciding to move forward and maintain the election on October 1,

---

Chapter written by Philippe-Antoine LUPIEN.
1 Launched in 1975 by violinist and conductor Yehudi Menuhin, International Music Day is celebrated on October 1 by the International Music Council and aims, in particular, to encourage "the promotion of music in all spheres of society; the application of the ideals promoted by Unesco in the fields of peace and friendship among peoples, the development of cultures, the exchange of experiences and the mutual appreciation of aesthetic values" (http://www.imc-cim.org/programme/international-music-day.html).

political parties and independence organizations had therefore placed themselves in an illegal position. In order to maintain the vote, the organizations and independence activists then resorted to a series of tactics and various strategies aimed at circumventing all forms of repression, including that of organizing *El dia de la música*, which aimed to replace any reference to the referendum with a musical vocabulary.

Here, we will focus on three "alternative media practices" (Landry *et al.* 2014) that contributed, in particular, to the dissemination, tactical communication and calls for mobilization[2] in the context of the illegal organization of the Catalan referendum vote on October 1, 2017. This case study is based on the observations of participants in Barcelona in September 2017 and an online literature search.

7.1. Context: the organization of Catalan civil society

The movement for Catalan independence has been growing since the mid-2000s, driven by civil society organizations (Crameri 2015), including Òmnium Cultural, a non-profit organization founded in 1961 and working to promote Catalan language and culture, and the Catalan National Assembly (*Assemblea Nacional Catalana*, ANC), an organization founded in 2012 and whose objective is to achieve Catalonia's independence. Each with approximately 100,000 members[3], these organizations have led a series of mobilizations and events since 2004 that have greatly contributed to supporting the Catalan government's political actions. Among these mobilizations, let us recall the two editions of the *Via Catalana*, organized on September 11, 2013 and 2014. The first edition consisted of a vast human chain of some 400 kilometers, with a number of participants, "in no case less than 1.6 million people"[4], according to the Ministry of the Interior[5]. The second edition brought together nearly 1.8 million people – according to the municipal police[6] – who formed a V along the streets of Diagonal and Gran Via in Barcelona, composing the Catalan flag with their layout and the color of their *samaretes* (t-shirts). These two

---

2 Here, and subsequently, we take up the typology of alternative media practices proposed by Landry *et al.* (2014).
3 In July 2018, Òmnium Cultural had nearly 120,000 members (https://www.Òmnium.cat/ca/presentacio/). According to the latest available sources, the ANC had nearly 71 members as of November 2017 (https://www.elnacional.cat/ca/politica/socis-omnium-anc_212289_102.html).
4 Free translation from: "*En cap cas inferior a 1,6 milions de persones*".
5 Cited in ARA (2013). La Via Catalana, minut a minut. *ara.cat* [Online]. Available at: https://www.ara.cat/politica/diada-onze_de_setembre-via_catalana-independencia_.12_9912 1220869.html.
6 Ara (2014). La Via Catalana, minut a minut. *ara.cat* [Online]. Available at: https://www. ara.cat/politica/diada-onze_de_setembre-via_catalana-independencia_12_991220869.html.

events, which used digital technologies and Web platforms to plan the availability of participants, are part of both the "image event", designed to produce impressive images that will be relayed in the media, and the "smart-mob" (Landry *et al.* 2014), with their organization based on the use of information and communication technologies.

In the 2017 referendum, it was these organizations – then led by Jordi Cuixart (Òmnium Cultural) and Jordi Sànchez (ANC)[7] – that had the mandate to campaign for independence, together with the independence political coalitions (*Junts per Catalunya, Esquerra Republicana* and *Candadidura of Unitat Popular*). The dynamism of these civil society organizations has led a large number of Catalans to characterize the independence movement as a grassroots phenomenon (Crameri 2015), unlike the Scottish and Quebec approaches, mainly led by political parties.

The ANC produced the main poster campaign for the *Sí* ("yes") campaign (Figure 7.1). However, when the Spanish government and its President, Mariano Rajoy, refused the referendum, the *Sí* camp found itself without a political opponent, without a *No*. Therefore, a completely different issue from that of achieving independence dominated the debate throughout the 15 days of the campaign: that of civil rights and the democratic right of the Catalan people. Òmnium Cultural illustrated this debate by producing a poster campaign featuring silhouettes of gagged faces highlighted with the word *democràcia* ("democracy") (Figure 7.2).

Figure 7.1. *ANC "Sí" flags*

---

7 They were the first to be remanded in custody on October 16, 2017, facing charges of sedition.

Figure 7.2. *Democràcia! poster of Òmnium Cultural (source: Wikimedia)*

With these organizations, a group of student unions, citizen movements, community groups and others participated in the mobilization and iconography of the campaign[8]. The decentralization of the mobilization of Catalan independence fighters was very well-expressed in the visual landscape of cities, where flags, posters, stickers and graffiti were displayed on balconies and on street furniture. A website[9] for downloading and printing posters at home was also put online anonymously to allow anyone to participate in voluntary posting operations (Figure 7.3). This method of distribution made it possible, among other advantages, to produce a large number of posters at low cost by sharing costs and facilitating their frequent replacement – posters were removed from street furniture rather quickly by municipal authorities throughout the referendum campaign[10].

The great graphic diversity and variety of messages conveyed by the organizations responsible for these campaigns illustrate the nature of Catalan independence mobilization, i.e. a decentralized popular involvement movement characterized both by the demonstrated ability of large civil society organizations to quickly mobilize very large crowds, and by the multiplication of small actions and the voluntary participation of a multitude of locally organized activists.

---

8 It should also be noted that almost all of this material was made using computers.
9 www.empaperem.com.
10 The slogan given, and generally respected by the activists, required respect for private property: the posters were thus mainly placed on street furniture and on companies that had positioned themselves against the referendum, such as financial institutions.

descarrega el teu cartell a **empaperem.cat**

Figure 7.3. Votem per se lliures, *example of a poster for project #empaperem (source: www.empaperem.com)*

However, in the context of the illegal organization of the elections, the constraints linked to the dissemination of information and the use of media technologies led the independence supporters to use certain alternative or circumventing media practices. Their aim was to support both the continued dissemination of information, messages and material aimed at organizing the referendum and the protection of the confidentiality of activists.

7.2. The alternative organization of the Catalan referendum

The complexity of organizing the October 1, 2017 referendum in a context of illegality led the organizations and activists involved in its implementation to use a variety of strategies and tactics to avoid repression and hide their activities. This was manifested, in particular, by the establishment of a vast enterprise of concealment and clandestine distribution of the electoral ballot boxes, which have become symbols of the democratic will of the Catalans (see Vincens Estaran and Tedó Gratacós 2018). The issues related to the organization of collective actions and the protection of the confidentiality of activists were also reflected in the technological organization of the election, and in activities related to the dissemination of election information and ballots and the management of the list of voters.

7.2.1. Broadcast: IPFS protocol to bypass censorship

The attitude of the Spanish central authorities towards the organization of the referendum was manifested, *inter alia*, by the pressure exerted on the media and the censorship of the communication mechanisms set up to plan the referendum on October 1 (Table 7.1).

September 9th	The *Guàrdia Civil* raided the newsroom of the newspaper *El Vallenç* in Valls in search of information on the organization of the referendum.
September 13th	The *Guàrdia Civil* raided the offices of CDMon and demanded the closure of the sites rather quickly of the *Generalitat de Catalunya* about the referendum.
September 15th	Armed agents in civilian clothes from the *Guàrdia Civil* "tour" some Catalan media including *NacióDigital*, *El Nacional.cat*, *VilaWeb*, *Racó Català*, *Llibertat.cat* and *El Punt Avui*.
September 20th	The *Guàrdia Civil* arrests the technological manager of the puntCAT foundation, orders him to close the sites linked to the referendum attached to the .cat domain and searches computer equipment.
September 22nd	Search of the residence of Dani Morales, who had published a list of mirror sites set up for the referendum. As a result of this intervention, many other students, draftsmen or activists will be arrested and investigated for the same reason.
September 30th	Search of the *Centre de Telecomunicacions i Tecnologies de la Informació* (CTTI) to retrieve the lists of voters and other material necessary for the organization of the elections.

Table 7.1. *Main police actions against the media and companies in the context of the 2017 Catalan referendum*

The closure of the site put online by the *Generalitat*[11] to disseminate information on the elections[12] on September 13 was accompanied by the closure of 20–140 other sites linked to the referendum, depending on the sources[13]. Immediately, copies will be read again on various servers and at different addresses, several of which are intended to make fun of the central authorities[14]. Some of the people responsible for these copies or the distribution of these sites would also be indicted and imprisoned, including Dani Morales, who was arrested on September 22 for sharing mirror sites and charged with rebellion. These sites were also "seized" – the addresses were diverted by Internet service providers to police servers – by the authorities as they appear (Figure 7.4), with the *Guàrdia Civil* having received authorization from the High Court of Justice of Catalonia (TSJC) to block access to any website without a prior authorization[15].

Este dominio ha sido intervenido y se encuentra a disposición de la Autoridad Judicial

This domain name has been seized pursuant to a seizure warrant under the Judicial Authority and is under its administration

Figure 7.4. *Landing page of sites closed by the Judicial Authority (source: www.marianorajoy.cat)*

---

11 The *Generalitat* is the institutional system formed by the Parliament, the Presidency, the Government and the other administrative institutions of Catalonia.

12 www.referendum.cat.

13 Molist, M. (2017). Aixì es van fer els ciberatacs contra el referèndum. *Naciódigital* [Online]. Available at: https://www.naciodigital.cat/noticia/140059/aixi/es/van/fer/ciberatacs/contra/referendum.

14 www.marianorajoy.cat, www.referendum.fun, guardiacivil.sexy.cat, etc.

15 ARA (2017). El TSJC autoritza la policia a bloquerjar qualsevol web sobre el referèndum que publiciti Puigdemont. *ara.cat* [Online]. Available at: https://www.ara.cat/politica/TSJC-autoritza-bloquejar-referendum-Puigdemont_0_1874812772.html.

In order to keep the information accessible, the referendum defenders –
including those linked to the Pirate Party of Catalonia [16] – then used the IPFS
(*Interplanetary File System*) protocol to create security copies. To simply put,
websites, as they are currently viewed on the Web, are based on the HTTP protocol,
which uses a single address that directs a request to a server where the site data is
hosted. The IPFS protocol is an open peer-to-peer protocol that fragments and stores
information in blocks and in a distributed manner. Not dependent on centralized
servers, IPFS makes it possible to make files virtually indelible and almost
impossible for Internet service providers to block. To make it impossible access to
these copies, the authorities therefore had to prevent access to gateways that allow
conventional browsers to access IPFS sites. In addition to these copies, a mobile
application was created and distributed on the Google Play store, before being
removed following a request from the TSJC[17].

7.2.2. Mobilization and tactical communication: Telegram Messenger, official ANC channel

In order to preserve the dissemination of electoral information (including
gateway addresses or access to copies of referendum sites) and to support
mobilization, independence organizations also sought to bypass conventional
communication mechanisms. In addition, although platforms such as Twitter and
Facebook have been widely used to disseminate the positions of organizations and
politicians or to maintain debate among activists of all persuasions, independence
supporters were aware of the need to guard against the false information, fake news
and trolls that abound on these platforms. It can also be noted that, in the daily
mobilization and tactical communication between militants, the WhatsApp
communication application – which is present on 98% of phones in Spain according
to the Spanish Commission on Markets and Competition[18] – quickly found itself
drowned in false information and swarming with trolls and hackers. The Telegram
Messenger application was used to maintain an official communication channel
between organizations and activists.

---

16 Bloc, General, Pirates de Catalunya. (2017). Pirates de Catalunya cola el web del
Referèndum tancada per la Guàrdia Civil. *Pirates* [Online]. Available at: http://pirata.cat/bloc/
pirates-de-catalunya-clona-el-web-del-referendum-tancada-per-la-guardia-civil/.
17 El País (2017). The TSJC asks Google to delete the app for voting in the referéndum
that Puigdemont has disseminated [Online]. Available at: https://elpais.com/ccaa/2017/09/29/
catalunya/1506700499_092932.html.
18 Gualteri, T. (2015). Why Spaniards are Europe's WhatsApp champions. *El País* [Online].
Available at: https://elpais.com/elpais/2015/02/16/inenglish/1424084620_570764.html.

Telegram Messenger is an encrypted messaging service hosted in the cloud created in 2013 by Nikolai and Pavel Dourov, also founders of the Russian social network VKontakte and now based in Berlin following the takeover of VKontakte by the Russian government. The application, blocked in Russia since April 13, 2018, is also tightly controlled by the Iranian government[19].

Telegram Messenger enabled ANC organizers to reach, through a direct channel, approximately 30,000 people every day in order to disseminate the addresses of websites created or copied on a daily basis, correct false information circulating in the media and other digital social networks, disseminate mobilization messages, advertising or promotional tools, etc. The use of technological devices – such as the IPFS protocol and the Telegram Messenger application – as part of the Catalan referendum campaign was therefore generally used to set up offline actions, such as posters, information tables and the organization of the referendum vote. Referendum organizers also used Telegram, for example, to program a robot to locate a polling station as an alternative to the referendum site, and distribute the official ballot (Figure 7.5), which voters could print at home. In fact, they were strongly encouraged to do so to facilitate logistics, especially since 9 million of the ballots that had been printed by printing houses had subsequently been confiscated by the police.

7.2.3. *Voting: the "computer heroes" of October 1*

For many Catalans, October 1, 2017 began very early, under light but constant rain, when dozens of members of the referendum defense committees (CDRs) gathered in front of the polling stations to protect access, as well as poll officials who had to arrive with the ballot boxes, which had hitherto been kept hidden to prevent them being seized. Shortly after 7 a.m., government spokesman Jordi Turull announced that the vote would be held using a single list of voters allowing Catalans to vote in any polling station[20], in order to prevent the police from closing polling stations in the future. To share the list of voters and allow it to be updated in real time, a group of IT experts not linked to the government set up a database hosted on Amazon's servers and protected by Cloudflare that was accessible to all polling officers[21].

---

19 Tual, M. (2018). L'application Telegram bloquée en Iran pour "maintenir l'ordre". *Le Monde* [Online]. Available at: https://www.lemonde.fr/pixels/article/2018/01/02/l-application-telegram-blocked-in-iran-to-maintain-order_5236831_4408996.html.
20 Agencia UO (2017). El Govern informa sobre l'existència d'un cens electrònic que permetrà votar a qualsevol col·legi electoral [Online]. Available at: https://agenciauo.org/govern-revela-lexistencia-dun-cens-electronic-que-permetra-votar-qualsevol-collegi-electoral/.
21 Molist, M. (2017). Així es van fer els ciberatacs contra el referèndum. *Naciódigital* [Online]. Available at: https://www.naciodigital.cat/noticia/140059/aixi/es/van/fer/ciberatacs/contra/referendum.

Mida: 105 mm x 148,5 mm

Figure 7.5. *Official voting form*[22]

However, as soon as the majority of polling stations installed in schools opened, Internet access was cut off by the body responsible for network management in schools and, quickly, the address allowing access to the electoral list[23] was blocked, *inter alia* through denial of service attacks[24]. Therefore, in order to share the database and maintain access from several alternative IP addresses, shared through social media and by a telephone number, many "computer heroes"[25] scattered throughout the polling stations connected to the voters list using the 3G and 4G

22 Source: https://drive.google.com/file/d/0B2lMi1igUvFcaFR4SU0xV1hvRjA/view.
23 www.registremeses.com.
24 *Quirium* (2017). Blocking techniques Catalunya [Online]. Available at: https://www. qurium.org/alerts/spain/blocking-techniques-catalunya/.
25 Torra, Q. (2017). S'ha parla poc dels herois informàtics [Online]. Available at: https:// twitter.com/QuimTorraiPla/status/914973921656627201?ref_src=twsrc%5Etfw.

frequencies of their cellular phones, or the Internet connections of their nearest neighbors, created relays in various places that allowed closed networks to be maintained. Furthermore, to reduce bandwidth, a watchword was circulated on September 29 in militant networks, encouraging people to activate the "flight mode" of cell phones in the vicinity of polling stations.

Around the polling stations, in order to allow people to communicate with each other, a peer-to-peer network was created, avoiding the Internet, using the FireChat application, which uses Bluetooth and short-range Wi-Fi. This short distance network was used, among other things, to exchange information, share images of other polling stations and prevent police interventions throughout the day.

7.3. Conclusion

In the light of the Catalan case, we are led to observe that digital technologies are inevitably present in contemporary political organization. However, in a context where democratic freedoms are constrained or repressed, or even here in a context of illegal mobilization, the most common communication devices – such as the Internet itself – may prove to be impossible to mobilize. In Catalonia, maintaining secure communication channels, allowing both the protection of anonymity and the dissemination of truthful information, proved to be a major challenge in mobilizing and organizing the referendum. In this regard, several bypass technologies, such as IPFS, Telegram Messenger and FireChat, have helped to support mobilization.

As part of the 2017 Catalan referendum mobilization, the many organizations and activists organized in a decentralized way "demonstrated the importance, sometimes a little forgotten, of the phenomena of ordinary socialization" (Granjon 2018) by using digital technologies to implement concrete, "in the flesh" actions (posters, local events, information tables, celebrations, etc.). Despite attempts to control the public authorities, the technologies used in the organization of the referendum made it possible to set up directories of collective actions (Landry 2012) aimed mainly at supporting the organization of the election and preserving the vote, rather than persuading people to vote *Sí*.

Remarkably, the actions carried out by Catalan independence fighters have drawn mainly from a repertoire of conventional actions (information, posters, etc.) and, to a lesser extent, from disruptive actions (coordination of public demonstrations, dissemination of opponents' abuses, etc.), but in no way from violent actions. The pacifism of Catalan independence activists was therefore reflected both in the major demonstrations on polling day and online. Even in the face of digital control and the attacks on freedom of expression and information against independence organizations, hacker communities have exemplarily respected the call for calm and have not taken any violent action against the sites and servers of the Spanish authorities, before the referendum at least.

This pacifism constitutes the main legitimacy of the independence movement's approach to international opinion and justice against a Spanish State whose repression has been highlighted and criticized, particularly with regard to the media and freedom of expression (see Amnesty International 2018; RSF 2017)[26]. This has led to the current political impasse, with seven politicians in exile and nine others still being held in "preventive" detention, accused of having organized the referendum of October 1, 2017 or rather *El Dia de la música*.

7.4. References

Amnesty International (2018). La situation des droits humains dans le monde. Report, Amnesty International, London [Online]. Available at: https://www.amnesty.org/download/Documents/POL1067002018FRENCH.PDF.

Crameri, K. (2015). Political power and civil counterpower: The complex dynamics of the catalan independence movement. *Nationalism and Ethnic Politics*, 21(1), 104–120.

Granjon, F. (2018). Mouvements sociaux, espaces publics et usages d'Internet. *Pouvoirs*, 1(164), 31–47.

Landry, N. (2012). Les mouvements sociaux, les technologies médiatiques et le pouvoir. In *Médias sociaux : enjeux pour la communication*, Proulx, S., Millette, M., and Heaton, L. (eds). Presses de l'Université du Québec, Quebec, 153–169.

Landry, N., Sénécal, M., Aubin, F., and George, É. (eds) (2014). *Cahiers du CRICIS. Luttes sociales et technologies médiatiques numériques : pratiques de mobilisation collectives*, 3. CRICIS, Montreal.

Reporters sans frontières (2017). *La liberté de la presse sous pression en Catalogne* [Online]. Available at: https://rsf.org/sites/default/files/enquete_catalogne.pdf.

Vincens Estaran, L. and Tedó Gratacós, X. (2018). *Operació Urnes*. Columna Edicions, Barcelona.

---

26 See, inter alia, Reporters sans frontières (2017). *La liberté de la presse sous pression en Catalogne;* Amnesty International (2018). Report 2017/18: *La situation des droits humains dans le monde.*

8

Digitalization and Civic Engagement for the Environment: New Trends

The widespread digitalization of civilization has led to many changes in the participation and involvement of social actors in civil society. The emblematic spaces of the contemporary Internet, particularly the social Web (Millerand *et al.* 2010), have facilitated the emergence of new civil society practices driven by "networks of indignation" and social movements, popular revolts (the Arab Spring, *Occupy Wall Street*, the *Indignados*, the student movement in Quebec, #MeToo, etc.) (Allagui and Kuebler 2011; Castells 2015; Gallant *et al.* 2015; Pipyrou 2018).

They have also led to "eco-citizenship" movements, a form of citizenship that, beyond respect for the environment (eco-citizenship), "is characterized by [...] its ability to create social ties and to integrate them into the fabric of a living environment" (Sauvé and van Steenberghe 2015, p. 284). The weaving of new "online social micro-ties" (Galibert 2013) would be the basis for a "distanced engagement" (Ion 1997).

Of course, citizen environmental initiatives have often emerged on an individual basis through different digital photo and video sharing platforms – for example, on Fotolia, Flickr, Dailymotion and YouTube – within blogs and digital social networks such as Facebook, Twitter and Instagram. Their aim is to influence public environmental policies by giving priority to the protection, preservation and resolution of socio-ecological problems (Douay 2014) such as climate change and melting glaciers or biodiversity, while not submitting to economic development projects. Examples include the *Coule pas chez nous* collective, which mobilizes

---

Chapter written by Ghada TOUIR.

citizens opposed to the transportation of oil in Quebec, the *Sauvons les belugas* collective, which mobilizes citizens to protect their habitat in the St. Lawrence River, and the Zero Waste initiative (almost everywhere in major cities in Quebec and across Canada), which is dedicated to disseminating environmental knowledge and skills to the public. These emblematic spaces of the contemporary Internet make it possible to facilitate exchanges between citizens and thereby encourage the formation of collectives around issues related to the environment.

The research in this area have largely focused on the use of social media for political purposes (Kahne and Bowyer 2018) by political parties, for example in Quebec (Verville 2012) or by non-profit institutions and organizations (Aykurt and Sesen 2017). But very few studies have focused on the environment and the use of digital platforms, including social media. Some researchers have undertaken work to identify emerging practices in social participation and significant trends in social and political engagement (Denouël *et al.* 2014), particularly in the environmental field (Ackland and O'Neil 2011). One of these trends is the phenomenon of "connective action" (Bennett and Segerberg 2012), based on the coordination of individual skills within personal action frameworks, where the sharing of personalized content via social media would play a central role.

In contrast to the standard ideal of traditional collective action based on the intermediary work of large organizational structures (trade unions, associations, etc.), working within collective frameworks of action, the logic of connective action, based on the coordination of individual skills, promotes participation through the circulation of political messages through networks of mutual trust. Digital social platforms (such as Facebook and Twitter) play a critical role as pivotal mechanisms for organization and coordination. The forms of activist action that are developing in social media give rise to different types of engagement – such as signing online petitions, producing photo reports or video clips, sending tweets, creating a blog, page or Facebook group, etc. (Segerberg and Bennett 2011). But, above all, they seem to favor the emergence of a new engagement culture of "ordinary citizens" that is anchored in their living environment for the conservation or protection of the environment and ecosystems (Scherman *et al.* 2015). This abandons the so-called traditional engagement within structured social groups and associations, or even political parties. Also, this new type of engagement can be observed on digital social platforms. These forms of engagement and action are all the more interesting to observe, as they seem to be specific to the digital context (Theviot and Mabi 2014). They are spontaneous collectives, totally online, emerging from the initiative of ordinary citizens without being experts in the field or even associate members of certain associative groups, but who play complementary roles in building online engagement and collective action. This engagement therefore leads to the predecessor courses describing this type of engagement as "slacktivism" (Morozov 2013) or "political consumerism" (Stolle and Micheletti 2013).

This chapter therefore proposes, on the basis of exploratory empirical research, an overview of the reality of digital engagement in Quebec for the environment. This is understood from the point of view engagement through online participation, i.e. a form of spontaneous, freely-consented and passionate individual action aimed at producing social change over a certain period of time (Amato and Boutin 2012; Bernard 2014). The central question that guided our research is the following: to what extent are we witnessing the emergence of new forms of eco-citizen engagement on the contemporary Internet, particularly in the environmental field?

8.1. Case study and methodology

In order to answer this question, we have followed an exploratory process to describe and analyze the renewal of individual citizens' social and political engagement to the environment, in the context of new practices developed around social media.

In the absence of a directory or mapping of online citizen environmental groups, they had to be found and identified first. We have therefore created our own directory of online citizen collectives related to environmental protection to capture them in all their diversity. Based on a keyword search related to environmental issues in Quebec (e.g. "citizen collective", "environment", "pipeline", "oil sands", etc.) and based on suggestions made by Google and Facebook search engines in March 2015, we have identified approximately 130 collectives in Quebec working for different environmental causes and issues. We selected 39 of them that we observed in more detail. These were chosen on the basis of several criteria of relevance (Pires 1997): the environmental cause or issue (to ensure diversity), the level of activity of the collective (the collective had to be active) and the ease of access and contact (with a view to possible interviews). However, only six collectives are included in our case study (Table 8.1). These were selected according to the same criteria of relevance, to which we added the criterion of the willingness of the collective and its representatives to collaborate in the research.

Name of the collective	Description	Digital platforms used
Ensemble contre les sables bitumineux	A collective of citizens (the first such Francophone collective) opposed to oil sands development, created in 2010.	The Facebook page* (https://www.facebook.com/eatenergie/) has more than 18,000 fans, the vast majority of whom come from Quebec. Video clips are available on YouTube.
Les citoyens au courant	A collective of citizens opposed to Enbridge's Line 9 B oil pipeline, created in February 2013. It is mainly composed of residents of the villages of Très-Saint-Rédempteur, Sainte-Justine-de-Newton, Rigaud and Pointe-Fortune.	The Facebook page (https://fr-fr.facebook.com/Les-Citoyens-au-Courant-529200363768200/) has 466 fans (mainly residents of the villages mentioned in this table). Since March 2015, it has been on Twitter, with more than 2,600 tweets. As part of its activities, it also produced video clips on YouTube.
Bric à bacs	A blog to "learn, demystify and reflect on residual materials" (https://bricabacs.com/).	It has a Facebook page (https://fr-ca.facebook.com/bricabacs/) *with 871 members, and he is also on Twitter.*
Citoyen du monde J.D	A blog for Outaouais residents, created in 2010 against urban sprawl and "developments that affect a better quality of life" (https://www.blogger.com/profile/06762795301340140153).	The blog has been inactive since late 2015, but the administrator is active on Facebook via his personal page, with a public profile of more than 3,000 friends.
Dans ma cour + Martinoutaouais	A blog dedicated to nature protection and bird conservation (http://dansmacour.quebec/)+A public group on Facebook (https://www.facebook.com/groups/Martinoutaouais/) dedicated to the chimney sweeper in the Outaouais with 41 members.	These two collectives were created by the same person. Video clips are also available on YouTube.
Zéro déchet Gatineau	A blog dedicated to the dissemination of Zero Waste knowledge and skills (https://zerodechetoutaouais.wordpress.com/)+a group (open) on Facebook.	The same person created these two online collectives.

"Ensemble accélerons la transition énergétique pour une transition énergétique", which has more than 44,136 subscribers as of the date of this chapter.

Table 8.1. *List and description of the six collectives studied*

Our research approach is based on a mixed inductive methodological strategy that is predominantly qualitative, while also including quantitative data analysis. The advantage of this approach is that it allows several data sources to be combined and linked in a triangulation logic. We have used three data collection techniques:

1) an online observation of 39 collectives, selected among the 130 identified between July 2015 and January 2016, and carried out from a perspective of online ethnography (Hine 2013)[1];

2) an analysis of the statistical data provided by the platforms (Facebook, Google, WordPress);

3) semi-structured individual interviews with the six people who created the collectives studied.

8.2. Results and analyses

Facebook is by far the platform with the largest number of citizen groups in the environmental field. These take various and varied forms, which can be distinguished, first of all, according to whether they are (1) open (public) or closed (private, requiring authentication) groups (*Mouvement Stop Oléoduc*, for example), (2) pages (*Contre les sables bitumineux*, for example) or (3) personal accounts (Marc Anticosti, for example).

Another differentiation element of these collectives is their purpose depending on whether they were created in a particular context, for example in response to an event (e.g. *"coule pas chez nous"* "Don't Go Home") or for promoting and defending a broader environmental cause (e.g. *pour un moratoire contre le gaz de schiste* (For a Moratorium Against Shale Gas")).

It should be noted that several significant current events took place during the observation period, leading to renewed activity among collectives: a scheduled discharge of waste water from the City of Montreal into the St. Lawrence River, the World Climate March, COP21, the Canadian federal elections, and the TransCanada and Eastern Energy oil pipeline crisis.

How does, then, environmental engagement manifests itself among the observed collectives? Our analyses lead us to identify several trends around four main types of activities.

---

1 Observations were made on a daily or weekly basis depending on the collectives and their level of activity. The news feed posted in the directory of environmental collectives in Quebec that the author had created on Facebook informed us about the activity of the page or group without the need to "like" the page. The observation notes were recorded in a dated logbook, with comments made following successive reviews.

8.2.1. News/monitoring

First, the dissemination of current news and the realization of a form of information monitoring constitute an important use within collectives. The objective is to select, relay and comment on information and other content from the information media (press, television, radio and online platforms) or other sources, including other online groups. This type of activity refers to the figure of the "citizen-informant" or, to a certain extent, the "citizen journalist" for the environment, who collects, analyzes and disseminates information – a figure that is also very close to the activist Internet user (Granjon 2014).

8.2.2. Contact/networking

Second, the interaction and networking opportunities offered on digital platforms (to criticize, discuss, get angry, comment, etc.) are considered as opportunities for connection between people and for the construction of a social capital as a set of "source-bearing" relationships on the network. This is both in terms of interpersonal relationships, as well as the level engagement and social participation. Collaborative networks are being formed and multiplied, promoting the dissemination of a message and its resonance in society. It should be recalled that networking, and the creation of exchange networks and online communities, are quite old, since they were present at the foundation of the Internet. However, they are currently the driving forces behind the development of the contemporary Web (Lefebvre 2005).

8.2.3. Mobilization/action

Third, two activities at the heart of engagement, mobilization and action, are among the most visible activities online. The responsiveness specific to socio-digital media and the opportunity they offer to reach a wider audience (Ellison and Boyd 2013) are assets that collectives are using to mobilize their members around specific events or actions. For example, during the World Climate March in Ottawa on November 29, 2015, the mobilization of online collectives, from all causes, played a key role in the dissemination and coordination of the thousands of people (approximately 25,000) who came to protest on Parliament Hill in Canada's capital. The same phenomenon was observed in the case of the June 2016 petition to the Quebec government against oil companies and hydrocarbon projects in Quebec.

8.2.4. Sharing of know-how and knowledge

Fourth, by observing the chains of interaction and exchange on digital platforms, we have seen the importance of sharing know-how and practical knowledge, ecological, economic and social, for example in terms of recycling, composting, zero waste, etc.

Sharing this type of know-how is a mobilizing, appreciated and emancipating activity within collectives, as evidenced by the intensity of activity around such publications (e.g. the publication of instructions on how to make an eco-friendly cleaning product or reusable bags).

In practice, these four activities (news/monitoring, contact/networking, mobilization/action, sharing of know-how and knowledge) are intertwined. For example, comments on current events may be accompanied by an editorial and political point of view, or by an incentive to act, as illustrated by a member of an online collective (Figure 8.1) on an article published in *Le Devoir*[2].

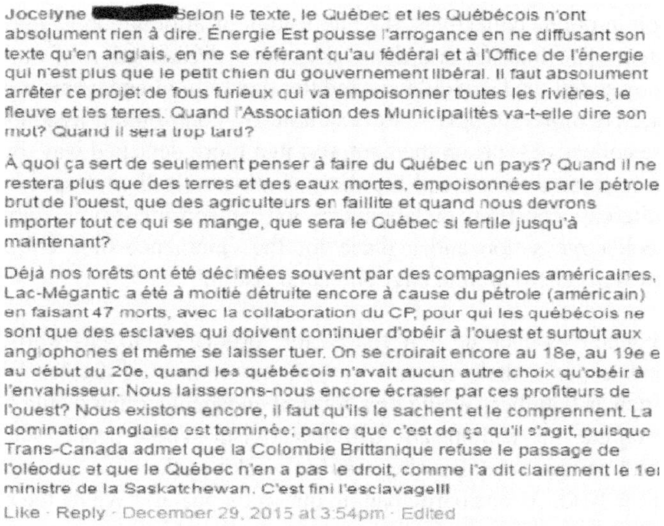

Jocelyne ▆▆▆▆▆▆Selon le texte, le Québec et les Québécois n'ont absolument rien à dire. Énergie Est pousse l'arrogance en ne diffusant son texte qu'en anglais, en ne se référant qu'au fédéral et à l'Office de l'énergie qui n'est plus que le petit chien du gouvernement libéral. Il faut absolument arrêter ce projet de fous furieux qui va empoisonner toutes les rivières, le fleuve et les terres. Quand l'Association des Municipalités va-t-elle dire son mot? Quand il sera trop tard?

À quoi ça sert de seulement penser à faire du Québec un pays? Quand il ne restera plus que des terres et des eaux mortes, empoisonnées par le pétrole brut de l'ouest, que des agriculteurs en faillite et quand nous devrons importer tout ce qui se mange, que sera le Québec si fertile jusqu'à maintenant?

Déjà nos forêts ont été décimées souvent par des compagnies américaines, Lac-Mégantic a été à moitié détruite encore à cause du pétrole (américain) en faisant 47 morts, avec la collaboration du CP, pour qui les québécois ne sont que des esclaves qui doivent continuer d'obéir à l'ouest et surtout aux anglophones et même se laisser tuer. On se croirait encore au 18e, au 19e e au début du 20e, quand les québécois n'avait aucun autre choix qu'obéir à l'envahisseur. Nous laisserons-nous encore écraser par ces profiteurs de l'ouest? Nous existons encore, il faut qu'ils le sachent et le comprennent. La domination anglaise est terminée; parce que c'est de ça qu'il s'agit, puisque Trans-Canada admet que la Colombie Brittanique refuse le passage de l'oléoduc et que le Québec n'en a pas le droit, comme l'a dit clairement le 1er ministre de la Saskatchewan. C'est fini l'esclavage!!!

Like · Reply · December 29, 2015 at 3:54pm · Edited

Figure 8.1. *Screenshot of the Facebook page of the "Ensemble contre les sables bitumineux" group (now renamed "Ensemble, accélérons la transition énergétique")*

In her remarks denouncing Énergie Est's project to build an oil pipeline across eastern Canada, the commentator highlighted the company's ties to the federal authorities and Anglophone Canada, while clearly expressing her ideological proximity to the Quebec sovereignty movement. She sees Énergie Est's decision to distribute its publications exclusively in English as discrimination against the

---

2 Shields, A. (2015). TransCanada présente la version finale de son projet de pipeline. *Le Devoir*, December 17.

French-speaking population of Canada, mainly in Quebec. While inviting Quebec to imitate British Columbia's position towards TransCanada in what may resemble a pan-Canadian environmentalist movement, this citizen links the issue of environmental protection in Quebec's territory to her political sovereignty.

8.3. Conclusion

Fundamentally, the nature of the activities around which collectives organize themselves (monitoring, networking, mobilization, sharing) is not so different from those that characterize activist groups (Touir 2015). However, some uses are specific to the digital environment and show an evolution in the way things are done. As a result, in addition to traditional militant practices (petition, marches, demonstrations, etc.), great importance is attached to the circulation of information and sharing it in online collectives; the publication of information is, in itself, a sign of engagement. The Internet and the "widespread digitalization of our societies", particularly by social media, would expand the spectrum of engagement by allowing to invest oneself more strongly – for example by contribution assiduously to the action of the collective – or, on the contrary, in a more detached way, by following current events from distance and regularly. Emblematic digital spaces, including Facebook, thereby constitute a laboratory for networking among citizens about connected collective action and a place for the emergence of a collective "we" (Bakardjieva *et al.* 2018) around environmental issues.

Online collectives open up new spaces for "ordinary" citizens who want to get involved and express their support for an environmental cause. What seems completely new is that there would be a form of engagement that would be deployed exclusively online, i.e. without any offline activism. These people show a strong ecological and environmental awareness, but weakly articulated around a practical approach in the field. As one participant in our study puts it: "We let the associations take care of the field". Among these citizens, digital engagement seems to be self-sufficient, as they find meaning in this exclusively online engagement. Most of the activity takes place in front of the screens and behind the keyboards. This form of participation refers to the notion of *distanced engagement* proposed by Ion (1997) to highlight the "flexible and unconstrained nature" (p. 62) of new militant practices, without, however, linking this distance to a scale of intensity. Again, the importance of online engagement can vary to the point where, in some cases, it can take the time of a full-time job.

The results of our research suggest, finally, a possible emerging trend: that of a stronger digital engagement to the environment among women. Is this because of a more general trend that would make digital engagement a more feminine practice?

8.4. References

Ackland, R. and O'Neil, M. (2011). Online collective identity: The case of the environmental movement. *Social Networks*, 33(3), 177–190.

Allagui, I. and Kuebler, J. (2011). The Arab Spring and the role of ICTs. Introduction. *International Journal of Communication*, 5, 1435–1442.

Amato, S. and Boutin, E. (2012). Engagement online et expérimentation en milieu naturel : retours d'expériences. In *Journée de recherche "L'engagement, de la société aux organisations"*. Propedia-IGS, Paris, 1–14.

Aykurt, A.Y. and Sesen, E. (2017). Social media in social organization. *European Scientific Journal*, 13 (20).

Bakardjieva, M., Felt, M., and Teruelle, R. (2018). Framing the pipeline problem: Civic claimsmakers and social media. *Canadian Journal of Communication*, 43(1).

Bennett, W.L. and Segerberg, A. (2012). The logic of connective action: Digital media and the personalization of contentious politics. *Information, Communication and Society*, 15(5), 739–768.

Bernard, F. (2014). Imaginaire, participation, engagement et empowerment. Des notions pour penser la relation entre risques et changements. *Communication et Organisation* (45), 87–98.

Castells, M. (2015). *Networks of Outrage and Hope: Social Movements in the Internet Age*. Polity Press, Cambridge.

Denouël, J., Granjon, F., and Aubert, A. (2014). *Médias numériques et participation. Entre engagement citoyen et production de soi*. Mare et Martin, Paris.

Douay, N. (2014). Les usages du numérique dans le débat public. In *Devenirs numériques*, Carmes, M. and Noyer, J.-M. (eds). Presses des Mines, Paris, 227–244.

Ellison, N.B. and Boyd, D. (2013). Sociality through social network sites. In *The Oxford Handbook of Internet Studies*, Dutton, W.H. (ed.). Oxford University Press, Oxford.

Galibert, O. (2013). L'injonction participative au débat environnemental en ligne : imaginaires d'Internet, démocratie environnementale et communication engageante. *Les Enjeux de l'information et de la communication*, 1(14), 35–49.

Gallant, N., Latzko-Toth, G., and Pastinelli, M. (2015). *Circulation de l'information sur les médias sociaux pendant la grève étudiante de 2012 au Québec*. Centre d'études sur les médias, Université Laval [Online]. Available at: http://cem.ulaval.ca/pdf/ CirculationInformation.pdf.

Granjon, F. (2014). Introduction. In *Médias numériques et participation. Entre engagement citoyen et production de soi*, Denouël, J., Granjon, F., and Aubert, A. (eds). Mare et Martin, Paris, 7–19.

Hine, C. (2013). *Virtual Research Methods (Four Volume Set)*. Sage Publications Limited, Oxford.

Ion, J. (1997). *La fin des militants ?* Éditions de l'Atelier/Éditions ouvrières, Paris.

Kahne, J. and Bowyer, B. (2018). The political significance of social media activity and social networks. *Political Communication*, 35(3), 1–24.

Lefebvre, A. (2005). *Les Réseaux sociaux : Pivot de l'Internet 2.0*. M21 Éditions, Paris.

Millerand, F., Proulx, S., and Rueff, J. (eds) (2010). *Web Social : mutation de la Communication*. Presses de l'Université du Québec, Quebec.

Morozov, E. (2013). *To Save Everything, Click Here: The Folly of Technological Solutionism*. Public Affairs, London.

Pipyrou, S. (2018). #MeToo is little more than mob rule//vs//#MeToo is a legitimate form of social justice. *HAU: Journal of Ethnographic Theory*, 8(3), 415–419.

Pires, A.P. (1997). Échantillonnage et recherche qualitative : essai théorique et méthodologique. In *La recherche qualitative. Enjeux épistémologiques et méthodologiques*, Poupart, J. *et al.* (eds). Gaëtan Morin, Montreal, 113–169.

Sauvé, L. and van Steenberghe, É. (2015). Identités et engagements : enjeux pour l'éducation relative à l'environnement. *Éducation relative à l'environnement. Regards-Recherches-Réflexions*, 12 [Online]. Available at: https://journals.openedition.org/ere/588.

Scherman, A., Arriagada, A., and Valenzuela, S. (2015). Student and environmental protests in Chile: The role of social media. *Politics*, 35(2), 151–171.

Segerberg, A. and Bennett, W.L. (2011). Social media and the organization of collective action: Using Twitter to explore the ecologies of two climate change protests. *The Communication Review*, 14(3), 197–215.

Stolle, D. and Micheletti, M. (2013). *Political Consumerism: Global Responsibility in Action*. Cambridge University Press, New York.

Théviot, A. and Mabi, C. (2014). Présentation du dossier : s'engager sur Internet. Mobilisations et pratiques politiques. *Politiques de Communication*, 3, 5–24.

Touir, G. (2015). S'approprier les technologies numériques : étude des dynamiques, des pratiques et des usages du Web de quatre associations environnementales québécoises. PhD thesis, Université Laval, Quebec.

Verville, M. (2012). Usages politiques des médias sociaux et du Web 2.0 : le cas des partis politiques provinciaux québécois. PhD thesis, Université Laval, Quebec.

9

Online Antifeminist Discourse and the Republican Left

For several decades, the French Republic, behind its motto of "Liberté, égalité, fraternité", (Liberty, equality, fraternity), has been suffering from an inability, or difficulty, to define the contours of its citizenship politically and inclusively. Whether it is a question of drawing the external borders of its people or guaranteeing to each and every citizen their fundamental rights, the French political system continually seeks to unite and centralize, not without violence, its power under the banner of republicanism and universalism (Guénif-Souilamas 2006).

That being said, the Republican model we are talking about is – as seen throughout its history – worked by a paradox. Indeed:

> "In the history of French republicanism, there is a surreal link between two contradictory universalisms: the universalism of individual political rights [...] and the universalism of sexual difference [...]. On the one hand, natural rights that transcend all differences; on the other hand, natural differences that cannot be transcended" (Scott 1998, p. 9).

This consideration leads us to reflect on the issues raised by feminist movement and gender studies scholars with regard not only to the articulation of these political struggles – the place of women in society and questions of citizenship – but also to the issues arising from the French colonial past and its influence on migratory movements, which result in cultural and religious diversity that the French political world is struggling to conceptualize.

Chapter written by Sklaerenn LE GALLO.

More precisely, this chapter aims to return to republican principles and, by extension, to the demands of so-called "republican" or "universalist" feminists with regard, in particular, to the question of secularism and its centrality in the process of national construction. By way of illustration, we will use the example of Jean-Luc Mélenchon and *la France insoumise* (a French left-leaning political party) to highlight certain contradictions that appear problematic to us in the discourse of this republican left-wing movement during the 2017 presidential election.

9.1. Republican feminism, universalist feminism

9.1.1. *Liberty, equality, fraternity*

The notion of universalism, through which we can relate to republican feminism, has been debated at length among various feminist and gender studies movements, notably by Judith Butler who, with the publication of Gender Trouble in 1990, put the cat among the pigeons. Drawing on the writings of several institutional feminists (Butler 2015), she underlines the idea that, for some, there is an identity of "woman" that guides feminist action. She wrote that:

> "[...] There is a political problem that feminism encounters in the assumption that the term *women* denotes a common identity. Rather than a stable signifier that commands the assent of those whom it purports to describe and represent, *women*, even in the plural, has become a troublesome term, a site of contest, a cause for anxiety" (Butler 2015, p. 4).

Butler's (2004, 2015) will is then to denaturalize the sexual binary, to question the framework of heteronormative power.

Through this idea, Butler deals with the materiality of the body and reaffirms the non-existence of a female or male essence at birth, and very rightly places the notions of gender and sex in a set of power struggles. She also notes that this universalist version of feminism also appears to be "efforts to colonize and appropriate non-Western cultures" (Butler 2015, p. 5). For her, Western cultures "support highly Western notions of oppression, but because they tend as well to construct a 'Third World' or even an 'Orient' in which gender oppression is subtly explained as symptomatic of an essential, non-Western barbarism".

This idea of building a particular otherness can also be seen through the promotion of the so-called "republican" model that France wishes to embody. Indeed, this model of citizenship, organized around the notion of equality, or even egalitarianism, is not experienced by everyone in the same way, in the sense that people of immigrant background are subject to a different perspective from society. Nacira Guénif-Souilamas (2006) then speak of "focus[ing] on the behavior of immigrants and their descendants, [which] leads to expectations of sexual and sexual hypercorrection from which French people of no particular origin derogate" (p. 19). This impossible egalitarianism is then expressed socially and economically, and here we can think of the crisis that took place in the French suburbs in 2005, triggered by the now infamous "Are you tired of this gang of scum? We'll get rid of them for you" from Nicolas Sarkozy to Argenteuil. It is thus read as a double lie, as Mucchielli (2006) states: "A lie in the promise of equal opportunities to be integrated into economic and social life, a lie in the promise of equality in value and dignity" (p. 58). The egalitarian promises of the Republic have thus not been kept for these young French people of a migrant background as social, economic and ethnic inequalities lead to a rejection of the integrationist perspective.

9.1.2. *Thinking about secularism*

In France, these issues, particularly those related to immigration, are also expressed in the context of secularism and the way in which it is considered by republicans, who, far from ensuring that the separation of Church and State is properly respected, are

> "far from the true values of secularism..... [They] have weakened the authority of politics when secularism aims to fully establish it, individual freedoms are violated when secularism enshrines freedom of conscience and freedom of worship, and the equality of citizens is violated when secularism presupposes it" (Roman 2006, p. 79).

Where the original spirit of the 1905 law is improperly extended to the private sphere, at the public level and, more particularly, at the level of the French State, breaches of this separation of Church and State are much more easily ignored.

In fact, in addition to the concept of the 1905 law, there is a new concept of secularism, known as "combat", "which willingly takes the stance of a fundamentalism or a republican fundamentalism" (Roman 2006, p. 75). Secularism is then perceived as "the means to put an end to *differentialism*, to reaffirm the criteria and conditions of integration, to ensure equality between men and women, to restore the sovereignty of the State" (p. 75). As a result, within this particular collective imagination, the idea of a Muslim population that cannot integrate into the republican citizen model because of its practice of Islam is emerging.

Within the French feminist movements, this concern was the cause of a fracture in March 2004, as noted in some of the debates surrounding the law to prevent the wearing of the veil in schools. This bill followed the expulsion of two high school students, Alma and Lila Lévy, who were wearing the veil. The event led several universalist feminist movements to develop a strategy of "defense" of the Republic, whose symbols and institutions were, according to them, in danger in the face of two female students wearing an Islamic veil. These movements, behind, among others, "*Ni putes ni soumises*" (Neither whores nor submissives), pointed to several elements considered problematic, namely the developments of Islamism, communitarianism or machismo, which would be orchestrated by minority groups. The "*Ni putes ni soumises*" movement, born from the publication of a manifesto in March 2003, is described by Guénif-Souilamas (2006) as "consensual, antifeminist, heterocentric, and reactionary" (p. 121) and will draw two central figures – that of the "beurette" victim (meaning a French woman of North African descent) and the Arab boy executioner. There will also be "secular" feminists, such as Caroline Fourest, for whom the 2003 law was "necessary to get out of each case and make the inside of the school a sanctuary" (2014), making the school, as Joël Roman (2006) puts it, the only institution responsible for educating citizens.

More recently, new voices have emerged advocating a universalist vision of feminism, as illustrated by the position of the *Comité laïcité République* (Republican Secularist Committee) (2016) on the *Marianne* website. There it states in particular the idea that "universalism, the key to individual and collective emancipation, is now denounced by an anti-republican [*sic*] movement as a 'colonialist' ideology". This qualification of anti-republicans attributed to feminist movements supporting, among other things, the wearing of the veil ultimately diverts the text of the 1905 law by proposing "the invention of a republican model, above all, to block demands for recognition and justice from categories of the population that are regularly suspected of being disloyal to national institutions and values" (Roman 2006, p. 78).

9.1.3. *A differentiated citizenship?*

This last point leads us to think of the question of communitarianism as a danger to the Republic. Indeed, as we have already discussed, republican demands for universalism and humanism aim to propose a society in which each and every citizen is integrated into a common culture, organized under the values of liberty, equality and fraternity.

This question of communitarianism can, first of all, be dealt with from a "territorial" perspective. Indeed, the individuals generally accused of such practices are people of an immigrant background, and even more so are young, racialized people living in the French suburbs. This territorial idea echoes, in particular, the above-mentioned quotation from Nicolas Sarkozy, which considers all people living in apartment blocks to be simply "scum" who can be "cleaned with a power hose" so that they stop bothering good, integrated French people. This trend stems, among other things, from a particular context which, put in a certain way, presents young people from colonial descent as living in a primarily working class neighborhood and then in a "ghetto", whose control is ensured sometimes by drug dealers and sometimes by fundamentalist imams. The discourse produced by SOS-Racisme and others makes the young suburbanite (*jeune de banlieue*), an expression that basically refers to black and Arab people, an actor of the ghettoization of the suburbs. They are, thus, considered "exogenous" to the nation and the suburbs themselves are considered to be "lost territories of the Republic" (Bouamama 2006).

The second form of communitarianism raised by the republican and universalist movements is that of non-mixing. Indeed, non-mixing – whether based on race, class or gender – is a political necessity, a necessary point of passage in the organization of struggles for self-determination, since it allows for a freer and safer discussion (Delphy 2016; Diallo 2017; Lallab 2018). For others, however, this militant practice is perceived as a refusal to accept or reject, as an exclusion of privileged populations, and is transformed into the expression of "anti-white racism" or a form of sexism against men. This point of view emerged in particular on the fringes of the organization of Nyansapo, an Afro-feminist festival organized by the Mwasi collective, which included a number of single-sex activities reserved for black women. Rokhaya Diallo (2017) summarizes the situation as follows:

> "This initiative was experienced as a formal attack on the white centrality so deeply embedded in the collective imagination. Indeed, when one is in a socially dominant and central position, when one's color has never been a barrier for anything, it is difficult to imagine people who are usually subordinate organizing spaces where one's presence is not desired."

The last point to address the question of communitarianism directly echoes the platform of the Comité laïcité République (2016), which considers universalism to be the only possible condition for emancipation, in this instance of the women who are veiled. This emancipatory concept of universalization is also found within the political agenda of *La France insoumise*. Communitarianism, here based on the criterion of cultural or religious affiliation, is based on a "refusal" to integrate on the part of people with a migrant background. According to some universalist feminists or republican movements, this refusal to integrate is in fact an inability or an incompatibility between Islamic beliefs and the values of the Republic. This is where we find the element that triggers legislation against the wearing of the veil in school. Indeed, in 2003, "gender equality became their constant, primary concern; the wearing of headscarves by a handful of adolescent girls became the only obstacle to gender equality in France" (Delphy 2006, p. 81). Under the guise of fighting sexism in favor of gender equality, the government pushed for legislation, leading to a political rupture and a fracture within feminist movements.

That being said, we can observe a vicious circle with regard to so-called communitarianist discourses, since people practicing Islam, for example, are considered to be living among themselves without the will to integrate and without being able to do so in any way, since Islam would not be compatible with republican principles. Thus, if they refuse to "renounce" the visible signs of their religious affiliation, they are not republicans. Consequently, these specificities are essentialized – Islam being represented as united and all Muslims being authoritarian men – and the resulting process of otherness only builds a figure of a violent, misogynistic, uncompromising inner enemy, whose legitimate precepts are considered archaic. This thus relegates Muslims to the margins, to a subordinate and external status that does not allow them to integrate into society in the same way as white people. In the land of the Enlightenment, the Republic and universalism then become the privileged weapons of certain people to "liberate" those who were victims of obscurantism.

9.2. The case of Jean-Luc Mélenchon

For this second part, we propose an illustration of some of the paradoxes mentioned above through some tweets by Jean-Luc Mélenchon. The choice of this particular person is not coincidental. He was indeed presented by several media as the most "feminist" candidate in the 2017 French presidential election. Despite these statements, and considering the poverty of other programs during this same political moment, we wish to question some of the events that were publicized via Jean-Luc Mélenchon's Twitter account, in order to highlight some antifeminist positions on the part of the leader of *La France insoumise*.

9.2.1. *On communitarianism*

La France insoumise ("France unbowed") defines itself as a humanist movement, using a universalist strategy to promote "emancipation". In this sense, the left-wing party is linked to a republican vision of politics behind the three ideals of freedom, equality and fraternity.

The first element of communication that interests us here is taken from the political platform of *La France insoumise* which, based on the issue of an irreproachable secular republic, addresses three points. The one we highlight is the following: "We will refuse to meet those who force our female ministers to wear clothing that are contrary to the republican dignity or who imprison people for their humanist and secular writings at the head of the state (Dupas and Sintes 2017, p. 17).

Two elements seem contradictory to us. First, this refusal to comply with the customs of the host country, which, as we have said before, is something that is something that blames certain immigrant populations and is exploited for political purposes. Second, the wearing of religious symbols, implying the Islamic headscarf, would be "contrary to republican dignity". We find here the same line of republican communication that regrets and wishes to combat the wearing of certain so-called "ostentatious" religious signs in order to defend the principles of the Republic and ensure the equality and freedom of its citizens – although here it is a question of wearing a cultural marker on foreign territory.

When asked about this point in his program as part of *L'Émission politique*, broadcast on France 2 on February 23, 2017, Mélenchon replied that he did not understand "how God would be interested in a rag on his head", adding: "As an activist linked to feminism, I fight, on a personal basis, the wearing of the veil. It is better to avoid ostentatious signs". These explanations tend to be in line with republican action, which, on the one hand, calls into question certain foundations relating to the wearing of the veil, which becomes nothing more than a "rag". On the other hand, we also find this idea of rejecting communitarianism for the sake of equality under the guise of a certain form of secularism. This translates into an invitation to no longer wear the veil in order to avoid displaying any ostentatious sign in the public space. While he stated that, in his opinion, the law does not have to impose how to dress on the street, the fact remains that the debate is then focused on the field of "values". The evocation of feminism is not fortuitous, since it allows him to refer, without naming it, to a certain struggle for the emancipation of women, equality between women and men, and thus entering into the myth of the veil as a means of oppression.

9.2.2. About Jeuxvideo.com's forum 18-25

That said, the point that caught our attention most during the 2017 campaign was the somewhat unexpected appeal of the candidate from *La France insoumise* to the 18-25 community of Jeuxvideo.com (jv.com). This forum is not unknown to feminists, since it has often been characterized by assertive misogyny since at least 2013, when alerts were issued by "feminist activists, online harassment victims and media [...] on the 18-25 hate culture" (Darmanin 2017). In addition to cyber-aggressions on the basis of gender, there are also many racist, anti-Semitic and homophobic statements, as this excerpt from a study conducted by *L'Obs* in 2015 (Petit 2015) shows.

Nevertheless, on November 29, 2016, in the middle of the presidential campaign, Jean-Luc Mélenchon, who then broadcasted his meetings on YouTube, thanked the 18-25 community by repeating some of the codes used by its users, or even "Yes We Canchon", a version of Obama's *Yes we can* to which is added Mélenchon's "chon". This addition can also be seen in various forum publications that address the slogan "Can't stenchon the Melenchon", taken from the 4chan community's "Can't stump the Trump" during the 2016 American elections.

On December 5, 2016, a blogger published a post on the *Simonae* blog noting the paradox of a Mélenchon claiming to be linked to feminism but thanking Forum 18-25 for its support during its meeting in Bordeaux. The author of the note, who has since been offline, has suffered numerous aggressive reactions and cyberstalking. She especially denounced the sexist and misogynistic nature of the forum, which was not well received by the members of the forum. Some considered it to have generalized the situation, while others were more direct and sent her insulting messages. A topic has been created on the forum in order to carry out an organized "response".

9.3. Conclusion

Whether it is a mistake or a real acknowledgment of the support of this platform (18-25 on jv.com), Mélenchon's positions suggest a lack of involvement, or at least a lack of reflection on the part of the leader of *La France insoumise*, and part of his political entourage, on certain anti-feminist issues. Thus, where the veil is merely a "rag" on the head and is part of a set of ostentatious signs that should not be worn under the guise of any feminist involvement, Jean-Luc Mélenchon's universalist position remains firmly rooted in this republican humanist will, at the expense of the people concerned who themselves make sense of their cultural and religious practices.

In conclusion, this republican idealism of a unified society in which all have the same rights and freedoms and apply them in the same way, without questioning themselves excessively, making the effort to integrate and thus erase any possible sign of a particular cultural belonging, tends, as Rancière (quoted in Aeschimann 2015) regrets, and as we mentioned with Guénif-Souilamas (2006) earlier, to create the figure of the internal enemy; to divide society between those who "accept" integration and those who, on the contrary, take the way of "communitarianism".

9.4. References

Aeschimann, É. (2015). Entretien avec Jacques Rancière : les idéaux républicains sont devenus des armes de discrimination et de mépris. *BibliObs* [Online]. Available at: https://bibliobs.nouvelobs.com/essais/20150403.OBS6427/les-ideaux-republicains-sont-devenus-des-armes-de-discrimination-et-de-mepris.html.

Bouamama, S. (2006). De la visibilisation à la suspicion : la fabrique républicaine d'une politisation. In *La république mise à nu par son immigration*, Guénif-Souilamas, N. (ed.). La Fabrique, Paris, 196–216.

Butler, J. (2004). *Undoing Gender*. Routledge, New York.

Butler, J. (2015). *Gender Trouble : Feminism and the Subversion of Identity*. Routledge, New York.

Comité Laïcité Républicain, Libres MarianneS et Association pour le droit international des femmes (2016). Pour un féminisme laïque et universaliste !. *Marianne* [Online]. Available at: https://www.marianne.net/debattons/tribunes/pour-un-feminisme-laique-et-universaliste.

Darmanin, J. (2017). Jeuxvidéo.com, des années de harcèlement misogyne et de laisser-faire. *Buzzfeed.News* [Online]. Available at: https://www.buzzfeed.com/julesdarmanin/jeuxvideocom-des-annees-de-harcelement-misogyne-et-de.

Delphy, C. (2006). Antisexisme ou antiracisme ? Un faux dilemme. In *La république mise à nu par son immigration*, Guénif-Souilamas, N. (ed.). La Fabrique, Paris, 81–106.

Delphy, C. (2016). La non-mixité : une nécessité politique. *Les mots sont importants. net* [Online]. Available at: http://lmsi.net/La-non-mixite-une-necessite.

Diallo, R. (2017). La non-mixité, un outil politique indispensable. *SlateFR* [Online]. Available at: http://www.slate.fr/story/146466/non-mixite-rokhaya-diallo.

Dupas, M. and Sintes, C. (2017). *Pour une République vraiment laïque*. France Insoumise, 3 [Online]. Available at: https://avenirencommun.fr/le-livret-laicite/.

Fourest, C. (2014). Pour le droit des mères voilées à accompagner les sorties scolaires. *Huffington Post France* [Online]. Available at: https://www.huffingtonpost.fr/caroline-fourest/voile-sorties-scolaires_b_6092800.html.

Guénif-Souilamas, N. (ed.) (2006). *La république mise à nu par son immigration*. La Fabrique, Paris.

Lallab (2018). 6 raisons pour lesquelles les réunions en non-mixité sont importantes. *Lallab Magazine* [Online]. Available at: http://www.lallab.org/6-raisons-pour-lesquelles-les-reunions-en-non-mixite-sont-importantes/.

Mucchielli, L. (2006). Immigration et délinquance : fantasmes et réalités. In *La république mise à nu par son immigration*, Guénif-Souilamas, N. (ed.). La Fabrique, Paris, 39–61.

Petit, T. (2015). Antisémitisme, homophobie, fanatisme : Jeuxvideo.com, la ruche à fiel. *Nouvel Obs* [Online]. Available at: https://www.nouvelobs.com/medias/20150924. OBS6430/antisemitisme-homophobie-fanatisme-jeuxvideo-com-la-ruche-a-fiel.html.

Roman, J. (2006). Pourquoi la laïcité ? In *La république mise à nu par son immigration*, Guénif-Souilamas, N. (ed.). La Fabrique, Paris, 62–80.

Scott, J.W. (1998). *La citoyenne paradoxale : les féministes françaises et les droits de l'homme*. Albin Michel, Paris.

10

Digital Social Media and Access to Public Sphere

The news media are going through an unprecedented financial crisis. Various 2016 reports all point towards a shift within advertising, from traditional media[1] to digital social media and search engines (Google). Despite recent (and late) government support, the number of journalism positions continues to decline and media outlets are closing their doors. In Quebec, where news media ownership already has one of the highest concentration rates in the West (George 2014), the diversity of voices seems seriously threatened.

However, the revision of the business model should not be the only concern of the news media. There is something more serious. It is the very legitimacy of the media as a key player in the public's right to information that is being challenged by new patterns of information consumption and the leveling of various sources. These range from partisan propaganda to news, duly validated according to proven ethical processes, including the crudest conspiracy theories and the diversion of attention to digital social media. In the end, "fake news" circulates faster and more widely than "real news"[2].

To survive, the news media must accept being the object of observation and criticism. That is, criticism that goes beyond detailed opinions on this or that temporary controversy, to explore the unthinking approach of so-called

---

Chapter written by Raymond CORRIVEAU and France AUBIN.

1 See, for example, Centre d'études sur les médias: http://www.cem.ulaval.ca/pdf/Donnees financial.pdf.

2 Agence France-Presse (2018). Les "fake news" circulent plus vite que les vraies infos. *La Presse.ca* [Online]. Available at: https://www.lapresse.ca/techno/reseaux-sociaux/201803/08/ 01-5156613-les-fake-news-circulate-more-fast-than-true-infos.php.

modern journalism, namely its mercantile nature. As long as we accept the idea that the primary purpose of an information enterprise is to make a profit, we will contribute to the weakening of the fourth power in democracy.

10.1. Research question

We therefore wrote an opinion letter on the right to information[3] and sent it to *Le Devoir*, the only media outlet that accepts letters of opinion of this length, but it remains unpublished. A format problem? A topical problem? We don't know: newspapers (which receive a large number of letters) never justify their decision not to publish. Nevertheless, in recent decades, the first author of this chapter, Raymond Corriveau, has written several letters of opinion and most of them have been published.

Faced with what we interpret as a possible media block[4] on a discourse that fundamentally challenges traditional media, we offered up our text for public discussion through digital social media. After all, some see digital social media as a vehicle for democratizing access to the public sphere (Cardon 2010). We have therefore sought to answer the following question: can these digital social media allow a text that criticizes the right to information and challenges the foundations of press enterprises to have access to the public sphere?

As our intention is to measure traffic from a given perspective, we focused on digital social media for text sharing (Facebook, Twitter), to which we added YouTube, because of its wide reach, as well as email. The website hosted the reference text (the unpublished letter) and the research protocol, and gave access to the main digital social media (Facebook, Twitter and YouTube). On YouTube, we produced a short video inviting the viewer to access the research process via a hyperlink. We used the email to directly address people who might be interested in the issue raised in the letter (but who may not necessarily agree). We wrote to people who were active in the university communications departments and community media. We saw them as potential influencers.

10.2. Public space and its challenges

According to Dacheux (2015), who largely takes up the Habermasian division, "the public sphere is a sphere of mediation with porous borders" (p. 148) composed in fact of three spheres: "the institutional public sphere, a place of decision-making;

---

3 The letter can be viewed at: https://oraprdnt.uqtr.uquebec.ca/pls/public/gscw030?owa_no_site=4991.
4 See "Faire sauter le verrou médiatique", issue 146 (April–May 2016) from *Manière de voir* (*Le Monde diplomatique*), edited by Pierre Rimbert.

the media public sphere, a place of visibility for the confrontation of opinions; the autonomous spheres of civil society, places where the communicative action specific to the lifeworld takes place" (p. 148). We conclude that the media can only play a key role if they are independent of systemic powers (money and the State) and open to the demands of civil society.

What happens to the mediation sphere if one of the spheres is short-circuited? How does the institutional public sphere judge the credibility of information/ argument, developed on digital social media, without having passed the filter of the media sphere, represented by traditional written media (Lavigne 2014)? Of the media sphere and digital social media, which Dacheux (2015) invites us to take into account, which will succeed in establishing a link with a civil society organization? What about the real potential of digital social media – where subjectivity reigns – as a deliberative place (Gonzalez Quijano 2012) and the attention economy, which directs participatory logic towards a perpetual quest for the consideration of the speaker (Citton 2013)? Do the modalities of recognition through the obligation of engagement in digital social media act as a filter for public discussion?

10.3. Methodological design

Engaging in a discussion in the public sphere of digital social media requires monitoring on multiple platforms, but how can we do this without engaging in the discussion ourselves? We did not intend to replace the public sphere, by creating a blog, for example, but rather to examine the possibility for our text to enter the public debate. As mentioned earlier, we chose to create an individual website, where we submitted the research protocol and a comment form. We have also made a monitoring matrix available to the public which allows them to follow the evolution of the research process. In this way, we wanted to create the necessary conditions of transparency with the least possible disruption to the process. To reduce the risk of influence that some comments might have had on the conduct of the research, we only made the results visible after a week.

To help us plan our presence strategy on social and digital media, we used three "good practice" guides[5]. The syncretism of these documents led us to develop a four-step approach:

1) observation and positioning;

---

5 See Wellcom Agency's *Guide social media 2015* (Paris, France) and Moz Agency's *Beginner's Guide to Social Media* (Seattle, USA), as well as Wikipedia's (n.d.) description of the term *social media*.

2) integration into digital social media;

3) presence;

4) measurement and follow-up

It should be noted that the implementation of the recommendations contained in these documents is not always easy. Some elements are difficult to adapt to an action-based research project like ours, since the logic behind all these approaches is marketing. However, we did not want to measure our personal fame on digital social media, but rather to evaluate the sharing of a viewpoint. We had to avoid the customization provided for in the proposed models, just as we had to put aside the matrices related to the marketing of commercial products.

The monitoring stage (1) was therefore used to determine our main potential relays, as well as the digital social media relevant to our approach. Monitoring had to continue throughout the research in order to identify possible reactions, particularly from media players. We used the positioning step, strongly influenced by marketing logic, only as a step in the installation of the measurement tools. We were not trying to measure our point of view among other points of view, as one brand can be compared to another. Integration with digital social media (2), as its name suggests, consisted of providing access to each of the selected media. The presence (3), on the other hand, consisted of launching the idea submitted to the public sphere for eventual public discussion. Measurement and follow-up (4) consisted of collecting data.

10.4. Demonstration of evidence

It remains very difficult to make any comparison of influence in the public sphere between what is (circulation through digital social media) and what could have been (circulation of an open letter in *Le Devoir*, for example). *Le Devoir* had a weekday circulation of 51,873 copies in April 2016. Would equivalent circulation on digital social media be a valid equivalence factor? In other words, are all modes of circulation equal? This is questionable: the readership of *Le Devoir* has a qualitative dimension because many political decision-makers pay particular attention to it. The value of a click of a high school student reading a document as a learning activity and that of a deputy minister will not be the same. The same goes for a click from outside Quebec society: how can we judge its role in the public debate in Quebec? There is also another major difference to consider. A publication in a daily newspaper reaches its audience in a single day. The strike force is multiplied. This improves the critical mass of an idea's exposure in the public sphere. Digital social media have difficulty doing the same thing unless they publish a spectacular image, which was not our case.

Steps to take	Actions	Means
Monitoring	Identification of potential contact persons	Klout (http://klout.com/)
	Identification of potential bridge organizations	Social authority
	Identification of relevant digital social media	Feedly (http://feedly.com/)
	Identification of influencers	Google + (https://plus.google.com)
	Identification of tools monitoring	Swayy (http://app.swayy.co/), Ifttt (https://ifttt.com/), Conversation drivers, Feeling, Influence
Positioning	Preparation of texts presented	Creation of the hosting website at UQTR on the Hublot platform
		Creation of accounts on digital social media (Facebook, Twitter, YouTube)
Integration with digital social media	Sending emails to bridge sources (individuals and organizations)	
	Launching invitations on Facebook, YouTube, Twitter and email	
Measurement	Visibility	Inventory of the number of clicks with platform measurement tools
	Consultation	Number (#) of visits on a Web page. At the end of the page, two hyperlinks, one to measure interaction and the other to measure tracking (Google Analytic and Google Search Console)
	Interaction	# of bounces; # of clicks on the search protocol; # of clicks on the comment form (last name, first name, email, comments); # of respondents to the form (Google Analytic and Google Search Console)
	Follow-up	Measurements are taken every week for two months to verify a long-tail phenomenon

Table 10.1. *Summary table*

In order to optimize our experience, we therefore launched our project in one go, in a short period of time, with as many bridge collaborators as possible. The first week's monitoring was designed to establish a parallel between the two options for access to the public sphere; the six-month monitoring was designed to verify the existence of a long tail. The bridge collaborators included about 20 civil society organizations working in social development or in the media, as well as a number of academic researchers.

We used various measures to assess the circulation of the reference text: a visibility measure, a consultation measure, an interaction measure and a follow-up measure. The whole process is clearly visible in the summary table (Table 10.1). The final step, the measurement, will be discussed in the results.

In addition to the computerized circulation monitoring just mentioned, we had planned to take into consideration a series of qualitative indicators. For example, we thought we would find references from the political world to our text, ideas taken up by citizens, academic or trade union organizations, or even troll attacks.

10.5. Results

We launched the project with the website on which the reference text was available on May 17, 2017, and completed the accounting for activities on November 17, 2017, six months later. As shown in Figure 10.1, the interface provided access to the reference text, research protocol, results and a comments page. The persons visiting the site also had at their disposal the most frequently used tools on digital social media, namely Facebook, Twitter and YouTube.

Figure 10.1. *Preview of the home page screen*

10.5.1. *Visibility and consultation*

The ratio of visits to the website compared to the potential readers of a daily newspaper remains considerably different. However, the effectiveness of the approach is greater than a university conference in terms of audience, considering the number of visitors (258) as well as the number of pages viewed (454). However, this in no way competes with the diffusion impact of a traditional media such as *Le Devoir* (51,000 potential readers versus 785 page views). It must be admitted, however, that there is no assurance that all potential readers of *Le Devoir* would have read the same article. To some extent, this is also the case for Internet users: clicking does not always mean "reading". The type of device most commonly used (175 for the "desktop" category) is also meaningful, because it reflects a content and culture of knowledge that is part of an academic approach. The data concerning the "visitor source" also corroborates the previous observation. The majority of those who consulted the text came from the Université du Québec à Trois-Rivières (UQTR). Moreover, it is not surprising to note that the page devoted to explaining the approach received very few visitors (4). *A priori*, our results therefore call into question the relevance of using a website to access the public sphere and suggest that a Facebook page to make the same kind of comments, for example, could have made consultation easier[6].

10.5.2. *The interaction*

Of the 97 emails sent, two people reacted and asked confirmation questions. We had 28 subscribers on the Twitter account associated with the project and the announcement of the project, 12 of them read the text and three issued a "like". On Facebook, among the 502 people reached, 77 consulted the reference text and 41 "likes" were given. On YouTube, no feedback was received from the 31 people who viewed the explanatory video. We have not received any comments on the website.

10.5.3. *The follow-up*

The monitoring of interactions leaves no doubt: the consultation of the reference text took place mainly during the first three weeks, as shown in Figure 10.2.

---

6 We then carried out a small experiment. During the 2017–2018 holiday season, we published a short Christmas story on Facebook. At a cost of 3 Canadian dollars, we benefited from visibility support offered by the company, which promised us up to 700 "friends". The result was lower (214). It should be noted that Facebook's technical equipment, while much simpler, gave similar results to those obtained in the search (258 visitors). This last experiment therefore suggests that the content would be the main filter.

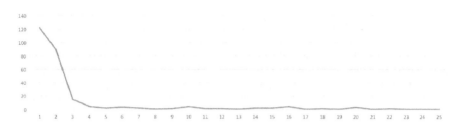

Figure 10.2. *Number of visits to the project Web page*

It is clear that the first few days were crucial, even if the text was not a news item as such. The figures also confirm this: no consultations were carried out in the last three weeks, and activity was extremely low throughout the last five months. The long-tail effect was therefore not observed.

10.6. Reminder of the approach

At this stage, it is important to recall the meaning of the approach and the methodological position used. We did not want to have a contest with *Le Devoir*, for example by accepting *ad nauseam* the people that Facebook offers. We would have created a fake audience. We wanted to see what digital social media could do without changing the situation of the individual who carries the reference text. For the same reason, we did not want to use the school period during which teachers could have made our reference text a compulsory activity. Here again, we would have misled our measurement reference.

This is also the reason why we did not send our text to journalists, since we wanted to know whether it would reach them through digital social media. We would have bypassed our own investigation. We wanted to measure the activity of a university professor who publishes in *Le Devoir* and make a comparison with reference to his usual situation. The same intellectual is faced with two different options for access to the public sphere. From this, we were able to draw conclusions.

10.7. Discussion

First, we have to admit that none of the parameters included in the analysis is applicable due to the low consultation rate[7]. Since digital social media have done very little to circulate our text in the public sphere, there has been no impact on civil society. At this point, we can postulate some reasons for this:

– The type of content and the form of academic presentation do not correspond to what seems to be the culture of digital social media;

– Among the people contacted by email, there were influencers. But, these influencers had an academic zone of influence as they influenced each other.

It is nevertheless relevant to note that it is very rare for an opinion text written by a newspaper reader to have an impact in the public sphere. In this sense, our initial comparison criteria would probably have to be reconsidered.

We therefore believe that the use of digital social media forces users to create their own media, or more precisely their own audience. To reach the level of knowledge, you need a sustained presence and a unifying activity. It is far from certain that media criticism and the right to information are part of the latter category.

The question of influencers is also a more complex element than it appears at first glance. Many people who are interested in information media and who are widely followed on social media (Patrick Legacé, Yves Boisvert, etc.) are indeed influencers because they have gained popularity by traditional media before. The identification of influencers is a very lucrative activity and not always discriminating because of its geographical deployment. Based on Google's automated alerts on "the right to information", only 10% reach Quebec. Without the introduction of two bills, one on the protection of sources and the other on the right to information, the relevance score would be even lower, at nearly 2%.

---

7 Our parameters were as follows: identification of "influencers"; use of ideas expressed by media players (journalist, columnist, editorialist, etc.) privately on their blogs, for example; use of ideas from the media (article); allusions to our text from the political world; ideas from citizens, academics, trade unions; use of ideas from bloggers outside the media sphere; use of diversions of ideas or troll attacks; use of age (if possible) of people who use the ideas; content of research criticism.

10.8. Conclusion

In our view, two main conclusions can be drawn. First, access to the public sphere through digital social media, without the help of traditional media and their influencers aimed at formulating university-style social criticism, is far from being achieved. Second, it becomes imperative to set up a civil society-led body to monitor digital social media, the media sphere and the public sphere. An observatory, for example, would have much more visibility in the public sphere than an approach such as ours; it would be a reference for journalists and, since it would be fed by several people, it could regularly contribute to improving our knowledge of the media and public sphere. In doing so, an observatory would have the opportunity to contribute significantly to social emancipation by proposing an understanding of reality that promotes the common good and, by proposing solutions to improve our potential for living together. The public sphere would be paved with new avenues and all of our worldviews could only benefit from it.

10.9. References

Agence Wellcom (2015). *Guide Social Media 2015* [Online]. Available at: https://www. wellcom.fr/guidesocialmedia/.

Cardon, D. (2010). *La démocratie Internet : promesses et limites.* Le Seuil, Paris.

Citton, Y. (2013). Le marketing entre économie de l'attention et exploitation culturelle. In *Marketing Remède ou Poison ?*, Bourgne, P. (ed.). Éditions Management et Société, Cormelles-le-Royal, 179–199.

Dacheux, E. (2015). Tic et espace public : les enseignements théoriques du printemps tunisien. In *Vers une culture médi@tic : médias, journalisme et espace public à l'épreuve de la numérisation*, Pelissier, N. and Mass, É. (eds). L'Harmattan, Paris, 147–156.

George, É. (2014). Concentration des entreprises et pluralisme de l'information dans le contexte des nouveaux médias : des enjeux toujours d'actualité. *Nouveaux cahiers du socialisme. Médias, journalisme et société*, 11, 15–30.

Gonzalez Quijano, Y. (2012). *Arabités numériques, le printemps web arabe.* Actes Sud, Arles.

Lavigne, A. (2014). Les interactions – sources, médias et publics – à l'ère des médias sociaux. *Les cahiers du journalisme*, 26, 56–71.

Moz (n.d.). The Beginner's Guide to Social Media [Online]. Available at: https://moz.com/ beginners-guide-to-social-media.

Wikipedia (n.d.). Médias sociaux [Online]. Available at: https://fr.wikipedia.org/wiki/ Médias_sociaux.

11

Civil Society and Online Exchanges: Some Digital Contingencies

This chapter is the result of a CRICIS (Centre de recherche interuniversitaire sur la communication, l'information et la société) research mandate to study the online communication practices of civil society. The organizations that make up the so-called "civil society" are trying to influence public debate by mobilizing citizens through digital tools. They deploy communication strategies (advertising campaigns, lobbying, awareness-raising actions, etc.), or even targeted interventions (boycotts, demonstrations, occupations, etc.). The research's aim was to understand how citizen groups are forced to adapt the form of their activities in order to ensure their circulation. From this perspective, the substance of the messages that are exchanged and consulted is less important than the form of their circulation as well as the wide disparities that mark their visibility. This chapter presents some constraints on online social movements and links them to three socio-technical aspects of digital technology. Without bowing to marketing speak, I think we can affirm that the mediation of social relationships implemented by the major digital players leads to profound changes in discussion between the individual and the collective.

11.1. Materialistic approach and transindividual communication *milieu*

I am inspired by works using a materialistic approach to online culture in the wake of post-Marxist studies (Laclau and Mouffe 2014; Storey 2009). These writings describe the influence of digital software and interfaces from an original perspective of their materiality. Beyond the ontological characteristics of digital media, they consider a set of constraints linked to the (ideological) choices governing their design, structure and daily functioning (Galloway 2012; Gillespie

---

Chapter written by Martin BONNARD.

et al. 2014; Loveluck 2015; Terranova 2004a). Following this same perspective and inspired, in particular, by the philosophy of technology (Simondon 2005; Stiegler 1996), a group of researchers have examined the influence of these constraints on the transindividual communication environment, i.e. what welcomes and supports exchanges, memory and aesthetic experiences (Hands 2013; Mager 2012; Munster 2014; Terranova 2004b; Thoburn 2007; Thomas 2012, 2013). I am particularly interested in the work of Tiziana Terranova (2004a).

In an article for the journal *Social Text*, published in 2004, Terranova (2004a) calls for an approach to communication as a *milieu*. Returning to the technical and mathematical sources of communication theories, it describes the sending of a message, not along a path from point A to point B, but through the crossing of a *milieu*. The information itself, its transmitter and its receiver are all specific to, as well as constituent parts of, this milieu. The objective of the person who wishes to convey a message will therefore be to interfere between noise and competing signals in order to guarantee the circulation of its content, give meaning to, or polarize, if you will, part of the information field, in order to ensure the propagation of his or her message. We will retain the idea of an underlying *milieu*, whose articulations can be modulated by the representations and processes associated with the development of digital technology.

This conceptualization makes it possible, as Alessandra Renzi (2015) points out, to apprehend the capitalist logics that compose and form an environment (the Web) where the dynamics of information – the form of its circulation, to use Will Straw's (2010) concept – take precedence over meaning. Neal Thomas (2013) provides some clarification on this point. A series of contingencies within the software platforms produce a specific *content plan* (Guattari 2012) in which the consultation of the elements presented and the exchanges between Internet users will take place.

11.2. *Apparatuses* and mediation through technology

Jean-Louis Déotte (2005, 2007, 2008), whose work is part of the philosophy of the arts, describes what he calls the *techniques of appearing*: "Knowledge and the arts are always equipped according to the technical devices of the time. With regards to the device, there is the function of 'making the same', 'matching': comparing what was previously heterogeneous" (Déotte 2007, p. 16.). He adds to the notion of power inherent in the Foucauldian idea of dispositive (Apparatus in English), the notion of apparat (in French). The Apparatuses, according to Déotte, equally determine the way in which content is made worthy to appear. This determination of the appearance is given as a *standardized system* – we will see that this point must be somewhat nuanced with regard to digital. Within this system, both what can and cannot be introduced into the cultural space of a society, and what forms this new contribution should take, are defined. You can associate an apparatus with an artifact (or a technical system), such as perspective and *camera obscura*, for example, but Déotte clearly underlines the need to distinguish between technique and apparatus. The *apparatus* designates, beyond artificial objects, the set of rules governing the creation and which, by helping to form a relatively homogenous group of works, techniques and representations – linked by the same principle of manifestation – make history.

In my opinion, this perspective can be applied to digital media. As we will soon see, these are governed by a set of standards, which, through their association with technical systems, constrain the visible within a precise framework. It is nevertheless necessary to note a small distinction between what we are dealing with today and the concept of *apparatus* developed by Jean-Louis Déotte. The selection of what is worthy of appearance is no longer made only within a "standardized system", a set of institutional rules or a mechanism, but also by the self-regulation of the participants in the exchange. I am thinking here of Maxime Ouellet's (2011) theses on *governance*. This may refer to the company-wide application of corporate management practices. Connecting individuals through technology ensures the stabilization of society through the self-regulation of its components. In this theoretical model, each individual and each institution use the information circulating on the network to rationally adapt its own actions. Using a genealogy of network development, Benjamin Loveluck (2015) observes that the norms embedded in digital networks and the determination of the exchanges that occur through them, contribute to the realization of this neoliberal ideal. It is, in a way, the strength of GAFAM to give individuals the responsibility for respecting and controlling the proper implementation of codes and processes for visibility on networks.

In an article on the ideological side of digital activism, Paolo Gerbaudo (2017) points out that the intercession of the GAFAM companies is carried out first and foremost through the mediation of social relationships using technology. What exactly do we mean, as far as we are concerned, by the term *social relationships*? In his book *La privation de l'intime*, Michael Foessel (2008) tries to describe a sphere of the intimate, which is neither private life nor a withdrawal into oneself. He refers to the intimate as "the freedom of ties": "the freedom to enter into relationships [with others] that we accept can transform us" (2017, p. 109). But he adds that this barely invented freedom is immediately assimilated in private. This possibility of transformation through the formation of social ties seems to be the subject of the mediation by technology, mentioned by Gerbaudo. Thanks to Jean-Louis Déotte's work, we can now understand the principle of manifestation as a set of standards that governs what is worthy of publication on digital networks, which means, in the case of these networks particularly, what deserves visibility.

This set of standards influences exchanges according to the governance modalities described by Maxime Ouellet (2011), i.e. participants adjust their practices to match the rules on their own. Bearing these different elements in mind, it is on the side of social relationships, and more particularly the discussions between the individual and the collective, that we can observe the effects of the constraints exerted on digital content by the standards just mentioned.

11.3. Three digital contingencies

The platforms, protocols, search and recommendation algorithms – three obvious components of digital networks – all result from a major software transformation:

"The Web has somehow evolved from a 'stock Web', where documents and data were stored on a server and 'frozen' by a URL, to a 'flow Web' where information flows, and is detached from its support and its initial form" (Ertzscheid et al. 2016, p. 130).

This change is both explained and encouraged by "pouring", or streaming logic, aimed at collecting as much data as possible within closed systems (Helmond 2015; Liu 2004; Plantin et al. 2016).

The term platform refers to the now canonical work of Tarleton Gillespie (2010). According to this author, the major players in the digital universe claim to be axiologically neutral when they present the role of the sharing spaces that they make available online. A front-end neutrality, of course, which allows them to serve several purposes and several audiences (if you will); among them shareholders, developers, Internet users and public authorities. However, the structure and functioning of the platforms developed by YouTube, Facebook, Microsoft and others influence the exchanges taking place within them. The phenomenon is also gaining momentum with the relative abandonment of emancipatory communication practices that create, through the development of parallel networks, self-managed spaces where civil society could communicate on its own terms (Gerbaudo 2017). Civil society organizations choose to, and are partly constrained to, operate with existing platforms and comply with various rules and obligations associated with them. As such, Kaun and Uldam (2017) note the progressive generalization of terms of use restricting the anonymity of contributions. Citing another article by Uldam (2016), the two authors refer to the closure by Wordpress of a blog criticizing BP, with the microblogging platform having justified its action by its policy of prohibiting anonymity. More broadly, we can imagine how no longer being able to communicate by masking one's identity can lead some individuals or groups not to make their voices heard for fear of repression or simply of the judgment of others.

The notion of *protocols* makes it possible to describe a form of organization that crosses, like the term *platform*, both software constructions and more or less transparent sets of rules. According to Alessandra Renzi (2015), protocols modulate the circulation of content by acting on their visibility, i.e. everything circulates within the digital universe, but within territories that are hierarchized and more or less marginalized, or placed in the shadows. We see here the relevance of the idea of *milieu* as proposed by Terranova (2004a, 2004b) and how this theoretical proposal highlights the form of modulation exercised by the protocols. Based on studies of mobilization through social networks, we can identify some concrete manifestations of these social and technical norms that govern the formulation of arguments, the functioning of mobilizations or the relationship between civil society and traditional media. Kaun and Stiernstedt (2017) note in particular that members of civil society organizations prefer photos and links to texts in a constantly renewed search for positive comments ("like") and recirculation of messages (sharing and retweets).

Such integration of the implicit rules of the functioning of socio-digital networks refers to a broader process of self-regulation of the expressive practices of organizations and individuals, as I mentioned earlier. We can also note the influence of protocols in the organization of publications within social movements. Swann and Husted (2017) observe changes in the message delivery structure of the Occupy movement as it withdraws from New York City's places of occupation to social networks. Members of pages and groups associated with the movement are thus more likely to relay messages written by a small number of individuals and produce less content on their own. Still, on the subject of hierarchies, Kaun and Uldam (2017) are interested in Facebook pages organizing the work of Swedish civil society to provide emergency assistance during the major wave of migration to Europe in 2015. The authors note a clear power relationship between good Samaritans, who are visible on networks, and migrants kept in the shadows (for various reasons, some of which are very legitimate and aimed at their protection). While the network is highly effective in the very short term – in the aid it provides quickly – as a media space, it replays the inequalities that exist in Western society. It should be noted that learning the codes related to the use of digital platforms can also be perceived positively. Jouët *et al* (2017) study the awareness campaigns and visibility actions carried out online by feminist activists. Their activities on digital networks enable them to acquire skills that can be used in the workplace: self-esteem training, public speaking, mastery of digital tools, etc. The authors also highlight the similarities between the strategies deployed online by these activist groups and those of marketing professionals.

On a more general level, the study of the expression of the network in terms of the notion of protocols also reveals, not only interactions and particular areas of attention, but also hypermedia structures that will allow us to return to the contents following a backward set of links, for example. These assemblies mimic and partly replace the transindividual *milieu* that underlies the acts of communication within the social body. This environment contributes to linking the future of individuals to the collective. As we can see, digital protocols, by assuming part of the regulation of exchanges, refer to a whole series of changes in their form.

Algorithms are programs that operate in an iterative mode and are designed to solve complex problems. Through the repetitive application of formal rules, they make it possible to transform datasets into outputs consisting of structuring patterns or correlations linking these sets together (Thomas 2012). They are used heavily to filter, sort and schedule digital content. Their function is often obscure, allowing platforms to pursue several objectives behind the scenes. Kaun and Uldam (2017) note, for example, that the organic reach of messages on the Facebook platform, i.e. the ability of content to move from one self-centered network to another through the actions of Internet users, is limited for monetization purposes. The algorithm ensures that the "natural" propagation of messages within the social network is restricted, so as not to overshadow the company's paid propagation offers. As for search engines, another field of application of algorithms, they collect information on the phases that have led a group of individuals to satisfy their desire for information and then produce a suitable response to other requests that they consider similar (Hosanagar *et al.* 2014; Thomas 2012). Astrid Mager (2012) emphasizes the role of users and various players in the digital economy in strengthening this mode of operation through consent (more or less informed, certainly) to the production of tracers and the optimization of referencing strategies, for example. This modeling of information needs – the collective requests and responses produced in return – is part of a substitution of collective choice processes. According to the concepts at work in the development and operation of these systems, algorithmic computation is intended to replace the collective search for consensus.

11.4. Conclusion

We can question the consequences of civil society's use of closed platforms and systems in which a set of (sometimes implicit) rules and mechanical processes influence the exchanges between users. If it turns out that the creation of parallel networks and self-managed spaces is less popular today, is it then possible to create spaces that are conducive to diversion and creation of new forms of mobilization from within the logic of the Net? The literature consulted does not really answer this question as it considers that online exchanges should be integrated into the dominant socio-technical context. It therefore envisages the adaptation of civil society mobilizations to the contingencies of the Net, in the form of a "DIY" attitude using what already exists. This stance leads researchers to note the transition from the constraints of the social world to the digital world, which in fact replays the contrasts in terms of access to public speech, power inequalities and socio-cultural inequalities. From this observation, the notion of *milieu*, as advanced by Terranova (2004a, 2004b), seems to deploy another way of understanding the logic of digital technology. Focusing on what underlies online exchanges and the elements that shape the circulation of messages (rather than the meaning they convey) makes it possible to take into account the possibilities of deviation, of emergence from the tensions that run through the media space itself. This does not mean considering only these logics in a kind of "immanentism" of the network. The fact that the network is far from solving the obstacles traditionally encountered by citizen movements is already a welcome step. The materialistic approach to online culture can, in my opinion, complement the tools for understanding the functioning of the digital universe and thus improve the chances of observing new (emancipatory) trends or, on the contrary, new constraints on the ability of civil society to express itself online.

11.5. References

Déotte, J.-L. (ed.) (2005). *Appareils et formes de la sensibilité*. L'Harmattan, Paris.

Déotte, J.-L. (2007). *Qu'est-ce qu'un appareil ? : Benjamin, Lyotard, Rancière*. L'Harmattan, Paris.

Déotte, J.-L. (ed.) (2004). The Differences Between Ranciere's Political Disagreement and Lyotard's Differend in *SubStance* - Issue 103, 33(1), 77–90

Déotte, J.-L. (ed.) (2008). *Le milieu des appareils*. L'Harmattan, Paris.

Ertzscheid, O., Gallezot, G., and Simonnot, B. (2016). À la recherche de la "mémoire" du Web : Sédiments, traces et temporalités des documents en ligne. In *Manuel d'analyse du Web en sciences humaines et sociales*, Barats, C. (ed.). Armand Colin, Paris, 121–160.

Foessel, M. (2008). *La privation de l'intime : mises en scènes politiques des sentiments*. Le Seuil, Paris.

Galloway, A. (2012). *The Interface Effect*. Polity Press, Cambridge/Malden.

Gerbaudo, P. (2017). From cyber-autonomism to cyber-populism: An ideological history of digital activism. *Triple C*, 15(2), 477–489.

Gillespie, T. (2010). The politics of "platforms". *New Media & Society*, 12(3), 347–364.

Gillespie, T., Boczkowski, P.J., and Foot, K.A. (2014). *Media Technologies: Essays on Communication, Materiality, and Society*. MIT Press, Cambridge.

Guattari, F. (2012). *La révolution moléculaire*. Les Prairies ordinaires, Paris.

Hands, J. (2013). Introduction: Politics, Power and 'Platformativity'. *Culture Machine*, 14, 1–9.

Helmond, A. (2015). The platformization of the web: Making web data platform ready. *Social Media + Society*, 1(2), 1–11.

Hosanagar, K., Fleder, D., Lee, D., and Buja, A. (2014). Will the global village fracture into tribes: Recommendation system and their effects on consumer fragmentation. *Management Science*, 60(4), 805–823.

Jouët, J., Niemeyer, K., and Pavard, B. (2017). Faire des vagues. Les mobilisations féministes en ligne. *Réseaux*, 201(1), 21–57.

Kaun, A. and Stiernstedt, F. (2014). Facebook time: Technological and institutional affordances for media memories. *New Media & Society*, 16(7), 1154–68.

Kaun, A. and Uldam, J. (2017). "Volunteering is like any other business": Civic participation and social media. *New Media & Society*, 20(6), 2186–2207.

Laclau, E. and Mouffe, C. (2014). *Hegemony and Socialist Strategy: Towards a Radical Democratic Politics*, 2nd edition. Verso, London/New York.

Liu, A. (2004). Transcendental Data: Toward a cultural history and aesthetics of the new encoded discourse. *Critical Inquiry*, 31, 49–84.

Loveluck, B. (2015). *Réseaux, libertés et contrôle : une généalogie politique d'Internet*. Armand Colin, Paris.

Mager, A. (2012). Algorithmic ideology. *Information, Communication & Society*, 15(5), 769–787.

Munster, A. (2014). Transmateriality. Toward an energetics of signal in contemporary mediatic assemblagee. *Cultural Studies Review*, 20(1), 150–167.

Ouellet, M. (2011). *Mutations du politique et capitalisme avancé : une généalogie "critique" de la gouvernance*. CRICIS, UQAM, Montreal.

Plantin, J.-C., Lagoze, C., Edwards, P.N., and Sandvig, C. (2016). Infrastructure studies meet platform studies in the age of Google and Facebook. *New Media & Society*, 20(1), 1–25.

Renzi, A. (2015). Info-capitalism and resistance: How information shapes social movements. *Interface: A Journal for and About Social Movements*, 7(2), 98–119.

Simondon, G. (2005). *Individuation à la lumière des notions de forme et d'information*. Jérôme Million, Paris.

Stiegler, B. (1996). *La technique et le temps*, vol. 2. Galilée, Paris.

Storey, J. (2009). Marxisms. In *Cultural Theory and Popular Culture: An Introduction*, 5th edition, Storey, J. (ed.). Pearson Longman Harlow, United Kingdom/New York, 59–89.

Straw, W. (2010). The circulatory turn. Dans *The Wireless Spectrum: The Politics, Practices, and Poetics of Mobile Media*, Crow, B., Longford, M., and Sawchuk, K. (eds). University of Toronto Press, Toronto, 17–28.

Swann, T. and Husted, E. (2017). Undermining anarchy: Facebook's influence on anarchist principles of organization in Occupy Wall Street. *The Information Society*, 33(4), 192–204.

Terranova, T. (2004a). Communication beyond meaning: On the cultural politics of information. *Social Text*, 22(3), 51–72.

Terranova, T. (2004b). *Network Culture: Politics for the Information Age*. Pluto Press, London/Ann Arbor.

Thoburn, N. (2007). Patterns of production: Cultural studies after hegemony. *Theory, Culture & Society*, 24(3), 79–94.

Thomas, N. (2012). Algorithmic subjectivity and the need to be informed. Dans *TEM 2012: Proceedings of the Technology & Emerging Media Track – Annual Conference of the Canadian Communication Association (Waterloo, May 30-June 1, 2012)*, Latzko Toth, G. and Millerand, F. (eds) [Online]. Available at: https://acc-cca.ca/index.php/actes-du-colloque-proceedings/.

Thomas, N. (2013). Social computing as a platform for memory. *Culture Machine*, 14, 1–16.

Uldam, J. (2016). Corporate management of visibility and the fantasy of the post-political: Social media and surveillance. *New Media & Society*, 18(2), 201–219.

PART 3

Digital: Some Major Issues to Conclude

12

Transparency, the Public's Right to Information versus Security and State Secrecy in the Digital Age

The problem addressed here refers to the theory of power relations or domination. However, contextualization is necessary to take into account an unavoidable phenomenon – globalization – which implies the mutation of the "fourth power" in the new structuring of the media offer now marked by the concentration and convergence of titles and content. Ignacio Ramonet (2003, p. 1) expresses this context in eloquent terms:

> "Globalization is therefore also the globalization of mass media, communication and information. Concerned above all by their continued gigantism, which forces them to court other powers, these major groups no longer propose, as their civic objective, to be a 'fourth estate', to denounce abuses against the law, or to correct the dysfunctions of democracy in order to polish and perfect the political system. They no longer even want to set themselves up as 'fourth estate', let alone act as a counter-power. When, if necessary, they can constitute a 'fourth estate', this one is added to the other existing powers – political and economic – to crush in its turn, as an additional power, as a media power, the citizens. The civic question that is now being asked is this: how to react? How can we defend ourselves? How can we resist the offensive nature of this new power, which has, in a way, betrayed the citizens and passed over, with its weapons and baggage, to the enemy?"

Chapter written by Ndiaga LOUM.

These concerns are recurrent in a context of informational change, as evidenced by the Leveson report (2012), and are all the more important as a reference for the public in its assessment of the real contribution of information professionals to the democratic game. It appears that the citizen arbitration that takes place within the framework of the public space (Habermas 1988) becomes essential when it comes to resolving conflicts between the different fields (Ramonet 2003). Since the "fourth media power", which should play its role as a counter-power, would have "discredited" itself by associating itself with the existing powers – especially with economic power – in "crushing" citizens, the only way to defend oneself, according to Ramonet, is to see the emergence of a "fifth citizen power". This fifth power of citizens will be a civic force that will oppose the coalition of dominant powers, and in this movement, the Internet could be an "opportunity" to be seized to correct what Julian Assange calls an "asymmetry of information" between public authorities and citizens (Lagasnerie 2015). However, the public should have access to the right information (Corriveau and Sirois 2012). As the media are no longer independent, is the Internet becoming a tool for citizens to enforce transparency? Would it therefore become possible to recreate, in a more "harmonious" way, the partnership of independence and transparency, as some defenders of freedom of expression increasingly claim?

Such an approach should take into account a process that has long been built around conflicts between actors with often conflicting interests, but who value their autonomy to operate (Bernier 2004; Corriveau 2015), so that any desire for a legislative and/or regulatory framework of the media has often been interpreted by information professionals as an attempt to silence the press, while the desire to know more about the actions of state leaders, in the name of a need for transparency, freedom and legitimate public interest in information, is perceived, on the other hand, as a threat to stability and public security. "It is clear", said Bourdieu, "that the various powers, and in particular government authorities, act not only in accordance with the economic constraints they are able to exert but also with all the pressures authorized by the legitimate monopoly of official sources in particular" (Bourdieu 1996 p. 82). For the strategies of self-defense of political power, in relation to pressure groups under direct or indirect state control, could undermine the balances on which the relative power of the media is based.

This chapter seeks to restore the historical dimension of the potential conflicts between political power and the media by postulating the possible inadequacy of legal and ethical frameworks depending on context and circumstance and by taking as practical cases the confirmation of a hypothesis based on the irreducibility of the opposition of principles two recent cases: the Daniel Leblanc case, or the sponsorship scandal[1] (Leblanc 2006; Bernheim 2004), and the WikiLeaks case (Leigh and Harding 2011). To this end, the objective here is not only to explain and analyze standards, nor to assess their usefulness and interest, but above all to examine the adaptability of certain provisions in the current context of the so-called "information and communication society in the digital age". The concern of theorization is in line with the clearly empirical nature of such an analysis, which questions the norms governing the communication sectors in general, and the media in particular, in a rapidly changing technical, political and ideological context.

12.1. Relationships of power and domination between fields: research questions

The theoretical approach based on power relations or domination-based relationships between politics and the media is inspired by Bourdieu's general field theory (1980). Bourdieu suggested that there are general laws of the fields:

> "Fields as different as the fields of politics and the field of religion have invariant laws of functioning, which is what makes the project of a general theory not foolish, and which, from now on, we can use what we learn about the functioning of each particular field to question and interpret other fields, thus exceeding the deadly and idiographical autonomy and the formal and empty theory" (p. 113).

We could have used the "journalistic field" as a term. However, in the context of a reflection on power relations, the expression "media field" is more appropriate in that it makes it possible to group those who proclaim their membership of this field under a generic name (see all those who enter the field of citizen journalism or digital social media) and who wish to offer an alternative to traditional media subject to concentration laws (Bernier 2004, 2008; Payette 2010), but who are challenged by the "purists" of the profession, who believe that assuming such a function is not without responsibility (Benkler 2011). It seems to us more prudent to maintain the expression "media field", which is less reductive than that of "journalistic field". As a result, what is most intriguing in the study of power relations between the different fields is the claim of these two actors of a democracy

---

1 The "sponsorship scandal" is a Canadian political case involving the use of public funds to finance a public relations operation aimed at thwarting the Parti Québécois' actions in favor of sovereignty. Significant funds were spent on communications companies that were supposed to promote federalism and fight the independence strategies of the sovereignist party, but they were not monitored to ensure that "the goods were delivered" in practice. Daniel Leblanc is the *Globe and Mail* journalist who broke the scandal through his media coverage. The public, outraged by such information, put pressure on the government to set up a public inquiry commission on the case in 2004.

(media and political power) to evoke the public interest to justify their "actions", whereas, paradoxically, the citizen seems increasingly far from their real concerns (Corriveau and Sirois 2012).

The case study favored here and associated with the qualitative approach augurs an original approach, justified by the novel nature of this theoretical reflection, which contrasts contradictory principles, specific to the functioning of different fields but of equal value in a democracy: the relationship between the preservation of state secrets and the public's right to information or democratic transparency, the protection of professional sources versus the requirement of truth in court and the obligation of testimony as a reasonable limit to the constitutional guarantee of freedom of the press. It is necessary to consider the potential risks of conflicts between rulers who have been legitimized in their function by popular suffrage and a media jealous of a freedom backed by more or less strict respect for the so-called ethical and deontological rules. To illustrate our point, we can refer here to concrete examples of open conflicts between the press and the government, such as the sponsorship scandal, or the case of journalist Daniel Leblanc, and the WikiLeaks case, which pit freedom of information against the transparency of the governance mechanisms of society and the need to protect state secrets.

It then becomes necessary to question the effectiveness of the legal mechanisms put in place by States to regulate the journalistic professions and the scope of ethical and deontological codes as sources of self-regulation. Can we hypothesize that media law is always relative and that the ethical and deontological framework of the media can be universalized? What happens when legal and ethical standards conflict? Should the desire for transparency to strengthen governance mechanisms in our societies and the legitimate public interest in information outweigh the need for security and the protection of state secrets? Do such notions of the principle of the traditional functioning of democracy resist the challenge of transparency imposed by the so-called "information society", where the Internet facilitates the circulation of information and its speed and makes censorship difficult, as the WikiLeaks site eloquently demonstrates? Does the misuse of granted and protected rights threaten the democratic balance? Are there appropriate solutions that reconcile opposing principles, such as the protection of sources and the need to establish the truth in court? How, for example, can we enforce the principle of source protection essential to press freedom and the legal provision that allows press companies to be searched and gives judges the ability to seize any document or computer data they deem necessary? And if, among the documents seized, was one that revealed the source, what should be done?

12.2. Illustrative case studies of power relationships

The Daniel Leblanc and sponsorship scandal cases and the difficult management of the information reported by WikiLeaks demonstrate the relevance of this debate while highlighting its ambiguity. They therefore multiply tenfold the scientific interest of analysis oriented towards this power conflict, which draws its source from opposing principles that are specific to each sphere (state and media) but of equal value in a democracy. The search for useful but often hidden information legitimizes the existence of investigative journalism, whose future depends, in large part, on the ethical and deontological protection of confidential sources and professional secrecy (Leblanc 2006; Woodward 2007).

The great challenge, wherever these questions arise, is to strike a balance between the principle of protecting journalistic sources, the need to establish the truth in court and the obligation to testify, as well as the legitimate interest of the public. If, today, the trend in the major democracies (Belgium in 2005, France in 2010, the United States in 2013, Canada in 2017) is to enshrine in law a principle of ethical and deontological origin, the problem raised by the Supreme Court of the United States (which reminds us that this privilege does not exist in Common Law) remains:

> "[While it] is not irrational to argue that the disclosure of sources may have an effect on the flow of information, it is also very difficult to establish precisely the nature and extent of this effect, given the differences and speculation that exist on this issue" (Langelier 2010, p. 11).

These questions, which have been debated at length in the literature and in democratic deliberative bodies (notably by the Council of Europe in 2011 and the *Fédération professionnelle des journalistes du Québec* in 1990), take on more concrete, and certainly more problematic, outlines when viewed from the perspective of power relations through case studies, as we propose.

12.2.1. *The sponsorship scandal: a Canadian case study*

Above all, it is a question of an opposition of principles on which the functioning of the political sphere, on the one hand, and the media field, on the other, is based: State secrecy and the protection of professional sources. On October 22, 2010, the Supreme Court of Canada issued an important decision concerning a fundamental value that refers to the public's right to information. The Supreme Court had to answer this question: can a court compel a journalist (Daniel Leblanc in this case) to answer questions about his anonymous source for the disclosure of information that is proven to be in the public interest, because it concerns taxpayer money (in this case, the sponsorship scandal)? In response, the Supreme Court issued a "half-decision", the essential aspect of which is the provisional preservation of the general principle of source protection, pending the Quebec Superior Court's reopening of the case based on its merits and reviewing whether a derogation from this professional "privilege" is relevant and justified in the circumstances. Our objective here is to restate the debate from both an ethical and a legal point of view in order to highlight its antinomic nature. Could we take the calculated risk of saying that if there is one area where the separation of ethics and law is most clear-cut, it is that of professional secrecy and its counterpart in journalism, the protection of confidential sources? What is the issue when it comes to the protection of confidential daily sources?

As far back as we can go, the texts that guide the practice of the journalistic profession are concerned with ensuring the protection of journalistic sources. One that is less controversial because it is expressed in the most diplomatic terms is that of UNESCO, known as the *Déclaration de l'Unesco sur les médias* (1983). The social role of the journalist requires that the profession maintains a high level of integrity. This includes the right of the journalist to refrain from working against his or her convictions or to reveal sources of information. The purpose of this provision is to be included in the section on the professional integrity of journalists (Principle IV). This means that the journalist's stated intention to refuse to reveal his sources is not only an act of bravery or respect for a pact made with his informant but also ethical behavior recommended by an international UN body.

From an international principle to a universal principle, the temptation to overcome this small difference is great. In addition to the UNESCO Declaration, there is the equally well-known "Bordeaux Declaration", adopted at the 2nd World Congress of the International Federation of Journalists (IFJ), held in Bordeaux in 1954, and revised in Helsingor in 1986. Article 6 of the Bordeaux Declaration states: "The journalist shall keep confidential the source of information obtained in confidence". And the Munich Declaration adds that the journalist must "maintain professional secrecy and not disclose the source of the information obtained in confidence" (art. 7). The *Pressekodex*, drawn up in 1973 and updated in 1990 by the German Press Council, provides unambiguously that "every person active in the press shall observe professional secrecy, shall exercise the right to refuse his testimony and shall disclose his sources only with their express consent" (art. 6). The British Complaints Commission's Code of Practice states this journalistic duty in terms of "a moral obligation to protect confidential sources of information" (art. 16). The *Guide de déontologie de la Fédération des journalistes du Québec* (which is not a code) states in article 6 b the following: "Journalists who have promised anonymity to a source must keep their promise, in any forum, unless the source has deliberately misled the journalist." Finally, the *Conseil de presse du Québec*, in its code of ethics, reinforces this right by providing the necessary guidelines (art. 2.1.7) and even published a white paper on the issue (1989). If such a principle is unanimously accepted, as we have tried to illustrate through the formal mention of ethical and deontological codes, we will have to ask ourselves why this should always be the case.

In the dynamics of power relations, it is up to the press to reveal everything that politicians hide, with the ultimate justification of the public's legitimate interest in the information. However, there is no fourth power except in the detailed investigative work in what is commonly referred to today as investigative journalism. It can only thrive in a context where information is gathered in confidence. This is the whole point of the ethical recommendation made to the journalist who has obtained information in a confidential manner and who must keep silent about its origin. It is natural that this ethical and deontological recommendation often leads him to cover his tracks to prevent the reader from identifying his source. This explains the "code names" given to protect informants, as illustrated by the most famous journalistic investigation that culminated in the political earthquake known as the Watergate scandal: "Deep Throat" was the code name of the informant of the two Washington Post journalists who broke the story (Carl Bernstein and Bob Woodward).

Daniel Leblanc's "*MaChouette*" is therefore in line with the same tradition of the investigative journalist, whose practice always reveals the interests of opposing powers: those of politics and those of the media. So would forcing the journalist to reveal his sources not amount to violating an ethical and deontological duty, the ultimate consequence of which is the end of investigative journalism and, consequently, the annihilation of the principle of a balance of power that guarantees the integrity of the democratic system? Is it up to politicians to keep changing the principle of the protection of sources until it disappears? Is it acceptable for judges to yield to pressure from unscrupulous political powers to the point of gutting such a provision by opposing it with principles of equal legal value? In applying this principle, should the freedom left to the journalist be broad, should it be an act of free conscience or an internal arbitration in order to achieve a balance between these different elements: the public's right to information, respect for a promise, the ethics of responsibility, the need to verify information?

Obviously, the practice of such a principle in the field of journalism is rich in potential minefields, hence its objective limitations. The ethical and deontological principle of protecting confidential sources should not be used to cover criminal sources or to place secrecy at the service of the search for a sensation. The principle would be distorted if it gave rise to an abusive practice of denunciation by third parties. The interest of mentioning such a principle also multiplies when it comes to a refusal to testify. The stakes are so high in this case that in many countries (Germany, Austria, France, the United States and, more recently, Canada and Quebec), an attempt has been made to include the ethical and deontological principle of source protection in the legal framework. In France, for example, legislation has been adopted with a simple formula, namely the addition of a provision to the Code of Criminal Procedure which stipulates that "[any] journalist heard as a witness on information gathered in the course of his or her activity is free not to reveal its origin" (art. 109, para. 2). Would procedural constraints that would oblige the journalist to testify have the effect of compromising the relationship of trust maintained with his sources and have consequences on the freedom of the press *lato sensu*?

These cases can be compared today to the sponsorship scandal and the subsequent one, now known as the "Daniel Leblanc case". By granting lawyers at the advertising firm Polygone the right to question journalist Leblanc about his anonymous source who revealed the sponsorship scandal, one may wonder whether the judge is not taking on the heavy responsibility of challenging a professional principle linked to press freedom, as guaranteed by the Canadian Charter of Rights and Freedoms. This fundamental text, while guaranteeing the freedom of the press (art. 2 (b)), does, however, provide for limits, but these must still be reasonable and justifiable in a free and democratic society (art. 1).

The question then arises as to whether the obligation to testify for the purpose of clarifying the truth or preserving the rights of defense of a party to a trial would be a reasonable limit opposable to the principle of the protection of sources and a corollary of the freedom of expression, within the meaning of section 1 of the Canadian Charter of Rights and Freedoms. By referring such a question to the Superior Court of Quebec while inviting it to take into account the reasons and recitals of its judgment, the Supreme Court is making only a "half-decision", whose merit is, however, to maintain, as it stands, the principle of the protection of confidential sources in journalism, which should therefore be assessed on a case-by-case basis[2]. But would not this be likely to weaken it because it reflects the ever-changing moods, circumstances and conjunctures, instead of being consolidated over time?

---

2 The Supreme Court of Canada is asking the judge of the Superior Court of Quebec to draw inspiration from the Wigmore principle or test, from the name of an American author, which consists of arbitrating between the principle of the administration of justice and the protection of sources, taking into account four criteria: 1) there must be an undertaking of confidentiality; 2) confidentiality must be essential to maintain the relationship between the journalist and his or her source; 3) these relationships must be of a nature that the community would like to see maintained; and 4) the harm to this journalist–source relationship must be greater than the judicial benefit of disclosing the source.

It is this kind of "legal uncertainty" that is supposed to be addressed by the new legal provisions adopted in Canada (2017) and Quebec (2018) to strengthen the protection of journalists' confidential sources, new provisions whose application will have to be monitored and evaluated in the light of case law practices in similar cases. However, we will not undertake this task here, and it would be premature to do so given the novelty of these legal provisions, both at the federal and provincial levels.

If these questions relate specifically to one of the cases studied (Daniel Leblanc case), they could arise everywhere, in terms that the lawyer Langelier eloquently summarizes in a research report submitted to the Task Force on Journalism and the Future of Information in Quebec:

> "A debate is still raging, he said, between those who fear that the imperfect protection of sources will have an inhibiting effect on the media's ability to play their role as the guardians of democratic processes and those who, on the other hand, fear that a press left to its own devices will disrupt judicial truth-seeking processes" (Langelier 2010, p. 11).

When the ethical and deontological principle of source protection is in line with the more clearly political concept of transparency as a justification or source of legitimization, the debate becomes more complicated and polemical. This is the difficulty that the WikiLeaks case singularly reveals.

12.2.2. *The unique and specific case of WikiLeaks: freedom of information versus the need for state security*

In the specific case of WikiLeaks, the question arises of the freedom to inform versus the imperative of state security with all its corollaries: state, defense, diplomatic secrets (Cohen 2012). Can we show and say everything in the name of transparency in a democracy (Boutaud 2005)? Does the Internet allow citizens to regain the freedom of expression suffocated by the complicity established between major media owners and governments (Bernatchez 2012)? Has WikiLeaks become a new kind of way to "right the wrongs"? What is certain is that with WikiLeaks, issues of transparency, state secrets and responsibility can no longer be approached in the same way (Deibert *et al.* 2010), especially in the context of the "information society", where communication technologies offer the possibility of having several platforms capable of promoting the circulation of information whose flows are increasingly difficult to control or even censor.

With WikiLeaks, we enter another type of journalism, which differs from traditional journalistic practices. Initially, news production was a construction business involving journalists, their media and sources. The WikiLeaks site illustrates the new phenomenon of collaborative journalism, Web 2.0. In a Web that is intended to be participatory, the collection of information is no longer the monopoly of the journalist, and the news gathered becomes accessible on the Internet and can be taken up by everyone, including by the major dailies[3]. The site's founder, Julian Assange, has become a theorist of transparency and explains the general principles on which he and his collaborators operate: the protection of the freedom of expression and dissemination through the media, the improvement of our shared history and the right of each person to create history. According to Assange, involving the general public anonymously allows for a more timely and transparent exchange. Moreover, most of the time, WikiLeaks issues information that the vast majority of the media would not make public (Assange 2011).

Consequently, WikiLeaks' operating principle runs counter to a phenomenon that is very present today, namely the convergence of the content and positions of the major mass media, which favor profitable content and participate in the general depoliticization of societies. We are still faced with the opposition of the principles conveyed by two spheres: one that defends freedom of expression and the legitimate interest of the public in information, and another that is based on the imperative of security and the protection of state secrets (Loum and Corriveau 2014; Ringmar 2007). Beyond the WikiLeaks case, there is the question of the disruption of norms that the Internet entails (Deibert *et al.* 2010; Loum 2015), access to which is considered by some to be a fundamental human right and whose restriction, for whatever reason, would be a regression (Assange *et al.* 2013). However, this is not the point of view of Vinton Cerf, considered one of the founding fathers of the Internet (co-inventor of the TCP/IP protocol in 1974, with Bob Kahn, and one of the founders of the *Internet Society* in 1992). In an article published in *The New York Times* on January 4, 2012, Cerf states: "Technology is an enabler of rights, not a right itself."

---

3 WikiLeaks is covered by five major publications around the world (*The New York Times, The Guardian, El País, Le Monde* and *Der Spiegel*), but its editorial line is considered irresponsible by other newspapers, such as *L'Est républicain*, which speaks of "despotic transparency", *Le Figaro*, which sees it as "worrying exhibitionism", and *The Washington Post*, which demands the closure of the wikileaks.org site, describing it as a "criminal enterprise" (Baillargeon 2010).

12.3. Conclusion

In theory, the positions expressed reflect the ambivalence between the need for transparency and the necessary limits of it in a democracy (Baillargeon 2010). For Marc Raboy (quoted in Baillargeon 2010):

"Anything that contributes to the transparency of the governance mechanisms of our societies is a good thing. It is precisely for this reason that media and information technologies exist: they equip citizens to enable them to monitor and intervene in things that concern them."

Anne-Marie Gingras finds it necessary to include nuance in the interpretation given to the principle of transparency in a democracy:

"I still observe in WikiLeaks the libertarian fantasy that can be found at all stages of Internet development. Transparency and accountability are not the same thing. Total transparency also means giving all ammunition to the enemy. Who tells us, for example, that in the documents disclosed, there is no coded information of a high level of danger that only experts can identify?" (quoted in Baillargeon 2010).

The main thing here is to note the strong impression of unlocking the secrets of political power. Returning to Stéphane Baillargeon's article, Anne-Marie Gingras recalls the political context of the birth and development of the WikiLeaks site since 2006:

"We no longer want the authorities to hide too much from us. In 1990 and 2003, both wars in Iraq were triggered by lies. A lot of people are angry because we are being lied to. So there is also, with WikiLeaks, the willingness to give a lesson in transparency. But I repeat: this display poses real problems."

These real problems are downplayed by Marc Raboy, who underlines the historical dimension of the information relayed by the controversial site in a democracy in search of more transparency:

"Within two or three years, when the researchers have taken the time to go through the thousands of pages, we will certainly obtain a beautiful synthesis. This is important information about the only superpower of our time. Its government and its way of making decisions concern everyone in the world. It is also in this regard that I welcome this transparency" (quoted in Baillargeon 2010).

This debate on contradictory legitimacy is longstanding, as we recalled above; it is recurrent and it is undoubtedly updated by the changes brought about by the new information and communication technologies and, above all, by the Internet, but particularly by the use made of it by freedom of expression "extremists" such as Julian Assange and the defenders of the WikiLeaks site. The legal battles that are beginning, the intense political debate between freedom of information advocates and the leaders of some Western states (notably the United States) and the contradictions between the norms that define the functioning of each sphere in the democratic space demonstrate the importance of this transdisciplinary reflection on this subject, which we can hope will shed a unique light on delicate issues.

12.4. References

Assange, J. (2011). *Julian Assange. The Unauthorized Autobiography*. Canongate, Edinburgh.

Assange, J., Appelbaum, J., Müller-Maguhn, A., and Zimmermann, J. (2013). *Menaces sur nos libertés. Comment Internet nous espionne. Comment résister*. Robert Laffont, Paris.

Baillargeon, S. (2010). La transparence en question : la mise en ligne des dossiers diplomatiques par WikiLeaks sert-elle la démocratie ?. *Le Devoir*, December 1st.

Benkler, Y. (2011). A free irresponsible press: Wikileaks and the battle over the soul of the networked fourth estate. *Harvard Civil Rights-Civil Liberties Law Review*, 46, 311–397.

Bernatchez, S. (2012). La signification du droit à la liberté d'expression au crépuscule de l'idéal. *Les Cahiers de droit*, 53(4), 687–713.

Bernheim, J.-C. (2004). *Le scandale des commandites : un crime d'État*. Méridien, Montreal.

Bernier, M.-F. (2004). *Éthique et déontologie du journalisme*. Presses de l'Université Laval, Quebec.

Bernier, M.-F. (2008). *Journalistes au pays de la convergence. Sérénité, malaise et détresse dans la profession*. Presses de l'Université Laval, Quebec.

Bourdieu, P. (1980). *Questions de sociologie*. Éditions de Minuit, Paris.

Bourdieu, P. (1994). L'emprise du journalisme. *Actes de la recherche en sciences sociales*, 101–102, 3–9.

Bourdieu, P. (1996). *Sur la télévision. Suivi de l'emprise du journalisme*. Liber-Raisons d'agir, Paris.

Boutaud, J.-J. (2005). *Transparence et communication*. L'Harmattan, Paris.

Cerf, V. (2012). Internet access is not a human right. *The New York Times*, January 4th.

Cohen, S. (2012). Official secrets act. *The Canadian Encyclopedia* [Online]. Available at: http://www.thecanadianencyclopedia.com/articles/official-secrets-act.

Conseil de presse du Québec (1989). *Livre Blanc sur la protection des sources confidentielles d'information et du matériel journalistique* [Online]. Available at: https://conseildepresse. qc.ca/publications/avis/avis-du-conseil-de-presse-du-quebec-livre-blanc-sur-la-protection-des-sources-confidentielles-dinformation-et-du-materiel-journalistique/.

Corriveau, R. (2015). La réplique Médias : les intouchables. *Le Devoir*, November 19th [Online]. Available at: http://www.ledevoir.com/societe/medias/455568/la-replique-medias-les-intouchables.

Corriveau, R. and Sirois, G. (2012). *L'information, la nécessaire perspective citoyenne.* Presses de l'Université du Québec, Quebec.

Deibert, R., Palfrey, J., Rohozinski, R., and Zittrain, J. (2010). *Access Controlled: The Shaping of Power, Rights and Rule in Cyberspace* [Online]. Available at: https://pdfs. semanticscholar.org/eec7/db21496f1327907b74f6914dd119647394a7.pdf.

Habermas, J. (1988). *L'espace public.* Payot, Paris.

de Lagasnerie, G. (2015). *L'art de la révolte, Snowden, Assange, Manning.* Fayard, Paris.

Langelier, R. (2010). Le statut professionnel du journaliste québécois. Éléments de réflexion à partir des débats historiques ayant entouré cette question et de l'expérience étrangère. Research report presented to the Task Force on Journalism and the Future of Information in Quebec [Online]. Available at: https://www.mcc.gouv.qc.ca/fileadmin/documents/ publications/media/Richard_E._Langelier_-_Statut_professionnel_du_journaliste_ quebecois-Experience-Internationale.pdf.

Leblanc, D. (2006). *Nom de code : MaChouette. L'enquête sur le scandale des commandites.* Libre Expression, Outremont.

Leigh, D. and Harding, L. (2011). *WikiLeaks: Inside Julian Assange's War on Secrecy.* Guardian Books, London.

Leveson, L.J. (2012). Leveson Inquiry - Report into the Culture, Practices and Ethics of the Press [Online]. Available at: https://www.gov.uk/government/publications/leveson-inquiry-report-into-the-culture-practices-and-ethics-of-the-press.

Loum, N. (2015). Repenser la régulation de l'information en ligne : nouveaux défis et nouvelles approches théoriques. *Revue africaine de communication*, 157–168.

Loum, N. and Corriveau, R. (2014). Bataille de légitimités et rapports de pouvoir entre les champs politique et médiatique. Pertinence des normes législatives et éthiques d'encadrement de la communication médiatique ?. *Les Cahiers du CRICIS*, 5 [Online]. Available at: http://www.archipel.uqam.ca/6475/.

Payette, D. (ed.) (2010). L'information au Québec : un intérêt public. Task Force on Journalism and the Future of Information in Quebec [Online]. Available at: http://www.mcc.gouv.qc.ca/fileadmin/documents/publications/media/rapport-Payette-2010.pdf.

Ramonet, I. (2003). Le cinquième pouvoir. *Le Monde diplomatique*, 1, 26, October.

Ringmar, E. (2007). *A Blogger's Manifesto: Free Speech and Censorship in the Age of the Internet*. Anthem Press, London/New York.

Woodward, B. (2017). *Mensonges d'État. Bush en guerre*. Denoël, Paris.

13

Information Commons and the Neoliberal State

In recent years, the notion of the *commons* has become increasingly popular. It can be seen both in contemporary activist practices and in critical reflections on financial capitalism (Karyotis 2018; Paranque and Perez 2015) and neoliberal attacks on democracy (Dardot and Laval 2016; Negri 2010). As a result, various claims and experiments have been placed under the banner of the commons or are designated as such.

In our opinion, the critical scope of this notion, and its ability to coalesce and bring together specific struggles, depends greatly on our ability to think in action, i.e. in our ability to grasp the meaning of the present, of current events based on history. Only then will it be possible to question, with nuance, the recent interest of the French State in the commons, which was particularly expressed in Article 8 of the Digital Republic Bill (2015) – an article which was eventually not adopted – and in Emmanuel Macron's speech on September 29, 2017 "financing common goods" at the European Digital Summit in Tallinn, Estonia.

This chapter will therefore be divided into two main parts: first, we will clarify what is meant by the notions of *common goods* in law and economics, and the *commons* and the *common*, and second, we will try to understand the interest of the French State in what is presented as an alternative to both the market and the State, namely information commons in a digital context in this specific case.

Chapter written by Lisiane LOMAZZI.

13.1. The history and evolution of the commons

13.1.1. *Legal and economic concepts of common goods*

The legal concept of common goods is rooted in the definition given in Roman law, more precisely in the *Institutes of Justinian* (533 AD), of *common resources*, which are public things that are not appropriable because of their nature and physical characteristics (e.g. air). The conception of common goods in economics is marked by Samuelson's (1954) theory of public goods. In his paper, Samuelson develops a typology of goods in terms of their intrinsic or production characteristics based on two variables: rivalry in use and exclusion in access. This matrix makes it possible to determine the most efficient organization of the production of goods and services between the market and the State. *Common-pool resources* are defined in terms of their rivalry – their consumption by one agent reduces the quantity available to others – and their non-exclusivity, as they are accessible to all (e.g. fisheries resources). This erroneous naturalistic definition – a common good as a resource for open access and common use without a governance structure – is found in Hardin's famous paper (1968). According to him, each rational individual tends to maximize his or her personal interest, which leads to overexploitation of the natural resource. For this reason, he assumes that common ownership does not work and advocates the introduction of private or, marginally, in case of market failures, public property rights. However, this deduction is based on an inaccurate vision of what a common good truly is. Indeed, Hardin confuses a *res nullius*, i.e. something that has no owner but is appropriable, with the commons, i.e. resources whose access, use and governance are governed by a set of rules established by a community to ensure its preservation and sustainability.

Until the return of the idea of commons in the 1990s, the notion of a common good in law and economics ignored the social dimension of the common by focusing on the resource considered as naturally common in view of certain physical characteristics that made it appropriable or not. However, what defines a common is not its natural properties, but its institutional dimension, i.e. "choices that are made concerning the conditions of access to the use of these goods, and more broadly a set of rules and practices that organize the conditions of use and possibly of production" (Weinstein 2015, pp. 72–73).

This thought of a common as an institution presents "two strategies of problematization" (Sauvêtre 2016): first, a political economy of the commons, which characterizes them in terms of institutional arrangements, and second, a socio-political concept of the common, which emphasizes the primacy of the activity that establishes it.

13.1.2. *Political economy of the commons: the commons as institutional arrangements*

The work of Ostrom and her colleagues (Ostrom 1986), first presented at the Anapolis conference in 1983, constitutes a "major turning point" in the theory of the commons. Empirical analysis of the diversity of collective resource management situations leads them to move away from Samuelson's conception and define the commons as institutional arrangements. Three criteria must be met for a common to be defined as such: a clearly identified resource, a legal regime that distributes the resource rights among *commoners* and a governance structure.

One of the main contributions of the political economy of the commons is to propose an alternative conception of property as a set of rights that breaks with the legal construction of modern Western property, as marked by the dichotomy between public and private property. By mobilizing this conception, Schlager and Ostrom (1992) aim to challenge the hegemonic interpretation of property as exclusive private property and to propose an alternative one. They break with the idea of ownership as possession in order to think of it in terms of use and governance: ownership of common property "can only be conceived as relative and shared between several actors [...] within the same community, [...] between the public authority and a community, or between communities and individuals, or even between the State and individuals" (Orsi 2015, p. 60–61).

The set of common property rights is divided into two categories of rights (user rights and governance rights) that are subdivided into five levels. The distribution of these rights defines specific statuses – from user to owner – in relation to the resource. In this sense, the legal regime of the commons prevails over the enjoyment of property, and user rights over the abuse of exclusive private property. This does not mean that the commons cannot be the subject of commercial uses decided by the governance structure. For example, some legal forms of information commons allow commercial uses (some GPL or Creative Commons licenses, for example), but they appear to be an exception and not the rule, thus it is the rights of use that prevail over the rest.

Subsequently, Hess and Ostrom (2011) extend the analysis to information commons which are different from common lands because of their non-rivalry and the ease of their digital capture. The work of Coriat and Bauwens (2015) aims to extend Ostrom and Hess' reflection on information commons. These are defined according to the same three definition criteria as those established by Ostrom (1999) for common lands (resource, legal regime, governance structure). First, "information commons deal with resource sets composed of non-rival and (generally) non-exclusive goods" (Coriat and Bauwens 2015, p. 40). Second, "[they] were made necessary by the effects of an artificially constructed 'exclusivity' due to specific property rights: the series of so-called 'intellectual property' rights" (p. 41). Therefore, they require the implementation of innovative legal regimes that "ensure access to resources and their allocation between commoners according to procedures that are not mainly based on price and market mechanisms" (p. 13), but also on cooperation. Third, "[the] governance of information commons is oriented not towards the conservation of resources, but towards their enrichment and multiplication" (p. 44).

13.1.3. *The socio-politics of the common: the common as a political principle*

The political economy of the commons focuses – exclusively in the work of Ostrom and mainly in that of Coriat and Bauwens (2015) – on the legal and economic dimensions of the commons. The socio-politics of the common (Dardot and Laval 2010, 2014; Hardt and Negri 2012) is giving thought to the socio-political aspects of the common defined as a political activity, an instituent *praxis*.

Dardot and Laval reclaim the Aristotelian concept of the institution of the common (*koinôn*), which is the result of an activity of communing (*koinônein*), i.e. the activity of deliberation by citizens on the common benefit (*koinê sumpheron*) which constitutes one of the pillars of the Athenian democracy. It is in this sense that "the common is to be thought of as a coactivity, and not as co-ownership, shared property or co-possession. [Only] the practical activity of humans … can make things common" (Dardot and Laval 2014, p. 48–49). The logic of the common, which characterizes a large number of contemporary social struggles, is therefore opposed to neoliberal rationality (Dardot and Laval 2010), because:

> "Once established, the common is inalienable and can't be appropriated. It opens a space within which common use prevails over property rights. It is therefore not a 'thing' even when it is related to a thing. […] the common is the living link between a thing, an object, a place, a natural entity (a river, a forest) or artificial reality (a theater, a public or private building, a service, a company, a square), and the activity of the collective that takes it on, preserves it, maintains it and takes care of it" (Cornu *et al.* 2017, p. 219–220).

The generalization of experiments to build "politics of the common", which consists of making the common a "principle of social transformation" (Dardot and Laval 2014, p. 463) and "the new meaning of social imagination" (p. 451), must lead to a revolution in the Castoriadian sense, i.e. to a new institution of society itself.

In conclusion, according to Weinstein (2015), the main difference between these two approaches is that the political economy of the commons sees "complementary and partially alternative configurations to the commercial and public forms of contemporary capitalism" (p. 69), while the socio-politics of the common is presented as "the basis for overcoming capitalism and for a real revolution leading to a new social order, or even a new communism" (p. 69). In either case, it is necessary to deal with the institutions in place, especially when they are closely interested in the commons, which seems to be the case of the French State. Indeed, while attempts to recover the commons from the market have been the subject of a number of reflections aimed at preventing the commons from becoming the common property of capital, the State's interest in the commons has so far been little considered.

13.2. The relationship between the commons and the neoliberal state

We have picked out two examples that can be of great help to study the French State's interest in information commons: first, the Digital Republic Bill (2015), under the presidency of François Hollande, and second, the speech "financing common goods" (*"Financer les biens communs"*) of the current French president Emmanuel Macron at the European Digital Summit in Tallinn, Estonia, on September 29, 2017.

13.2.1. *Article 8 of the Digital Republic Bill*

The eighth article "Positive definition of common domain information" of the Digital Republic Bill (2015) – of the law proposal of the government led by Manuel Valls and the Secretary of State for Digital Affairs, Axelle Lemaire, under the presidency of François Hollande – aimed to "[p]rotect the resources common to all in the public domain against appropriation practices that lead to the denial of access to these". As a reminder, the public domain can be summarily defined as what is not or is no longer protected by intellectual property rights. In this sense, inventions or works of information in the public domain are common goods under the meaning of Article 714 of the Civil Code: "There are things that belong to no one and whose use is common to all". Article 8 was intended to combat the creation of abusive exclusivities in the public domain and, at the same time, in a data economy, to promote open innovation through the free flow of information. The purpose of this article was therefore twofold:

1) the positive definition of common goods currently in the public domain to protect them from abusive and exclusive appropriation;

2) ensuring the flow of information essential for data-based innovations.

The online consultation conducted from September 26 to October 18, 2015 was marked by an outcry from collective societies for the rights of rights holders whose strategy to persuade the public and members of the National Assembly consisted of making people believe that copyright was being attacked, even though, by definition, what is in the public domain is not or is no longer subject to copyright in its proprietary dimension[1]. This uproar led to the setting up of an information mission urgently entrusted to lawyer Jean Martin, which resulted in a 10-page report entitled *"Rapport de la mission sur les enjeux de la définition et de la protection d'un domaine commun informationnel au regard de la propriété littéraire et artistique"* [Report on the challenges of defining and protecting a shared informational domain in relation to literary and artistic property] (*Conseil supérieur de la propriété littéraire et artistique* 2015).

During the examination of Article 8 in the National Assembly in November 2015, the deputies considered that, as it stood, the provisions contained in the text were insufficient to ensure that it did not constitute potential copyright infringement. It is worth mentioning here the important lobbying work that has been done on members of Parliament, which may be related to this conclusion.

The government finally decided to remove Article 8 from the text to be voted on, despite almost 80% of Internet users voting in favor of the article. The promise of a new information mission to *"propose, in conjunction with all stakeholders and with transparency towards the general public, measures to enhance the value of the public domain and encourage the creation of common values, essential for innovation and growth"* (Berne 2018) has not been fulfilled.

13.2.2. *The European Digital Summit*

At the European Digital Summit in Tallinn, Estonia, the President of the French Republic, Emmanuel Macron, delivered a speech at a press conference on September 29, 2017, which presented a digital strategy for the European Union based on four pillars; the fourth focused on "financing common goods". In particular, he said:

> "Digital technology is profoundly shaking up our economies and societies. But it also means financing things that no private actor finances. A significant proportion of our populations do not have access to digital technology today, because they do not have access to

---

1 Indeed, the moral right in a work may continue to be exercised by the creator or his successors in title even though it has fallen into the public domain.

broadband, because they do not have access in terms of knowledge or capacity, and this is a real challenge for all societies and democracies in the European Union [*sic*]. It is an investment that operators do not make, because it is not profitable. It is up to the public to do so" (Macron 2017).

This discourse is problematic in many ways. First, Emmanuel Macron does not define what he means by "common goods". Second, as Lionel Maurel points out:

"What Emmanuel Macron cites as an example of these 'common goods' to be financed is *a priori* quite surprising. These are, on the one hand, the physical infrastructure of the network (broadband) and, on the other hand, the digital education of citizens. These resources would constitute 'common goods' because they would not be supported by private actors because they lack sufficient incentives in terms of profitability. This is true for digital training, if we consider it to be provided by the French Ministry of Education, universities and continuing education. It is already less so for broadband, and overall, for the entire physical infrastructure of the Internet's 'pipes', the development of which is largely carried out by telecom operators" (Calimaq 2017).

As a result, "there is a great ambiguity in Macron's speech between common goods and public goods or public services" (Calimaq 2017). Third, the means of "financing common goods" are equally inaccurate since Macron states:

"I support the initiative taken by several Finance Ministers to introduce a tax on the value created in our countries. This tax will make it possible to raise fair financing for these common goods by taxing actors who compete with European actors and who, today, do not participate sufficiently or at all in this financing" (quoted in Calimaq 2017).

He does not specify how this tax will eventually be redistributed. By making "common goods" a synonym for public goods, Emmanuel Macron's speech allows us to observe two things. On the one hand, his definition of common goods does not correspond in any way to Ostrom's (resource + legal regime + governance structure). On the other hand, it seems to redefine the semantic content of the notion of *common goods* and maintain confusion with the subversive notion of *the commons*.

This might seem anecdotal if it had not appeared four months earlier, in the magazine *Esprit*, in an article by Henri Verdier[2] and Charles Murciano (2017) entitled *"Les communs numériques, socle d'une nouvelle économie politique"* [Digital commons, a basis for a new political economy]. In this article, the authors write that "digital commons reveal a window of opportunity for public action: digital technology is not signing the death certificate of the State, but rather making it possible to redefine its intervention" (p. 134). "In its confrontation with the Valley, the French State must appropriate the rules and methods of the digital age to accomplish its main mission: the defense of the general interest" (p. 145). While this article does not provide a definition of digital commons, a report on the State platform published the same year states that "a common good is a public good (accessible to all), cultivated jointly by those who use it" (Pezziardi and Verdier 2017, p. 30). The challenge now is to turn the entrepreneurial State (Dardot and Laval 2010) into a platform State, i.e. "a public authority that can act in a similar way [to platforms such as Google and Uber,] but in the general interest […] by facilitating access to different resources, public goods, common goods and cognitive infrastructure, instead of pretending to regulate through prohibition" (Pezziardi and Verdier 2017, page 31).

13.3. Conclusion

The theory of the common(s) does not provide tools to understand the French government decision to intervene in order to legislate in the area of information commons. The political economy of the commons, on the one hand, considers the State as a potential partner without taking into consideration the neoliberal turn of the State, which began in the 1980s. The socio-politics of the common, on the other hand, is aware of this transformation of public action, but opts for a political strategy of relativization of the State by affirming that the State is only one particular form of political organization. According to Dardot and Laval (2010, 2014), it is therefore a question of relativizing the neoliberal state at all levels through the multiplication of counter-hegemonic institutions guided by the political principle of the common.

In our opinion, the desire to escape the control of the State by simply keeping it at a distance is an illusion *a fortiori* in the digital environment, as shown by the two examples mentioned above concerning information commons. As we can see, the information commons in the digital environment constitute counter-hegemonic institutions that nevertheless remain fragile and are likely to be the object of covetousness on the part of both private and public actors. Their sustainability depends, among other things, on our ability to think about the role of the State in the

2 Interministerial director of digital and information systems for the French State; he is also general data administrator.

economic organization of digital capitalism and to consider the struggles for the commons both outside and inside the State.

13.4. References

Berne, X. (2018). Comment le gouvernement Valls a enterré la mission sur les Communs. *Next Inpact*, 26 April [Online]. Available at: https://www.nextinpact.com/news/106522-comment-gouvernement-valls-a-enterre-mission-sur-communs.htm.

Calimaq (2017). Les "biens communs" d'Emmanuel Macron ne sont pas les nôtres !. *S.I.Lex*, 2 October [Online]. Available at: https://scinfolex.com/2017/10/02/les-biens-communs-demmanuel-macron-ne-sont-pas-les-notres/.

Conseil supérieur de la propriété littéraire et artistique (2015). Mission du CSPLA sur le domaine commun informationnel. Ministère de la Culture, France, 12 October [Online]. Available at: http://www.culture.gouv.fr/Thematiques/Propriete-litteraire-et-artistique/Conseil-superieur-de-la-propriete-litteraire-et-artistique/Travaux/Missions/Mission-du-CSPLA-sur-le-domaine-commun-informationnel.

Coriat, B. and Bauwens, M. (2015). *Le retour des communs : la crise de l'idéologie propriétaire*. Les liens qui libèrent, Paris.

Cornu, M., Orsi, F., and Rochfeld, J. (2017). *Dictionnaire des biens communs*. Presses universitaires de France, Paris.

Dardot, P. and Laval, C. (2010). *La nouvelle raison du monde : Essai sur la société néolibérale*. La Découverte, Paris.

Dardot, P. and Laval, C. (2014). *Commun. Essai sur la révolution du XXIe siècle.* La Découverte, Paris.

Dardot, P. and Laval, C. (2016). *Ce cauchemar qui n'en finit pas : Comment le néolibéralisme défait la démocratie*. La Découverte, Paris.

Hardin, G. (1968). The tragedy of the commons. *Science*, 162(3859), 1243–1248.

Hardt, M. and Negri, A. (2012). *Commonwealth*. Stock, Paris.

Hess, C. and Ostrom, E. (2011). *Understanding Knowledge as a Commons: From Theory to Practice*. MIT Press, Cambridge.

Karyotis, C. (2018) Bien public ou bien commun : Pour une finance au service de la société. In *Vers une république des biens communs ?*, Alix, N., Bancel, J.-L., Coriat, B., and Sultan, F. (eds). Les liens qui libèrent, Paris, 259–266.

Macron, E. (2017). Conférence de presse du président de la République, Emmanuel Macron, lors du sommet du numérique à Tallinn, Estonie. *elysee.fr* [Online]. Available at: http://www.elysee.fr/communiques-de-presse/article/conference-de-presse-du-president-de-la-republique-emmanuel-macron-lors-du-sommet-du-numerique-a-tallinn-estonie/.

Negri, A. (2010). *Inventer le commun des hommes*. Bayard, Paris.

Orsi, F. (2015). Reconquérir la propriété : un enjeu déterminant pour l'avenir des communs. *Les Possibles*, 5 [Online]. Available at: https://france.attac.org/nos-publications/les-possibles/numero-5-hiver-2015/dossier-les-biens-communs/article/reconquerir-la-propriete.

Ostrom, E. (1986). Issues of definition and theory: Some conclusions and hypotheses. In *Proceedings of the Conference on Common Property Resource Management, Annapolis Maryland, April 21–26, 1985*, National Research Council (ed.). National Academy Press, Washington, 597–614.

Ostrom, E. (1999). *Governing the Commons: The Evolution of Institutions for Collective Action*. Cambridge University Press, Cambridge.

Paranque, B. and Perez, R. (2015). *La finance autrement ? Réflexions critiques et perspectives sur la finance moderne*. Presses universitaires du Septentrion, Villeneuve d'Ascq.

Pezziardi, P. and Verdier, H. (2017). *Des startups d'État à l'État plateforme*. Fondapol [Online]. Available at: http://www.fondapol.org/etude/pierre-pezziardi-et-henri-verdier-des-startups-detat-a-letat-plateforme/.

République française (2015). Projet de loi pour une République numérique [Online]. Available at: https://www.republique-numerique.fr/pages/projet-de-loi-pour-une-republique-numerique.

Samuelson, P.A. (1954). The pure theory of public expenditure. *The Review of Economics and Statistics*, 36(4), 387–389.

Sauvêtre, P. (2016). Les politiques du commun dans l'Europe du Sud (Grèce, Italie, Espagne). Pratiques citoyennes et restructuration du champ politique. *Actuel Marx*, 59(1), 123–138.

Schlager, E. and Ostrom, E. (1992). Property-rights regimes and natural resources: A conceptual analysis. *Land Economics*, 68(3), 249–262.

Verdier, H. and Murciano, C. (2017). Les communs numériques, socle d'une nouvelle économie politique. *Esprit*, (5), 132–145.

Weinstein, O. (2015). Comment se construisent les communs : Questions à partir d'Ostrom. In *Le retour des communs : la crise de l'idéologie propriétaire*, Coriat, B., Bauwens, M., Bellivier, F., and Benhamou, F. (eds). Les liens qui libèrent, Paris, 69–86.

14

Digitalization of Society: Elements for an Ecology of Solicitation?

The following few pages provide an opportunity to extend a reflection that has been underway for many years on the process of social computerization and then on what is now called the "digitalization of society", even though, in our opinion, it only forms, as we will see, the same process of rationalizing activities through technology. Before beginning the analysis, a few clarifications are required.

The first is that the research we conduct is less concerned with (digital) computer technology, even though it is necessary to understand its operating methods and material logics concerning software and networks, than with social computerization and the long-term historical process that has fostered the diffusion of information technology in society, while taking into account the technical, organizational, social, economic, legal and cultural dimensions, not to mention the communication mechanisms at work.

The second is that my investigations have not focused on the vast scope that digital technology represents today, but mainly on a more limited scope restricted to Digital Information and Communication Technologies (DICT) and only touching on connected objects in the field of well-being and health.

The third is that having studied the main stages of this social information process at different times (telematics, information highways, generalized digitalization) allows me to provide some reflexive elements that contribute to a better understanding of the current digitalization of society.

Chapter written by Dominique CARRÉ.

14.1. Social computerization, digitalization of society: two different processes or a new step in the same rationalization process?

The results of the research carried out tend to perceive the digitalization of today's society not as a different process or a break with what has previously taken place with the computerization of society, but rather as a new stage in the general process of social computerization that began in the 1960s and 1970s. To illustrate our point, let us take two examples. First, the study of the way in which the computerization of society is thought and conducted (Carré 1996), and then the generalized digitalization since the 1990s, reveals constants already encountered at other major stages of this process, particularly during the implementation of telematics (1970s–1980s), or the development of information highways (1990s– 2000): the notion of a major project, the inflation of discursive production, the unavoidable role of the State and the centrality of the notion of *convergence*. All this makes it possible to affirm that we are indeed confronted with the renewal of a major project that is not simply technical, but, above all, societal: the generalized digitalization of society (Carré 2016a). Digitalization is therefore only one more step in a long process of social computerization that began more than 50 years ago.

The second point concerns the establishment of a pivotal communication system linking digital platforms and social networks, which extends the industrialization of information and communication processing to a field that, until now, had escaped this massive process: networking. The place of a main technical configuration had already been identified when telematics was introduced and, later, when the information highways were disseminated. The importance taken, for some time, by the proliferation of intermediation platforms (Web and, let us not forget, increasingly mobile platforms) suggests that we are confronted with the "platformization" of society that articulates: a form of production, matching; a technical rationalization of linking; a socioeconomic model, brokerage; substantial discursive productions and utopias that accompany the ideologization at work (Carré 2016b).

14.2. Relevance of communication studies to understand the process of social computerization (digitalization)

Until recently, most communications research in the field of social computerization has consisted of joint or separate questions on: the constitution of supply, industrial strategies, public policies and marketing, conditions of acceptability and social appropriation, conditions for the dissemination of what was called, some time ago, ICT and its usage, and even the study of social control methods.

The digitalization of society has undermined the relevance of certain analyses that focused on the anteriority of the offer and a long time frame for the construction of uses and studies that had made it possible to highlight the main stages that punctuated the implementation of telematics and the formation of usage. The article by Jean-Guy Lacroix, Gaëtan Tremblay and Gilles Pronovost (1993) is quite symptomatic. As a reminder, these researchers had identified six steps over a long period of time in the process of social computerization:

1) the development of the social IT project in which the State plays the central role;

2) the establishment of a technical standard and industrial actors taking care of implementing the project;

3) the development of a prototype and its social testing to refine the technical proposal;

4) the beginning of the socialization of the new technology through large-scale experiments with the general public, which marks the arrival of users as truly active actors in the process;

5) the first marketing phase, during which the development of the offer continues, particularly in terms of content, and through which the offer builds a critical mass of consumers, which will legitimize its generalization efforts;

6) the generalization that is occurring without affecting the entire population and that is confused with a movement of diversification and penetration into a broader set of social practices.

The miniaturization and multiplication of media devices adapted to mobility (portable microcomputers, tablets, multifunctional telephones), the renewed implementation and distribution methods, the fact that digital technology is an integral part of our daily lives, the unbridled marketing of globalized products and services, most often free for users, and the very highly competitive context now require other research areas to be developed in order to analyze the widespread digitalization of society (Carré 2012). Without being exhaustive, it is possible to identify three main areas still emerging in information and communication sciences:

1) studies devoted to the trio of Big Data, algorithms and machine learning (Cardon 2015), which sometimes follow on from previous reflections on informationalization (Miège and Tremblay 1999) and question both the decoding of society and the way in which society functions;

2) studies dealing with the economics of attention[1] (Goldhaber 1997; Simon 1971), the basis of online commerce, attempts to articulate socioeconomic models, communication strategies and relational marketing to capture the attention of individuals using new forms of advertising on a large scale. Is the economy of attention a new horizon for capitalism? Indeed, paying attention to information, to a proposal, also consists of giving it value, as Citton (2014a; 2014b)[2] rightly reminds us;

3) studies which, under the generic term of "digital humanities", offer the possibility of conducting research based on large amounts of data (Cultural Analytics) or creating specific methods for understanding digital objects (Digital Methods) in order to observe online and at a distance, and in a generally invisible way, the usage of DICT and social practices in the digital world, and which challenge studies in communication both through the research objects studied and in terms of how to relate science to digital technology (Bourdeloie 2013).

These three orientations are interesting. But they too often bear a very utilitarian vision, or deal only with one dimension of the current process. They do not contribute to a more transversal and global understanding of the generalized digitalization of society that is very often "disruptive" as well as the challenges that result from it. Hence, we wish, for all these reasons briefly mentioned, and in the given format, to outline another research perspective that does not neglect the more generic understanding of this global process.

14.3. Outline of a new research orientation: moving towards an ecology of solicitation?

The originality of the proposed orientation is based on the principle that the process of social computerization must henceforth be approached through the prism of studying relational and communicational practices while incorporating them into

---

1 It should be noted that the economy of attention is based on the principle that the attention of an individual (a consumer) is a rare source, especially if the latter is very widely solicited. The objective is to seek relevant modalities to attract or retain attention. It is a supply economy. It differs from the economy of intention, which is in a way an alternative to the economy of attention, since it is a demand-oriented economy and depends on the diffusion of the needs of individuals to businesses so that any individual is able to control his relationship according to the principle of *intentcasting*, i.e. the client advertises and publicly announces his wishes and needs. In this case, the salespeople are listening. This latter orientation is based on the observation that consumers who are free in their choices are more available than those who are solicited (see Searls 2012).

2 It should be noted that it was economist Georg Franck who proposed an initial analysis of the economics of attention, even though it is reported that sociologist Gabriel Tarde conducted an initial reflection on an economy of attention to deal with industrial overproduction, thus forcing the use of advertising forms promoting attention.

a critical approach designed to question incessant and highly productionist demands from multiple actors: communication manufacturers, advertisers, communication agencies and the most diverse groups, without forgetting anyone, since any user can become a receiver and contributor.

The hypothesis on which our research work is based can be summarized as follows: the Internet, a tangible instrument of exchange, promotes an important relational habitus and numerous requests from a wide variety of applications and services that contribute to the increase in life rhythms, which results in an increase in the number of episodes of action and/or experience per unit of time and in the resulting feeling of urgency – immediacy, reactivity, interactivity (Rosa 2010, 2012). As for the mode of activation, it results from the incessant, and if possible uninterrupted, solicitations to multiply the number of connections to such an extent that some individuals without connections find themselves deprived of, if not disqualified from, the social scene.

Why start from the concrete analysis of communicational action and, in particular, from the importance of relational opulence and hyperconnectivity to study the generalized digitalization of society, and not from the technological offer, applications or online services? There are four elements to consider.

– First of all, after exploring the realities, let us remember that at every moment, network users must make choices, between acceptance and subordination, in order to access new online services, in return for the tracking of their data; all data that will then be processed, exploited and marketed (Carré and Vidal 2018).

– Let us then point out the need to take into account two interrelated issues. The first one is the subject and his emancipation, or at least the subjectivity of liberation dear to André Gorz, which animates individuals, as François Gollain (2018) reminds us. The second is the advent of neoliberalism, which must be understood less as a new stage of capitalism than as a type of governance of conduct, as Michel Foucault (Laval 2018) put it, and that the Internet user is required to respond to requests, needs and commands according to increasingly pre-established forms and norms, perhaps referring to what Bernard Stiegler (2017) seems to call an "impulsive economy"[3].

– Let us then specify the interest of identifying, beyond just usage, the social practices (friendly, professional, cultural) and mediations that are organized around the following triptych: free access and/or content[4], very productive and sometimes

3 Promotion and exaltation of the self, development of hedonism, perpetual agitation of desire, singular aspirations and passions, as well as sometimes heightened sociability.
4 It should be recalled that, faced with the failure of online service marketing in the 1990s, manufacturers gradually transformed many paid services into services that are "free" for the user, but are therefore subsidized by advertising. As a result, the marketing of applications and services to the general public is largely free of charge. However, we should note the current emergence of paid digital social networks.

unsustainable individualized requests, thereby making it possible to account for the impact of the devices on the modes of subjectivation and thirdly, let us not forget, of course, the production of traces or data.

– Finally, we must stress the need to analyze the mechanisms induced by highly productive relational and communicative practices. They are, in fact, far from virtual, and have very material consequences, which are too often ignored. They have an impact on the production of greenhouse gases, a source of global warming/disruption (Carré 2013; Carré and Vidal 2018).

The objective is to contribute to a better understanding of the widespread process of digitalizing society at the beginning of the 21st Century and to understand the interrelationships between economic dimensions (the socioeconomic model), social dimensions (social uses and practices) and environmental aspects (electricity consumption, greenhouse gas production and global warming).

14.4. Which approach should be adopted?

To reflect what is happening on the Internet scene, it is possible to adopt a Marxist approach. It would very definitely be seen as an alienation and an extension of commodification, because from this point of view, capitalist logic tells us so. However, this approach has a major disadvantage: it does not really make it possible to explain this hyperconnectivity, which forces individuals to solicit and be constantly solicited (Carré and Vidal 2018). For this reason, the Foucauldian approach seemed more relevant and operational to us, particularly when it shows that the project of neoliberalism consists of generalizing the "form-enterprise" to all aspects of existence. The company must therefore no longer be perceived simply as an institution, but above all as a "social model" that subjects society to competitive dynamics (Foucault 2004; Laval 2013). In this context, the individual must be an entrepreneur for himself. Entrepreneurship is an economic force, but, above all, a moral and political force.

The incessant solicitations would therefore comply with the imposition of the competitive norm obliging all individuals to stand out, while allowing them to seize new opportunities, make encounters possible, fight inhibitions, renew their knowledge, share concerns and fears and cultivate the same hopes. Above all, the injunction is to not remain anonymous; to make oneself visible and distinguish oneself are the main characteristics of the neoliberal social norm that advocates competition as an ideology (Carré and Panico 2013; Carré and Vidal 2018). The other interest is that the chosen orientation makes it possible to study the daily mechanisms at the borders of the individual and the collective, the economic and the social, without denying the environmental dimension. This needs to be made somewhat explicit. The aim is to take into account the four main characteristics of DICT and their associated uses: the materiality of their immateriality; their technical and programmed marketing obsolescence; the origin of the energy source (renewable or not, carbon-free or not) to produce electricity and the carbon footprint of highly productive information and relational and communication practices when billions of people use these techniques on a daily basis (Carré and Vidal 2018, Chapter 5).

14.5. Conclusion

Communication studies that have been conducted for some time no longer enable us to understand the global process of social computerization (generalized digitalization) and all the associated issues. We have therefore proposed a new research orientation: an ecology of solicitation, the purpose of which is to study the ecosystem of cross-relationships produced from DICT by industrialists and users and by users among themselves, while taking into account social, economic and environmental interactions. This orientation invites us to abandon studies that are too often fragmented in order to provide a more global framework for intelligibility and the interpretation of the process of a generalized digitalization of society. These first elements will have to be completed more broadly in order to better formalize the orientation that has been, too briefly, outlined here.

14.6. References

Bourdeloie, H. (ed.) (2013). Mondes numériques : Nouvelles perspectives de la recherche. tic&société, 7(2) [Online]. Available at: https://journals.openedition.org/ticetsociete/1362.

Cardon, D. (2015). À quoi rêvent les algorithmes. Le Seuil/La République des Idées, Paris.

Carré, D. (1996). Télématique et autoroutes de l'information. Manières de penser et de conduire l'information de la société. In AILF-Lexi Praxi 96: Société de l'information : les enjeux culturels, Proceedings, Paris, December 11th, 17–24.

Carré, D. (2012). Étudier les usages, est-ce encore nécessaire ?. In La sociologie des usages. Continuités et transformations, Vidal, G. (ed.). Hermès-Lavoisier, Cachan, 61–85.

Carré, D. (2013). Approche critique et techniques numériques d'info-communication. Vers la prise en compte d'une nouvelle dimension ?. In *Proceedings, Où (en) est la critique en communication ?*, Kane, O. and George, É. (eds), 61–73 [Online]. Available at: http://www.archipel.uqam.ca/5557/2/carre.pdf.

Carré, D. (2016a). Le numérique. À nouveau le grand projet reconduit ?. International symposium proceedings, ACFAS, *Métamorphoses numériques de la culture et des médias*, Montreal: 9–10th May. 14–25 [Online]. Available at: https://www.cricis.uqam.ca/wp-content/uploads/2017/10/Cahiers2017_VF.pdf.

Carré, D. (2016b). Plateformes numériques ou plateformisation de la société ?. In *XXe Congrès de l'AISLF : Sociétés en mouvement, sociologie en changement*, CR33 proceedings "Sociologie de la communication", Montreal, July 5–7th [Online]. Available at: https://web.univ-pau.fr/RECHERCHE/SET/AISLFCR33/DOCS_SOCIO/2016/Actes_AISLF_CR33_2016_Montreal.pdf.

Carré, D. and Panico, R. (2013). Puissance d'agir à l'ère du Web social. In *Réseaux socionumériques et médiations humaines. Le social est-il soluble dans le web ?*, Rojas, E. (ed.). Hermès-Lavoisier, Paris, 177–197.

Carré, D. and Vidal, G. (2018). *Hyperconnectivity: Economical, Social and Environmental Challenges*. ISTE Ltd., London and John Wiley & Sons, New York.

Citton, Y. (ed.) (2014a). *L'économie de l'attention. Nouvel horizon du capitalisme ?* La Découverte, Paris.

Citton, Y. (2014b). *Pour une écologie de l'attention*. Le Seuil, Paris.

Foucault, M. (2004). *Naissance de la biopolitique*. Le Seuil, Paris.

Goldhaber, M.H. (1997). The attention economy and the net. *First Monday*, 2(4) [Online]. Available at: http://firstmonday.org/ojs/index.php/fm/issue/ view/79.

Gollain, F. (2018). *André Gorz. Une philosophie de l'émancipation*. L'Harmattan, Paris.

Lacroix, J.-G., Tremblay, G., and Pronovost, G. (1993). La mise en œuvre de l'offre et la formation des usages des NTIC. Les cas de Videoway et de Télétel. *Cahiers de recherche sociologique*, 21, 79–122.

Laval, C. (2013). L'entreprise, comme nouvelle forme de gouvernement. Usages et mésusages de Michel Foucault. In *Usages de Foucault*, Oulc'hen, H. (ed.). Presses universitaires de France, Paris, 143–158.

Laval, C. (2018). *Foucault, Bourdieu et la question néolibérale*. La Découverte, Paris.

Miège, B. and Tremblay, G. (1999). Pour une grille de lecture du développement des techniques de l'information et de la communication. *Sciences de la Société*, 47, 9–22.

Rosa, H. (2010). *Accélération, une critique sociale du temps*. La Découverte, Paris.

Rosa, H. (2012). *Aliénation et accélération, vers une théorie critique de la modernité tardive*. La Découverte, Paris.

Searls, D. (2012). *The Intention Economy: When Customers Take Charge*. Harvard Business Review Press, Boston.

Simon, H.A. (1971). Designing organizations for an information-rich world. In *Computers, Communication, and the Public Interest*, Greenberger M. (ed.). The Johns Hopkins Press, Baltimore, 38–72.

Stiegler, B. (2017). Entretien avec Bernard Stiegler. *Rue Descartes*, 91, 119–140.

15

What is the Concept of Humanities in Francophone Digital Humanities?

While unreflective scientification increasingly ostracizes spirit as a kind of extraneous nonsense, it also entangles itself ever more deeply in the contradiction between the content of its activity and the task it sets itself. If the universities are to change their orientation, then there is no less reason to intervene in the human sciences than in the disciplines they falsely imagine to be backward in spirit.

T.W. Adorno, Critical Models.

15.1. The emergence of Francophone digital humanities

Although relatively unstable and covering changing and disparate realities, according to the authors (Alvarado 2012; Terras 2011), the phrase Digital Humanities (DH) has nevertheless been used extensively in higher education and research for the past 15 years. A unifying label, it has been used to create departments, units and research chairs, as well as specialized courses and a large number of scientific gatherings and events. Since their introduction in France at the end of the 2000s, DH have been of particular interest in the discipline of information and communication sciences (ICS), which has recently pushed for an institutional position towards them. In addition to journal issues on the study of the ICS/DH overlap (Bonaccorci *et al.* 2016), and in response to a "manifesto" for a positioning of the discipline towards DH (Paquienséguy 2017), a symposium was organized in March 2018.

Chapter written by Christophe MAGIS.

Presented as a new interdisciplinary field of research considering both the study of the introduction of digital tools in the procedures of the human and social sciences (HSS) and the production of such tools and their usage, the integration of DH into ICS is sometimes considered as "going without saying" (Massou 2017). However, if these statements within ICS are sometimes an opportunity to reaffirm certain epistemological anchors of the discipline (e.g. the principle of interdisciplinarity or the study of social relations to technology), it is regrettable that it does not always apply its most critical expectations to its reading of the emergence of DH and its own need for positioning. In many respects, in fact, we can read the proliferation of such a term in the academic field, as well as that of those who preceded it (e.g. convergence, collaborative Web, creative economy): the renewal of a mythical discourse presenting communication as a solution for overcoming the various phases of crisis that accompany the last mutations of capitalism according to its particular technical, social and economic features. Working on a critique of one of the most persistent of these myths, the "information society", Bernard Miège (2008, paragraph 1) reminds us that "the strength of a phrase or term is to be forgotten and to be used without a clear awareness of the issues of all kinds involved in its use or even without a minimal knowledge of the previous steps that were necessary to forge it". This can largely be applied to DH, and the use of the expression or some of its most prominent slogans far exceeds its theoretical strength or reflexive feedback on its emergence.

Of course, over the past 15 years, several theoretical investments have been carried out to give some substance to such a syntagma and elevate it to the rank of a new field of research. An official history has been written: DH are integrated into the suite of humanities computing, which is generally traced back to the first attempts by the HSS to use computer resources and, in particular, to the work of Father Roberto Busa in 1949 to automatically index the work of Saint Thomas Aquinas. The following work involved the automated creation of corpora and dictionaries and was mainly the work of librarians and research technicians (McCarty 2005). The rest is less clear. The first projects systematically labeled "Digital Humanities" have had as their point of origin a Textual Scholarship department at the University of Virginia since the end of the 1980s. The challenge is then to use computer techniques to edit translations of ancient texts, in an "anti-interpretive" tradition, assisted by technology (Allington et al. 2016). The term, however, is popularized when American language and literature departments within different universities, kept up, in a fairly rootless manner, by integrating academic paths that proposed competencies on some of these techniques in information technologies for publishing, thus attracting new recruits.

As the term emerges and is recognized, it brings together a group of disparate researchers, often in a precarious position on the margins of their disciplines and working *on* or *with* technology. It is then that it takes care of the imaginations coming from the subcultures and that the "hacker's ethos" will become essential to the first Digital Humanities Manifesto, as well as to the various manifestations of the "HSS 2.0", like the *THATCamp* (Broca 2016). These imaginations, which, in addition to those from the history of the humanities, bring some extra glamor to the field, and are reminiscent of those who, in their time, fueled other phrases, such as "collaboration" or "creativity". The latter are also integrated into DH as part of new ways of producing knowledge, thanks to the new modalities allowed by digital technology (data mining, crowdsourcing, etc.). It was at this time of expansion that the term was imported into French-language works, from the late 2000s onwards, when it encountered a number of imperatives affecting the field of higher education and research.

15.2. Digital humanities in the changing world of universities and HSS

It must be noted that the proliferation of the Digital Humanities syntagma in the English-speaking world is taking place in a very particular period of increased commodification of research and higher education (Allmer and Bulut 2018; Grusin 2013), which sees a continuing crisis in HSS in particular. They are now struggling to maintain their recognition at a time of continued disaffection and suspicion, a recent radical development of which was the Japanese Minister of Education's call for the closure of several Japanese social science faculties – "not sufficiently 'useful'" – in 2015[1]. The injunction to pragmatize HSS and align them with the natural sciences' model is obviously not recent. However, in a globalized race to finance research and university training, the call to account for their social utility and the production of valid and sustainable knowledge, always measured through quantitative and mathematical criteria, now leaves Damocles' sword hovering over entire areas of knowledge production.

When it recalls the possibilities offered by automated information processing systems in the work of HSS, the phrase "digital humanities" makes it possible to offer them some publicity by displaying results of a more "serious" appeal and measurable appearance. Subsequently, particularly in the English-speaking world, the major research funding foundations (Mellon Foundation, Ford Foundation,

---

1 Grove, J. (2015). Social sciences and humanities faculties 'to close' in Japan after ministerial intervention. *Times Higher Education*, September 14th 2015 [Online]. Available at: https://www.timeshighereducation.com/news/social-sciences-and-humanities-faculties-close-japan-after-ministerial-intervention.

Google, etc.) quickly reoriented several of their HSS funding offers towards DH (Allington *et al.* 2016).

The breakthrough of the syntagma in the French-speaking world has also seen a similar movement, with the introduction of specific DH themes in research-funding agencies (SSHRC in Canada, ANR and PIA in France, etc.), inviting HSS to take a rapid stand in favor of the digital and its tools. Hence, in 2013, Michel Wievorka spoke of the "pioneering role" of the *Maisons des sciences de l'homme* foundation – which he led – in the implementation of computerized processing applied to HSS:

> "Computers were installed very early and math applied to the social sciences was done with them. Today, we are preparing a digital pole and a vast programme of digital humanities, with the idea of putting digital at the service of the humanities."[2]

Elsewhere, it is also by highlighting the syntagma that in 2015, Jean-Michel Blanquer, then director of the *École supérieure des sciences économiques et sociales*, who, two years later, became French Minister of National Education, defended the human sciences (particularly the study of ancient culture): "Digital humanities contribute to reinventing both historical and sociological or linguistic approaches."[3] In this "reinvention", it is the very image of HSS that aims to be modified, towards the production of results that are perhaps not so much *sustainable* as *visible* and *demonstrable*. As a result, since the establishment of the "digital humanities" chair at the *École polytechnique fédérale de Lausanne* (Switzerland) in 2012, its holder, Frédéric Kaplan, has tended to be (at least for a period) the media representative of HSS in several Swiss media outlets, such as *Le Temps* and *La Tribune de Genève*. In addition to several interviews in which Kaplan or some of his colleagues have presented several of the DH projects on which they are involved (such as the very recent large-scale Venice Time Machine project aimed at the virtual reconstruction of Venice in past times[4], projects on selfies[5], etc.), Kaplan is given forums or interviews on subjects embracing HSS as a whole, as diverse as the analysis of the bankruptcy of the Encyclopædia Universalis[6], Montaigne's work[7],

---

2 Interview with Michel Wieviorka: Mettre le numérique au service des humanités, *Libération*, May 11th, 2013, p. 8.
3 Blanquer, J.-M. (2015). Les humanités, avenir de l'humanité. *LePoint.fr*, April 4th, 2015 [Online]. Available at: https://www.lepoint.fr/chroniques/les-humanites-avenir-de-l-humanite-04-04-2015-1918618_2.php.
4 Dubuc, D. (2017). Venice Time Machine, un canal à remonter le temps. *LeMonde.fr*, December 13th, 2017 [Online]. Available at: https://www.lemonde.fr/tant-de-temps/article/2017/12/13/venice-time-machine-one-channel-a-rise the time_5229068_4598196.html.
5 Danthe, M. (2014). Le selfie, cette testostérone de l'être. *Le Temps*, March 26th.
6 Stevan, C. (2014). Le Web est l'incarnation de l'encyclopédie. *Le Temps*, November 27th.
7 Le Temps (2017). Montaigne incarne une lecture joyeuse et libre. *Le Temps*, January 18th.

the question of the right to forget[8] or the analysis of the success of certain popular music hits[9].

In the end, the momentum in favor of DH tends to give HSS the benefit of the current sociopolitical aura of digital technology as much as it marks how much HSS must organize themselves in working order after it. A recurring object of several myths about emerging from the crisis of industrial capitalism, digital technology is therefore at the center of many political and economic projects; DH serve to materialize part of such impulses in the field of knowledge production and dissemination. The question, for example, of the place of digital technology in schools is reinterpreted through the phrase. During an interview in the *Challenges* magazine in 2018, the French Secretary of State for Digital Affairs, Mounir Mahjoubi, described the government's policy on the issue of digital training as follows: "If we want to become leaders in artificial intelligence, we need more people to enroll in computer science and mathematics masters, otherwise we will continue to be subjected to the innovations of those who are advancing faster in the field."[10] It is therefore a question of proposing a program capable of offering digital training in high school, training that would integrate DH into HSS courses. This resolution is based on a number of speeches and studies by researchers claiming to follow DH to support how many such digital training courses are able to meet two social challenges. On the one hand, learning about the dangers of digital technology:

> "Some young people are naive about digital screens and services. As a result, they are subject to the offers of large platforms. [...] The greatest danger of this digital naivety is [...] that people will only have access to information or technology because they are presented with it, without critical thinking."

And, on the other hand, the issue of social equality:

> "Today, the children of executives in private institutions have access to coding and computer courses. And on the other hand, in the working class, it is often the children who explain to parents how these new technologies work, from what they have learned by themselves."[11]

---

8 Le Temps (2014). Mémorable "droit à l'oubli". *Le Temps*, May 21st.
9 Kaplan, F. (2014). Les hits métamorphiques, *Le Temps*, March 19th.
10 de Neuville, H. (2018). Mounir Mahjoubi : "Pourquoi il est urgent de former les jeunes au numérique". *Challenges*. February 23rd, 2018 [Online]. Available at: https://www.challenges.fr/education/mounir-mahjoubi-pourquoi-il-est-urgent-de-former-les-jeunes-au-numerique_569097.
11 *Op. cit.*

These statements follow other references to the phrase in reports or ministerial committees. In France, for example, the *Jules Ferry 3.0* report of the National Digital Council, published in October 2014, advocates the establishment of a "digital humanities" stream in the general baccalaureate, with the aim of "reducing the gap within equal opportunities"[12].

In the face of changes in the higher education and research system, DH are invoked as a solution to economic, social or political problems, through the magic of the combination of digital technology with the humanist imagination, all sprinkled with some hacker's glamor. However, their breakthrough is not without carrying, in addition to this tendency to "pragmatize" the HSS, several other missteps that digital technology brought with it when it was introduced into other fields, in the current movement of neoliberal capitalism. This is the case, for example, of the injunction to implement branding practices for HSS researchers, which, through the use of Web 2.0 tools (blogs, electronic columns, tweets, etc.), is increasingly necessary for career development (Allmer and Bulut 2018). Academics claiming to be involved in DH are expected to be able to embrace these new tools, to such an extent that one of them wondered, in 2016, in *The Guardian*, about his status: "serious academic" or "professional Instagrammer"?[13]

This injunction, which parallels the declining number of tenured positions in universities, the multiplication of MOOCs[14] and the precariousness of academic life – particularly for HSS – tends to make DH what some see as the Trojan horse of neoliberalism in universities (Allington *et al.* 2016; Grusin 2013). The term and its accompanying discourses, which articulate the humanist imagination with pragmatic common sense as to the need to make some academic paths and certain research works "useful", complete the rise of technical expertise and quantitative methodologies as a superior form of academic knowledge, following the positivist traditions that nevertheless need to be further criticized.

15.3. Towards a critical theory of the humanities in the digital age: experience, interpretation and speculative thinking

It therefore seems that our reflection must be oriented in this direction. It is not a question of simply abandoning the phrase. Indeed, although mythical in nature, it also serves, like many other myths of information capitalism (Mosco 2004), as a

---

12 Tassel, F. (2014). Le numérique à l'école pour l'égalité des chances. *Libération*, October 4th, 19.
13 Academics Anonymous (2016). I'm a serious academic, not a professional Instagrammer. *The Guardian*, August 5th [Online]. Available at: https://www.theguardian.com/higher-education-network/2016/aug/05/im-a-serious-academic-not-a-professional-instagrammer.
14 Massive Online Open Courses.

unifying banner for a set of strictly critical proposals (Citton 2015; Mounier 2015), most of which did not need the institutional framework of this or that discipline to be deployed. From the margins of certain disciplines or research institutions, rather than at the heart of their institutional frameworks, DH sometimes serve to reinterpret a number of the expectations of critique in the digital age (e.g. around the question of interdisciplinarity or the theoretical/practical articulation or the critique of the political economy of knowledge regimes) (Granjon and Magis 2016). They have also served as a melting pot for the movements of people in unstable jobs and non-teachers in higher education and research – generally relegated to undergraduate teaching and technical tasks, which have been devalued – towards large-scale mobilization (e.g. the *alternative academics* movement) (Magis 2018). In addition, the need for some DHers (i.e. researcher engaged in the digital humanities practices) to usually include HSS in public debates should be an essential social issue in critical research.

DH could thus potentially be the place for radical critical reflection on the very role of theory in the digital age, following the Frankfurt School's Critical Theory project. However, it seems that it is not the direction that is currently being taken in Francophone discussions, while debates, particularly within ICS, are more concerned with the second term of the phrase than with the first. Concerns arise asking if we should rather translate it to "*humanités digitales*" in French instead of "*humanités numériques*" to refer to digits, the technical dimension and the importance of indexes in the work of initial *Humanities Computing* (Le Deuff 2015). Lost in such debates, French ICS is reaffirming the importance of this *digital* dimension, which seems to represent the essential issue of the debate. Thus, when it is not viewed with suspicion, critique is considered at most as incorporated in the hacker ethics or "geek attitude".

On the contrary, we believe that the deployment of DH in the French-speaking world should be a means of rethinking, in the digital age, the critical role of the "humanities"[15]. In this respect, a return to the work of Critical Theory, which has played a large role in the critique of positivist pragmatism, is essential. Indeed, the researchers in this area have continuously sought to reflect on the integration and safeguarding of the proposals of the *Aufklärung*, which, in its time, had claimed to bring together philosophy and HSS by developing categories such as that of *humanity*. If "'man' and the common humanity, which wants every human being to be considered human on an equal footing, stand out as one of the most active backgrounds of the *Aufklärung*" (Corcuff 2001, p. 161), this background has been somewhat eroded by the search for scientific claims in the so-called "social sciences". The formulation of methodologies, aimed at the purest possible

---

15 This idea sometimes crosses some work on DH, especially in ICS (Clivaz 2012; Le Deuff 2015), but it never leads to a thorough reflexive development.

objectivity – understood as what remains once the subject has been evacuated (Adorno 2005b) – has resulted in a set of formulas that allow an "intellectual economy", disconnecting research from experience: "Complicated logical operations are carried out without actual performance of all the intellectual acts upon which the mathematical and logical symbols are based" (Horkheimer 1947, p. 23). In this respect, the situation reported by Adorno about his sociological work in the United States – when invited to produce hypotheses for an investigation on jazz, he formulated, after rapid reflection, proposals that proved to be accurate to the great suspicious surprise of his interlocutor[16] – also reminds us of the limitations presented in the report of the very "DH" works of Erez Aiden and Jean-Baptiste Michel (2013). Creators of a tool to query the Google Books database and ecstatic about the possibilities offered by Big Data to HSS, the authors note that the facts they have established by querying their tool could be predicted by a colleague, an academic who has never had access to the data! If digital technology amplifies, as we have seen, this movement, by which research ensures, through the application of automated methodologies, that nothing will be thought of that is not already known, a challenge for critical DH would be to dialectically pose the construction of research methods, using digital tools, in applications that would not disconnect from *experience*. The point would then be not to judge the rigor of the research by its ability to translate into operational questions for computer machinery, but to subordinate the very creation of the tools to the research questions.

This category of experience, which must be reflected on from the perspective of the development of critical DH, is articulated in a second category, that of interpretation. We have seen how computerized procedures, even in some of the projects that gave rise to DH, have been used against the role of interpretation in HSS, a category that positivism has long sought to remove by focusing only on "the facts":

> "Ultimately it is positivism's most profound moment of truth – even if it is one against which positivism rebels as it does against the word which holds it in its spell – that the facts, that which exists in this manner and not in any other, have only attained that impenetrable power which is then reinforced by the scientist cult of facts in scientific thought, in a society without freedom of which its own subjects are not masters" (Adorno 1976, p. 64).

It is therefore necessary to be able to disconnect the phases of interpretation of the results in DH from the only mappings that the tools offer. Otherwise, research on

---

16 "My young colleague did not attribute the result, say, to my simple reasoning, but rather to a kind of magical capacity for intuition. [...] [He] preferred deeming me a medicine man to conceding validity to something that lay under the taboo of 'speculation'." (Adorno 2005a, p. 373).

digital technology, carried out *with* digital technology, will be subject only to the possibilities offered *by* digital technology and the operations it embodies. The risk then becomes subjecting the work to the lack of freedom that already characterizes the administered society, by a reifying logic of which we already find the trace in these operations (Berry 2014).

Finally, we come to a third category that must be reinterpreted in the context of critical DH: that of speculation (or speculative thinking). And there would be an important reflection to be had around the following question: what can speculative thinking mean at a time when research methodologies, as well as many of the situations in social life, are subject to digital procedures? Generally, advocates of the technical status quo and the use of information and communication technologies by researchers without questioning them argue that, since society is now digitalized from one end of the spectrum to the other, it is quite normal for research to be affected in its turn[17]. It is then a question, without wishing to defend an illusory (and otherwise undesirable) autonomy of HSS research from the society it questions, of reflecting on the modalities of a way of thinking which, while not abandoning its scientific claim, would not be limited in advance to this kind of tautology.

In a radio conference on the theme "psychoanalysis and sociology" given in May 1948 in the United States, Adorno lists a number of characteristics of Freud's work that, according to him, put him among the thinkers of the philosophical tradition of the *Aufklärung* – although he may have defended himself against it elsewhere. Among these characteristics, one

> "is today in jeopardy: [Freud] dared to think. Despite all his passion for empirical data he never curtailed his spontaneity of speculation; there was no taboo on thinking! Nowadays we are constantly asked: where is the evidence? The verification? It is my feeling that in this particular respect Freud is of utmost importance for our thinking. The thing that makes him so outstanding is that his intellectual phantasy was never stunted or stilted. It is quite legitimate to ask whether any of the Freudian concepts could have been evolved under our present way of intellectual work. [...] The unique position of Freud in today's intellectual situation is that he is the only thinker who combined an extremely close relationship to the empirical data with autonomous thinking" (Adorno, 1948).

---

17 This argument was used by Dean Burnett in response to the debate in 2016 in *The Guardian* on the case of the "serious academic", presented above, in a mocking reply. See https://www.theguardian.com/science/brain-flapping/2016/aug/05/im-a-non-serious-academic-i-make-no-apologies-for-this.

15.4. Conclusion

Simplistic in appearance and usually claimed by any self-respecting researcher, this is the ambitious horizon for a critical reflection within the DH field. It is a question of maintaining the theory up to its very concept, as formulated by the tradition of the Enlightenment, as well as by the advances in the social sciences that followed it, but without ever letting the instituted methodological routines dictate either our research objects or hypotheses, and therefore exempt from the work of reflection by relying on automated procedures. This in no way means, of course, that we must be satisfied with confining ourselves to a theoricism that speculates outside of the world. The historical survival of an idealistic temptation is just as problematic as mechanistic empiricism (whether or not it is helped by digital tools). It is important to embrace the narrow line of "equal distance from the horrors of unconceptual empiricism and theoricism which lacks the administration of proof" (Granjon 2012, p. 76), but with the knowledge that, in the current debates around DH, it is the former that presents the biggest risk.

15.5. References

Adorno, T.W. (1948). Psychoanalysis and sociology. AdornoArchiv, TWAA Vt_018_ Psychoanalysis and Sociology-2st. Akademie der Künste, Berlin.

Adorno, T.W. (1976). Introduction. In *The Positivist Dispute in German Sociology*, Adorno, T.W. (ed.). Heinemann, London, 1–67.

Adorno, T.W. (2005a). *Critical Models*. Columbia University Press, New York.

Adorno, T.W. (2005b). *Minima Moralia*. London, Verso.

Aiden, E. and Michel, J.-B. (2013). *Uncharted*. Penguin, New York.

Allington, D., Brouillette, S., and Golumbia, D. (2016). Neoliberal tools (and archives): A political history of digital humanities. *Los Angeles Review of Books* [Online]. Available at: https://lareviewofbooks.org/article/neoliberal-tools-archives-political-history-digital-humanities/#!.

Allmer, T. and Bulut, E. (eds) (2018). Academic labour, digital media and capitalism. *tripleC*, special edition 16(1).

Alvarado, R.C. (2012). The digital humanities situation. In *Debates in the Digital Humanities*, Gold, M.K. (ed.). University of Minnesota Press, Minneapolis, 50–55.

Berry, D.M. (2014). *Critical Theory and the Digital*. Bloomsbury, New York.

Bonaccorci, J., Carayol, V., and Domenget, J.-C. (eds) (2016). Humanités numériques et sciences de l'information et de la communication. *Revue française des sciences de l'information et de la communication*, special edition 8.

Broca, S. (2016). Épistémologie du code et imaginaire des "SHS 2.0". *Variations*, 19.

Citton, Y. (2015). Humanités numériques. Une médiapolitique des savoirs encore à inventer. *Multitudes*, 59, 171–180.

Clivaz, C. (2012). "Humanités Digitales" : mais oui, un néologisme consciemment choisi ! [Online]. Available at: https://claireclivaz.hypotheses.org/114.

Corcuff, P. (2001). Les lumières tamisées des constructivismes l'humanité, la raison et le progrès comme transcendances relatives. *Revue du MAUSS*, 17(1), 158–179.

Granjon, F. (2012). La critique est-elle indigne de la sociologie ?. *Sociologie*, 3(1), 75–86.

Granjon, F. and Magis, C. (2016). Critique et humanités numériques. Pour une approche matérialiste de l'immatériel. *Variations*, 19.

Grusin, R. (2013). The dark side of the digital humanities – Part 2. *Thinking C21*, January 9th [Online]. Available at: https://www.c21uwm.com/2013/01/09/dark-side-of-the-digital-humanities-part-2/.

Horkheimer, M. (1947). *Eclipse of Reason*. Oxford University Press, New York.

Le Deuff, O. (2015). Les humanités digitales précèdent-elles le numérique ?. In *Le numérique à l'ère de l'Internet des objets, de l'hypertexte à l'hyper-objet*, Saleh, I. *et al.* (eds). ISTE Editions, London, 421–432.

Magis, C. (2018). Manual labour, intellectual labour and digital (academic) labour. The practice/theory debate in the digital humanities. *tripleC*, 16(1).

Massou, L. (2017). SIC et humanités numériques : un allant de soi à valoriser. *Revue française des sciences de l'information et de la communication*, 10.

McCarty, W. (2005). *Humanities Computing*. Palgrave MacMillian, Basingstoke.

Miège, B. (2008). L'imposition d'un syntagme : la société de l'information. *tic&société*, 2(2).

Mosco, V. (2004). *The Digital Sublime*. MIT Press, Cambridge.

Mounier, P. (2015). Une "utopie politique" pour les humanités numériques ?. *Socio*, 4, 97–112.

Paquienséguy, F. (2017). Manifeste pour un positionnement des sciences de l'information communication (SIC) vis-à-vis des *Digital Studies* (DS) et autres mutations du numérique. *Revue française des sciences de l'information et de la communication*, 10 [Online]. Available at: https://journals.openedition.org/ rfsic/2630.

Terras, M. (2011). Peering inside the big tent: Digital humanities and the crisis of inclusion. *Melissa Terras' Blog* [Online]. Available at: http://melissaterras.blog-spot.com/2011/07/peering-inside-big-tent-digital.html.

16

The Digital Humanities as a Sign of Their Time

The digital humanities deal extensively with the roles of information technology in the production of knowledge. In any case, this is the common backdrop to various debates on the relationship between digital technologies and knowledge, which has developed from the 1960s onwards[1], involving a technology-based "theory" of social change, but which seems to ignore the theories that deal centrally with the technological dimension. Moreover, the approach is generally optimistic, even naïve, because no negative effects appear to have any place in the analyses of knowledge production. Fans of the digital humanities seem to ignore the ambiguity of the effects of technology and the criticisms posed by the philosophy of technology, as if these technologies were presented only for the good of all. Obviously, there is something strange about this "hemiplegia of meaning" (Nietzsche).

For some, "true digital humanists are those who build systems (*hack*) rather than those who theorize them (*yack*)" (Montfort 2016, p. 127). There would be a supposed superiority of technology over theory, as well as of the new over the traditional, the digital humanities would be replacing an obsolete form of thought – science (understood as a troublesome educational system and an authoritarian organization of power). Moreover, what is also significant is the way in which they dismiss their criticisms. Against the digital humanities, they are said to be centered on themselves and on the present, pamphleteers, messianic in vocation, anti-theoretical, a disordered and dispersed field of study. These are serious, but insignificant

---

Chapter written by Luiz C. MARTINO.
1 For an overview of the history of the digital humanities and the universe of issues raised by this current of thought, see Berra (2015).

considerations, given that these criticisms are made by those who would represent the old forms of thought. To take just one example, Warwick (2016) does not hesitate to use an incredible *ad hominem* argument to get rid of the criticisms raised by Stanley Fish: "He seems to betray a certain level of concern that the next generation chooses to focus on an area in which he [Fish] is not a central figure", while reminding us that he is a "highly theorized" post-modernist "star" (Warwick 2016, p. 539). There is a contempt for theory and a blockage of argumentation, signs of a value system and ethos that are not part of the academic universe (philosophy, social sciences)[2].

These indices – and we could multiply them – then lead us to think of the digital humanities as an intellectual movement rather than as an epistemological rupture[3], as claimed by its defenders. There is indeed something to "marvel at" in the methodological contributions made possible by computer technologies, but this is an integral part of the "normal" movement of science. We know that research and knowledge transfer work is directly linked to technological conditions. From the time of the emergence of modern science in the 18th Century, letter exchanges (the first network of collaboration among scientists) and publications in the journals of emerging academies of science (*Philosophical Transactions*, *Le Journal des Savants*, 1665) were at the origin of the development of technical networks for the circulation of knowledge, whereas in the Middle Ages, it was the students who circulated, not the letters or books, with handwritten books being rare and too expensive. The system later became more complex, but from Descartes to Einstein, evolution was characterized by a series of improvements, with exchanges and collaborations between scholars still taking place through letters and publications still being printed. Change would not be felt until the middle of the 20th Century, when the knowledge revolution movements began. At that time, digital technologies were barely emerging, but other symbolic technologies were already well consolidated and the communication system, which served as the basis for science, was blending with that of society. Philosophy, science and all academic knowledge have found themselves being discussed in the public sphere, which affects their ethos and has consequences on academic practices.

---

2 Without an ethos, scientific knowledge is confused with information. On the scientific ethos, see Merton and Storer (1979).

3 For Le Deuff (2017), an analysis of long-term history shows that "digital humanities are not so recent and that the question of renewal is in fact only the consequence of approaches that have been discussed for a very long time" (p. 9). They "are based more on convergence than on revolution" (p. 10) and, above all, they are part of a "desire for transdisciplinary refoundation" (p. 10).

As a result, the digital humanities will be taken as a socio-historical formation, the symptom of a certain epistemology or a certain paradigm linked to intellectual practices of interdisciplinary movements that developed in the second half of the 20th Century. Digital humanists argue that digital technologies generate an ethos that revolutionizes knowledge. We will take the opposite path to show that the social sciences and philosophy had already been shaken by the non-digital communication system and that the digital humanities are rather the ethos that flows from that system.

16.1. Breaking down the barriers between digital humanities

The digital humanities are not an isolated phenomenon, neither as a revolutionary epistemology nor as a cultural movement. They follow the evolution of academic and intellectual practices. Let us take a very significant example. In the 1970s, a new type of magazine shook philosophy. Louis Pinto (1994) described the action of these media and how they have interfered in the processes of building authority in this field of knowledge. The fundamental question is not about the possible benefits of the "democratization" of knowledge, but rather raises the following debate: do we still talk about philosophy when it is mediatized? Would not philosophical thinking and the mediatization of the debate by the media be incompatible processes?

The emergence of the so-called New Philosophers led to the struggle for recognition. Two different concepts of philosophy were formed and opposed: on the one hand, academic philosophy, the heir to the Greek tradition, and, on the other hand, popular philosophy, focused on current problems (or problems of actuality), which would make it accessible to the general public. Nevertheless, the media arena, more than any other, favors making a spectacle of such exchanges; it encourages radical combat; the theses are unconditionally defended, which transforms their nature, the arguments being evaluated on the basis of their ability to be understandable and to attract a non-specialized audience.

The transposition of the academic world into the world of technological mediation imposes new rules about knowledge. The confrontation of theses is no longer regulated by argued reasoning; there is a new "logic", where success (visibility, recognition) becomes the main objective and where in-depth research work can be replaced by striking sentences and attractive presentations, adapted to the communication media (spectacle). The epistemological criteria give way to those of "intellectual marketing": it is in this new field, and not in that of knowledge production, that the confrontation takes place. It is a question of performing, obtaining a certain success with the public and ensuring its media sustainability. This is not a completely new phenomenon, as we know. It can be compared to others, such as the sophist movement in ancient Greece or, more recently, the problem of intellectual impostors, worked on by Sokal and Bricmont. However, unlike them, the idea of "intellectual marketing" is not necessarily pejorative and does not necessarily amount to "deviance". It is an ethos, an adaptation of the intellectual to a new communications architecture, an epistemology, to which all are subject and which everyone must face. There is no "offside" position but various possible positions.

The case of the New Philosophers allows us to draw important conclusions: it shows that new intellectual practices[4] are not limited to technologies described as digital; they are predecessors to them. Moreover, these new intellectual practices (which refer to logic, ethics and the conception of the knowledge that accompanies them) are linked to the media system (and not to a single technology) and to the *actuality*, as we will see.

16.2. Actuality

According to Foucault (1994), actuality is one of the two sources of modern philosophy. He defines it as an *ontology of the present* as opposed to an analysis of truth. It is a form of reflection that takes into account its historical condition, inscribed in a field of possibilities given by the present to which the thinker belongs. Kant would have been the first to realize the present as a condition of knowledge[5].

Foucault draws attention to an original way of raising the issue of knowledge. It can be said that it is neither the relationship with things (seeking to know what they are) nor a relationship with the other (convincing him, establishing a power relationship). Nor is there any question of the condition of the possibility of knowledge, i.e. of knowing what makes it possible (the approach that made Kant

---

4 Other directories of these practices can be found in several authors. For a critical perspective, see Reynoso's (2000) observations of cultural studies; for a committed interpretation, see Geertz (1980).
5 At the very least, the idea of current events as a source of knowledge has already been around for almost a century. The reflection began with the emergence of the newspaper in the 18th Century (Tobias Peucer in 1690 and Caspar von Stieler in 1695). In an anthological article, "*Escritos Recientes sobre el Concepto de Atualidad*", Wilmont Haack (1969) gives a presentation of the first five decades of the 20th Century devoted to the remarkable progress on the subject in Germany. In France, the problem attracted attention when the American historian Daniel Boorstin (1961) discussed the concept of a *pseudo-event* and published a remarkable article by his colleague Pierre Nora (1972).

famous). Actuality establishes the relationship of thought with the historically situated world, placing the human being in the *circumstances* of his existence (as Ortega y Gasset, a prominent 20th-Century philosopher, journalist, grandson and son of newspaper owners and publishers).

Actuality is therefore the possible knowledge of a state of affairs at a given time. It is the condition of time and place that accompanies a situation and that we cannot separate from our existence without reducing it to a vague abstraction. In this sense, it is essential, and conditions what we can know and what it is important to know. The actuality is the present as an *event*, the latter gives it a face, the concrete form it takes for a community. Kant captures the structure of the actuality, but its content, of course, can only be given in a situated way, as a *significant event*, which, in relation to his time, was the French Revolution.

The notion of event separates the paths of the philosopher and the researchers in communication and media studies. For the former, the event is a revelation (phenomenon) that comes without anyone can indicate its cause (its reason for being, the intention that supports it), either because it is not known or because it transcends humankind. In this sense, the event is not a human order. It is existence in a pure state and refers to an impersonal "action", like verbs without a grammatical subject. The theory of communication follows the general features of the social sciences. The event is the result of the actions of social agents without being confused with them. It is not the action of an individual but of a whole (society, historical period, market, etc.) of which the action is a part. The event is of the order of the totality. In addition, it results from other events. Causality must always be sought in other events, i.e. in a relationship between events. The totality is that of the communication system.

The means of communication provide a representation of the social and propose a non-theoretical conception of the social totality, the actuality. It is not just any representation, we inhabit it. There is no discontinuity between real life and the media dimension, with the two constituting the objective-symbolic set of human reality. As such, the media system crosses all other social systems so that, through direct or diffuse effects, it plays a fundamental role in the production of all kinds of knowledge, especially when the boundaries between university and society, theory and public opinion, reflection and social action are becoming increasingly unclear. The media must therefore be seen as an active force in this process of the dissolution and recomposition of institutions and of the mental frameworks of knowledge.

From a communications point of view, the 20th Century has seen a structural change in the actuality: significant events are no longer revealed by history, but they receive this qualification of "significant" because they are transmitted through the media (Nora 1972). They, the media outlets, are the ones who bring us the events. News from the media takes on a different meaning: if, before, we had to wait for something to happen, with the *Révolution graphique*, Daniel Boorstin (1961) tells us, the novelty is invented and we live in the age of the pseudo-event. We live with people we have never seen before, with facts we cannot verify. Reality goes beyond our senses, without being able to establish the limits of our immediate experiences and those of the media. They nourish the experience, as well as transform its nature.

Foucault sees the actuality as a way of philosophizing. He does not relate it to its material conditions of possibility, to the newspaper (and to the media system), and he does not recognize in it a technical reality that introduces a new form of knowledge allowing the common man to see society and perceive his present life as part of History. The actuality is not conjecture; it is itself factual and accessible to all. Seen in this way, its transformations can be monitored by observing the evolution of the media system and its structural changes when it becomes the main reference point of social life. As a result, its influence extends to all forms of knowledge and even to the notion of theory.

16.3. Theory and practices

What characterizes the digital humanities and distinguishes them from other interdisciplinary approaches is the use of computer technologies to organize the production of knowledge. The use of electronic lists, Web pages, blogs and the digital social network Twitter, according to digital humanities, has produced values of collaboration and sharing (sharing culture), from which a new epistemology emerges. According to Davidson (2008), this is manifested in theory through the mobilization of decentralized concepts, free from fearful constraints and power structures. Knowledge therefore acquires the same properties as technical support. Similarly, Warwick (2016) emphasizes the importance of the nature of the means by which these ideas are disseminated. Warwick's analysis is therefore similar to Davidson's: the form of the debate of ideas is closely linked to the structure of the medium through which the debate takes place. Therefore, theory is what emerges from practice, as ethics and ethos immanent in interactions in communication networks.

But why should we believe that abandoning the "traditional" structures of knowledge production will lead us to greater knowledge? Is the free market of ideas self-regulated? Would the order emanating from the practices of digital communities really be unambiguous? The point here is not to insist on the existence of negative effects but to arouse suspicion that the epistemological revolution claimed by the digital humanities may not come from the positive effects of symbolic technologies.

Like the most recent trends in the sociology of knowledge, the reflection of the digital humanities takes as its starting point the practices of social agents. However, these impose an excessively artificial division of the communication components present in knowledge production practices. For digital humanists, the new ethos that shapes these practices results from the use of computer technologies: researchers spend their time working in networks, which stimulates collaboration and sharing. While this thesis repeats some aspects of communication theory established since the 1950s[6], it does not capture its complexity or other well-recognized principles, such as the integration of social communication circuits (or subsystems). As a result, since oral communication is not isolated from media communication (television, radio, newspapers, books, etc.), there is no reason to assume that this would not be the case for digital media.

In reality, the effect of media action cannot be seen as a mere consequence of media use. These effects are integrated into the experience so that social life – in all its aspects, including the bodies that serve as social matrices for the production of knowledge – is affected by the influence of symbolic technologies. Media action cannot then be taken solely in the form of learning, as claimed by digital humanists. Symbolic technologies reach deeper levels, such as our perception of the world and our way of thinking. As Foucault points out, in modernity, individual experience is related to current events, which, as we have seen, is the product of a technological system. The media is therefore part of the forces that shape experience, and their effects are present in the context that frames the social action and not just in social action itself. They are not simply the "result" of social practices.

In short, a too closed notion of practice can only offer a rather partial description of the action of symbolic technologies. Reducing knowledge to what its social actors do eliminates theoretical reflection, unless – and this is the "solution" of the digital humanities – theory is assimilated to a practice, to *doing*, which is equivalent to saying that there would be, in practices, a virtual epistemology. But would the practices carry an epistemological proposal *per se*?

---

6 For Innis (1951), the materiality of media (heavy, light) gives rise to the clash of two communication biases closely linked to culture, time and space, hence the clash between tradition and the culture of the present. Havelock (1963) has shown that we should not overemphasize the opposition between oral and media communication, because there is no longer pure oral communication. Finally, for McLuhan (1962), contemporary culture results from a mixture, more or less conflictual, of media.

This situation of theory was already described by Geertz in *Blurred Genres* in the early 1980s, a decade after the interdisciplinary movement gained momentum:

> "... we more and more see ourselves surrounded by a vast, almost continuous field of variously intended and diversely constructed works we can order only practically, relationally, and as our purposes prompt us. It is not that we no longer have conventions of interpretation; we have more than ever, built – often enough jerry-built – to accommodate a situation at once fluid, plural, uncentered, and ineradicably untidy" (Geertz 1980, p. 166).

Intellectual practices would have broken down borders and created a unified field for the humanities and the social sciences. They have canceled out the disciplinary contexts, which serve as a framework for the meaning of theories, hence the enormous and heterogeneous mass of information. Without these frameworks, we would only have to take pragmatic action. It is the properties of this chaotic field that would lead to the "loss of meaning" of the theory. It would not be a question of the death or disappearance of the latter; on the contrary, the theory would multiply – for example, in the form of studies in Anglophone countries – to adapt to precise, specific situations, but the content produced would be as fluid as the various situations analyzed. It is therefore difficult to grasp the theory outside of practice.

It should be noted that Geertz's description refers to both contemporary culture and journalistic information: fluid, plural, dispersed and inevitably chaotic. The theoretical field has the same properties as the news of actuality. Structural homology is not accidental, and it could indicate the mixing of two forms of knowledge that have developed since the 17th Century: science and the press. If, as Foucault pointed out, actuality becomes a reference point for philosophical thought – and for the social sciences – then the communication circuits of actuality and science are getting closer and even inevitably mixed in the public space, which means that scientific knowledge is exposed to the influence of the media ethos.

What would become of theory in such circumstances? Would theoretical thinking only be a reflection on immanence, a permanent reaction to actuality, to events isolated and scheduled by the media, creating the risk of becoming an automatic reflex rather than a reflection on its purpose?

16.4. Conclusion

Among the various epistemological revolutionary movements that multiplied in the mid-20th Century, the digital humanities are characterized by the attention paid to intelligence and communication technologies. Rather than auxiliary methodologies, they would have revolutionized knowledge. If some justify this phenomenon with a naive and anti-theoretical technological determinism, a more sophisticated version defends the formation of an immanent ethos for the formation of networks of thinkers and collaborative work. However, the movement away from these two points prevents us from seeing that the communications system can also constitute an epistemological obstacle. A better understanding of the impact of digital technologies should take into account factors such as the diversity of the types of media used, their functioning as a system and the ambiguity of their effects.

It is not difficult to see that the culture of sharing is not the only value that emerges from digital technologies. We also have processes inherent in the structure of social communication, such as the struggle for visibility, the dispute over the setting of agendas and many other practices and values that were in place before the advent of digital technologies. As we have seen, these traces are part of the media news communication system and concern all media, not only digital media. It is therefore to this system that we must be accountable for the ethics of the digital humanities.

In addition, the digital humanities, although recent, respond to an old problem, that of the complexity of knowledge, by asking how to deal with an excessive and growing mass of information. While digital technologies have introduced new methods that can help reduce complexity, the praxis and understanding that prevails in the digital humanities are not in complete contrast to previous solutions. Just as the publishing industry and scientific journalism, they testify to the existence of a *pathos* favorable to what is new, an inclination for the present, which plays a function of filtering information through the rupture with the past. It is the same solution given by the newspaper to the complexity of social life: what matters is current information. The present time functions as a way to break down and reduce information.

In short, symbolic technologies play a dual role: they sometimes constitute the conditions for the possibility of knowledge, while they can also make the classical concept of knowledge impracticable. The very notion of theory is replaced by the analysis of immanence, by a way of reacting "in real time" to events, with conceptual resources specially shaped for the facts, in their absolute singularity of novelty. The new intellectual ethos would correspond to a *historical situation of theory*, which must be associated more with media events than with new epistemological paradigms of science or philosophy. As a sociocultural phenomenon, the digital humanities can be seen as an indicator of a system of values and meaning, an epistemology that crosses intellectual practices and shapes the frameworks of knowledge production in a contemporary way. This is a dated and emblematic form of knowledge for our time.

16.5. References

Berra, A. (2015). Pour une histoire des humanités numériques. *Critique*, 8–9(819–820), 613–626.

Boorstin, D. (1961). *The Image: Or What Happened to the American Dream*. Weidenfeld and Nicolson, London.

Davidson, C.N. (2008). Humanities 2.0. Promise, Perils, Predictions. *PMLA*, 123(3), 707–717.

Foucault, M. (1994). *Dits et écrits*, vol. 4. Gallimard, Paris.

Geertz, C. (1980). Blurred genres: The refiguration of social thought. *The American Scholar*, 49, 165–189.

Haacke, W. (1969). Escritos recientes sobre el concepto de actualidad. *Revista Española de la Opinión Publica*, 18, 169–193.

Havelock, E. (1963). *Preface to Plato*. Belknap Press of the Harvard University Press, Cambridge-London.

Innis, H.A. (2003). *The Bias of Communication*. University of Toronto Press, Toronto.

Le Deuff, O. (2018). Digital Humanities. ISTE Ltd., London, and Wiley, New York.

Martino, L.C. (2017). A Atualidade Mediática: O conceito e suas dimensões. In *Escritos sobre Epistemologia da Comunicação*, Martino, L.C. (ed.) Editora Sulina, Porto Alegre, 96–110.

McLuhan, M. (1962). *The Galaxy of Gutenberg: The Making of the Typographic Man*. University of Toronto Press, Toronto.

Merton, R.K. and Storer, N.W. (eds) (1979). *The Sociology of Science: Theoretical and Empirical Investigations*. University of Chicago Press, Chicago.

Montfort, N. (2016). Exploratory programming in digital humanities pedagogy and research. In *A New Companion to Digital Humanities*, Schreibman, S., Siemens, R., and Unsworth, J. (eds). Blackwell, Oxford, 98–109.

Nora, P. (1972). L'Événement Monstre. *Communications,* 18, 162–172.

Pinto, L. (1994). Le journalisme philosophique. *Actes de la Recherche,* 101–102, 25–38.

Reynoso, C. (2000). *Apogeo y Decadencia de los Estudios Culturales : una visión antropológica.* Gedisa Editorial, Barcelona.

Warwick, C. (2016). Building theories or theories of building? A tension at the heart of digital humanities. In *A New Companion to Digital Humanities*, Schreibman, S., Siemens, R., and Unsworth, J. (eds). Blackwell, Oxford, 538–552.

Conclusion

Widespread Digitalization of Society: A (in)Complete Process?

Culture, the economy, schools, health and many other social components are now systematically labeled with the digital adjective, thus representing many diversified results of the deployment throughout society of what has been rightly or wrongly called the "digital revolution", as if they were *a priori* sectors separated from each other and which, as time goes by, were affected by the progression within all spheres of activity of a phenomenon too often characterized primarily by its technological nature. In short, it is a phenomenon that would appear at first sight to be exogenous and which, moreover, would be deterministic, not primarily because of its technical dimension, but also because of its socially inexorable progress. What if it were otherwise? If, on the contrary, all these sectors had long been prepared to participate in the process of a generalized digitalization of society, which itself is the bearer of the generalization of the techno-capitalist logic that today would no longer tolerate sectoral, territorial, legal or cultural borders. And if they still existed, they would have become increasingly porous, to the point that no field of activity could escape this dynamic. Consequently, no sector would want to be excluded from it, as it would seem necessary to actively contribute to its ramification, in order to be able to benefit from the so-called advanced level of progress it would symbolize.

The famous digital revolution, if there is one, cannot be understood as a single phenomenon, isolated and hanging over society, since it is part of a more global socio-historical movement that is extended from capitalism and whose widespread digitalization would be a new stage, rather than the absolute end goal. In this respect, it is more a process that should be understood in its entirety, including in the long term, rather than an attempt to carry out a post-mortem on it as a completed, definitive reality, captured at a specific moment.

Conclusion written by Michel SÉNÉCAL.

And even if the generalized digitalization of society has a high volume of technological compounds, it cannot in itself be limited to them because the generalization of the phenomenon cannot be effective without its resonances, observed in a variety of sectors, whose combination reinforces it in its entirety. Often focused on its computer and communication origins, the analysis of the generalized digitalization process has tended to focus on the (infra)structural, i.e. economic and technological aspects. On the other hand, the phenomenon is just as decisive in terms of its ideological dimensions, since it simultaneously invigorates and connects other important spheres of society: culture, education, health, security, etc.

Armand Mattelart (2015) rightly demonstrated that the phenomenon of the globalization of culture and communication, the beginning of which is too often confined to the early 1980s, is, in fact, only the evolution of an ancient process, which has certainly, but not only, been based on advances in the means of communication in the capacities of the media to circulate information, goods, people and capital, so that no horizon was unattainable and the speed of banking transactions far surpassed that of land transport. Globalization would therefore be the product of a convergence of factors, each as decisive as the next, at the origin of the project to create a global market.

What is called digital is therefore the most recent of all the paradigm shifts (mechanical, chemical, electrical, electronic, computer-based) that have taken place over the 19th and 20th Centuries, without one or the other replacing the rest completely. On the contrary, their combination has given rise to unprecedented results, often the result of hybridization, which has led to ever-increasing progress in the development of socio-technical systems, while their growing role in society was to become increasingly visible and decisive. Today, the convergence of technologies, which was not a new concept when it appeared to be crucial in the mid-1990s, is no longer to be proven, since the current systems have definitively integrated this process.

While it is often said that the generalized digitalization of society began with the emergence of digital networks and technologies, the genealogy of this process confirms, on the contrary, that it is a long-term phenomenon, developed in accordance with the relationships and production conditions of the different historical periods through which it has evolved and which have given it its materiality. For this reason, it is important to consider the generalization of the digitalization process not as an end in itself, but as a phase of a longer-term process, whose socio-historical and geopolitical origins must be taken into account to better understand both current issues and future directions, regardless of the semantic packaging it may adopt in the future.

C.1. Learning from the past

In preparing my closing text for the conference on the generalized digitalization of society (*Numérisation généralisée de la société : acteurs, discours, pratiques et enjeux*), I had intended to identify the dimensions and structuring conditions of the generalized digitalization of society that would be applied under various approaches and perspectives during the event, in order to highlight that it is indeed a process that has deep historical roots that are only seeking to expand ever further. I then remembered a documentary film entitled *Origins of a Meal*, released 40 years ago, in 1978, and directed by Luc Moullet, a French critic and filmmaker who regularly contributed, from 1956, to the *Cahiers du cinéma* (Dilorio 2005), a French film magazine, and who was very closely associated with the New Wave filmmakers, including Godard, Truffaut, Rivette, Chabrol, Rohmer, Resnais and Varda.

Origins of a Meal is a low-budget film, made by craftsmen on a shoestring, which is visible when you watch it. This does not, in any way, diminish its purpose. According to several analysts, Moullet has considerably contributed to the renewal of French political cinema of that time and even political film in general. It is in a way counter-current, the filmmaker himself says that "[his] film is the opposite of activist cinema that only aims to realize an action without showing the complex aspects of reality" (Moullet 1980). In May 1968, he added that "political films flourished, but they often lacked precision: they spoke of oppression and conflict without returning to the source: work" (quoted in Blottière 2010). In fact, as Audrey Evrard (2015) points out in her excellent article on this film[1]:

> "[Where] political cinema focused mainly on local conditions and the emancipation of workers through strikes and better political organization, *Origins of a Meal* chooses to highlight the effects of global capitalism on the political unification of the working classes and the dehumanization of production and consumption."

In several respects, this film, *Origins of a Meal*, recalls the work of analysis, explanation and awareness that we have collectively begun in the two volumes of this book about the process of the generalized digitalization of society, especially in regard to the need to grasp both the complexity of the phenomena observed and the multiplicity of actors and social issues involved. Indeed, this film, which proposes a "holistic" approach, could certainly inspire us in the pursuit of our collective reflection.

---

1 This is a very relevant article for understanding the work of filmmaker Luc Moullet and, in particular, for examining his film *Origins of a Meal*. The analysis developed by the author helped me considerably in structuring this chapter based on the narrative framing of the film, which she explained so well.

Moullet begins his film with a sequence in which he directs himself, sharing with his wife a frugal meal consisting of an omelette, canned tuna and bananas for dessert. From there, the filmmaker embarked on an intercontinental investigation between France, Senegal and Ecuador, seeking to trace and analyze the relationships, conditions and means of production of these products from their origins to their consumption. It focuses on circuits that, in the end, have become invisible because of the distance and intermediaries between the workers who produce these products and consumers:

> "The film thus presents us with a multiplicity of points of view. For the most part, these men, women and children describe social, ethnic and economic divisions that are deeply rooted in the social and political fabric of their respective countries. These inequalities facilitate the exploitation of labor [*sic*] at each level of the food production chain – local, national and international" (Evrard 2015).

Consequently, "Senegalese, Ecuadorian and French representatives of all levels share their experiences and analyses of their trade. They describe power struggles that intensify racial, socio-economic [and socio-political] divisions" (*ibid.*).

Moullet's film, which is amusing at times, claims an analytical and dialectical approach that unfolds in three ways and as many narrative lines that help to expose here some of the ideas voiced during the conference on the generalized digitalization of society: 1) it dialectically reframes the process of globalization in the colonial structures of the past; 2) it challenges the viewer as a citizen, but first and foremost as a consumer; and 3) it operates a subjective repositioning of the filmmaker within political documentary cinema.

C.2. Dialectical reframing

The first task Moullet is therefore working on is to *dialectically reframe the process of globalization within the colonialist structures of the past*. It investigates the origin and itinerary of these three products (eggs, tuna, bananas) before consumption: from production to distribution, including the various processing industries. The food circuit reveals itself to be extraordinarily complex, which means that it is already necessary to demonstrate the diversity of the national and international actors involved, the alliances and confrontations between the interests of each and the power of some actors over others. In other words, we are talking here about "demystifying the dimension of global capitalism" (Evrard 2015). To this end, the filmmaker will restore the production and distribution circuits of these products to the dialectical continuity existing between the colonial structures of the past and the globalization of the neoliberal economic model already at work in the 1970s. Therefore:

"The three food chains (banana, tuna and eggs) are skillfully intertwined [so that] the film as a whole gradually builds a historical continuity [...] between the structures that supported the expansion of European colonialism, North American imperialism and more recently the globalization of neoliberal capitalism" (Evrard 2015).

Moullet will finally show that multinationals hunt in ever larger territories and ever more varied sectors to accumulate profits, territories that have already long been marked out by colonial and even imperialist powers. These paths are now taken by transnational companies, assuming the role of States and their strategy of territorial conquest; there is therefore no need, as in the past, to invade foreign territories militarily in order to gain control of them. Consequently, there is, in the film, "a certain continuity and striking parallels between the former colonial structures governing the exploitation of land and people and the global expansion of the market economy" (Evrard 2015).

The exercise of revisiting the genesis of the process of the generalized digitalization of society thus obliges me to revisit certain aspects of the development of local and international social realities that are intertwined, or even confused, in the same way as the sectors retraced and analyzed by Luc Moullet in his film. For the exercise, I will only mention four of them, although others can be added to give more depth to the analysis.

First, it seems to me crucial to (re)build the fabric of the socio-technical evolution of the means of communication – as means of circulation of goods, persons, ideas, information, capital – in which the digital paradigm is embedded, which is in addition to, and does not replace, as has been said, other past scientific and technological advances (mechanical, electrical, electronic, etc.) that have ensured that there is a continuity of hybridization, mimicry, reproduction, emergence, integration and realignment. Moreover, so-called "new" media technologies have often emerged in periods of social crises or war, having been conducive to their implementation by States, particularly imperialists, as was the case with many information, control and monitoring systems deployed over the past two centuries (Mattelart 1992). Clearly, technological results must be considered the historical materiality of social relationships and social conflicts, and the digital means of communication of the present are no exception.

Secondly, in a synchronous way, it would be relevant to follow the development trajectory of transnational companies, any combined sector of activity (from agri-food to communication) and their strategies in the deployment of a globalized economy that they want to be without borders in every sense of the word (territorial, regulatory or fiscal). These multinationals take up, in their own way, an adage I learned from Mexican friends that translates as: "It is easier to ask for forgiveness than to ask for permission". To be convinced, it is enough to trace the many excuses of the bosses of multinational Internet companies regarding, among other things, the misuse of users' personal data. This approach literally challenges States that, in the absence of a rapid response, are quickly overwhelmed by new challenges and power struggles, which explains why they end up in a weak position. The case of the implementation of digital platforms (Google, Netflix, etc.) in Canada and Quebec is a good example (Sénécal and George 2018).

States must therefore either rely on alliances and agreements with multinationals that are in the interests of existing governments, or defend the interests of their populations in general in the face of various threats to privacy, sovereignty and cultural diversity, as well as the maintenance of public services. This implies a significant transformation of the State from a major actor to an accompanier of large corporations, particularly through its political, legal and economic interventionism. Moreover, the bridges between States and companies have become multiple (staff exchanges, lobbying, bilateral confidential agreements, etc.), to the point of considering the independence and integrity of government authorities problematic.

Thirdly, a framework integrating the updating of older business economic models for value chain control would also be interesting to analyze from a socio-historical point of view. For example, film majors have long controlled the value chain, from production studios to theaters, until anti-trust laws were put in place by the State. Despite legal and political obstacles, however, these models were hybridized and adjusted throughout the 20th Century to the various sectors of culture, media and communication. As a result, there is still a tendency to have more control over all the stages of the trading process, to have all the machinery and to escape the regulations in force in national territories for as long as possible.

Furthermore, and as a result, the evolution and transformation of the relationships of confrontation and alliances between the major social actors, namely companies or corporations, the State (States) and social movements (civil society), as well as between their visions of society on different aspects of social organization including governance, democracy, citizenship, the common good, general interest, and the definition and satisfaction of basic needs (health, food, education, information, concept and model of access to culture) must not be omitted. In short, how, for example, does the hegemonic capitalist ambition of Web multinationals today constitute a social project in itself, against which, to take up Armand

Mattelart's proposal in the chapter earlier in this book, it is necessary to multiply the sources of resistance, or even to lay the foundations for a fully-fledged counter-hegemonic social project?

Lastly, exploring these various avenues would be a question of examining more closely how multinationals, regardless of their sector of activity, are transforming international labor organization and production chains, thereby taking up Moullet's ambition, which was "to compare working conditions, but also to illustrate the ways in which capitalism benefits from transnational trade and can thus capitalize on national disparities to redefine workers' rights to its own advantage" (Evrard 2015). Because there is also, in this film, a prototypical aspect in the way he deconstructs the workings of globalization, which, in this case, then targets the risks of the industrialization of food resources (Shafto 2010), but whose framework could just as easily be replicated in other sectors of the globalized capitalist economy, including those of culture, communication and the media, which are of particular concern to us.

C.3. Interpreting the spectator/consumer

Another narrative line taken by Moullet is of *wanting to appeal to the spectator as a citizen, as well as primarily as a consumer*. To do this, he directly inserts "spectators into the production chain and the centrality of their role as consumers in the monetary and critical evaluation process" (Evrard 2015). By interweaving economic, political and geographical considerations, the filmmaker wants to interest the viewer/consumer "in the profound injustices that guarantee the viability of the system" in which they operate, because, ultimately, "as consumers, viewers are inevitably part of the system criticized by the film" (*ibid.*), thereby breaking down the traditional border between the exploiter and the exploited. Consequently, the director insists that consumerism would be the ultimate goal of this operating system, because "the globalization of the operating system and Western consumerism [are] presented as inextricable developments" (*ibid.*).

From the perspective of the viewer/consumer, what would then be the lessons produced in this respect in the context of the two volumes of this book? For my part, I see a democratization of means of communication to varying extents: from market access to citizen appropriation, including the notion of public service.

Make money, make value: the stuff of dreams! Since the beginning of the implementation of the first mass media coverage devices, the main goal of media companies has been to increase their number, by attracting the attention of their audience for an ever longer period of time (audience ratings), by gaining an ever greater market share (thanks to advertising and the industry that has been built with it), while remaining as attractive as ever for the financial market (stock market rating). To achieve this, it was necessary to cover ever larger territories (broadcasting areas), bridge time gaps between time zones and, consequently, invent technologies that enabled widespread broadcasting over the air, or an increase in distribution channels (cable, satellite and the Internet). And to increase the number even more, it is always necessary to increase one's knowledge of the profiles of consumers, develop ways to keep their attention and loyalty, or continuously increase and individualize the offer. Finally, the experience must be sufficiently fun and pleasant to the point that users/consumers recommend it to others and that, consequently, this satisfaction is used, in turn, in a circular process, to orientate production and establish programming or catalogs. The historical links between mass media coverage, the advertising industry and suppliers of goods and services are continuing, expanding and diversifying with the strategies deployed by the industrial players in digital networks.

It is also essential to return to the genesis of the act of consuming information and communication goods and services, which *de facto* requires, for example, in the case of access to digital networks, the purchase or rental of devices and the required subscriptions. For this reason alone, we are far from the myths of free or non-market democratization, as there are barriers to entry, before even having access to a telephone conversation or a simple e-mail. These are barriers that consumers are willing to overcome by investing a significant portion of their personal budgets in expenses related to telecommunication services (cordless telephone, cable, Internet, etc.). Significantly, in Canada, "Internet spending increased by an average of 7.7% each year between 2011 and 2015 and is the fastest growing category of spending for households" (CRTC 2017, p. 42), averaging $218 per month in 2015 for each household to cover Internet, television, landline and wireless costs alone (CRTC 2017). This is not to mention the sums paid for the costs of various services offered by streaming Internet platforms (radio, music, audiovisual, etc.) and knowing that, ultimately, all these expenses combined in telecommunications and subscriptions weigh much more heavily on lower income households.

A second aspect of this problem is, in my opinion, the dialectical tension between the image of the consumer and that of the citizen. Recalling some of the contributions to the conference about the modalities of individual expressions, I asked myself an old question about participative ideology: how does a certain ideology of participation (injunction to collaborate, to share, to produce collectively) hide the place and the real role of consumers in the process of network expansion and, ultimately, in the operating system of various kinds mentioned above and of which the various articles in the two volumes of this book are a part of? To paraphrase Jean Baudrillard (1972), wouldn't power be in the hands of those who give the floor rather than those who take it? Hence, there is a historical need for anti-hegemony actors not simply to insert themselves into the traditional media (also known as "dominant"), but to autonomously and critically appropriate the means of communication and invent new forms of interaction. In this respect, wouldn't socio-digital media, under the guise of total democratization, be something other than a new generation of dominant media?

As a corollary, it is important to remember that the actors of alternative media practices have always been in a constant struggle to appropriate and control their own means of production (press, radio, television, video, cinema, etc.). Digital social networks are said to have the potential for this appropriation, but sooner or later, it comes up against limits, hence the importance of debates on Internet neutrality and governance. It should also be pointed out that, for the actors of the alternative media, very often, the production process (and all the stages of creating and negotiating, as well as the interactions between the individuals participating in the collective project) was as important, if not more so, than the resulting product. It should not be forgotten that these actors continue their activities by working with tools, also digital, in an autonomous way and without necessarily depending on networks. And that is why it is important to avoid any form of network-centrism, i.e. to claim that (socio)digital networks are essential and that, without them, it would be impossible to develop oppositional cultural and media spaces.

C.4. Subjective repositioning of the filmmaker/critic

In addition, in his film, Luc Moullet invites *a subjective repositioning of the filmmaker within the documentary policy*. In the form of critical reflexivity, Moullet questions himself as a Western filmmaker, referring to the very economy of the film, exposing his own contradictions, as well as the filmic devices he uses. For him, it is a question of insisting on "the need to recognize the personal and subjective investment of the filmmaker in each of his projects" (Evrard 2015), because, ultimately, the film dissects a system of exploitation and domination from which no one escapes, neither the director nor the spectators. In fact:

> "[Luc Moullet's] voiceover conclusions at the end of the film challenge his problematic position as a French filmmaker and the more general ethical dilemma he faces as his investigation reproduces the social and economic structures and inequalities he specifically seeks to expose" (*ibid.*).

Following the example of Moullet's questioning of his own cinematographic practice, would it not be appropriate to share this reflexive approach and question, at the end of these two volumes, the place of researchers in the reproduction of the system that is criticized here, the reasons for taking an interest in issues of generalized digitalization and, especially, the conditions for using the results of the research carried out, particularly outside university circles? It is interesting to note that, four decades ago, a film that retraced the circuitous routes of international food production can now serve as a reference point for configuring what can be a dialectical and totalizing critical analysis of phenomena that, in short, apply not only to agri-food activities but also, among other sectors subject to the same dynamic, to communication and the media.

I would like to conclude my remarks with this quote, found a few years ago in a San Francisco museum dedicated to the American-Chinese community – which says a lot about the longevity and persistence of the rhetoric of endless accumulation and exploitation linked to colonialist and imperialist forces – and which still seems to be the credo of globalized capitalist thought today. This is a fragment of a note from a British merchant in Shanghai addressed to Sir Rutherford Alcock, then consul in Fuchow, China, during the 1840s:

"We are money-making, practical men. Our business is to make money, as much and as fast as we can and for this end all modes and means are good which the law permits".

C.5. References

Baudrillard, J. (1972). *Pour une critique de l'économie politique du signe*. Gallimard, Paris.

Blottière, M. (2010). Luc Moullet : "J'aime la manière dont mon frère, assez primitif de nature, découpe son steak". *Télérama*, 11 January [Online]. Available at: https://www. telerama.fr/cinema/luc-moullet-j-aime-la-maniere-dont-mon-frere-assez-primitif-de-nature-decoupe-son-steak,51511.php.

Conseil de la radiodiffusion et des télécommunications canadiennes (2017). Rapport de surveillance des communications 2017. *Gouvernement du Canada*, Ottawa [Online]. Available at: https://crtc.gc.ca/fra/publications/reports/policymonitoring/2017/rsc2017.pdf.

Dilorio, S. (2005). The woodcutter's gaze: Luc Moullet and Cahiers du Cinéma. 1956–1969. *SubStance*, 34(3), 79–95 [Online]. Available at: https://www.jstor.org/stable/3685733.

Evrard, A. (2015). Genèse d'un repas, ou l'économie mondiale dans une boîte de thon. *Période*, 8 January [Online]. Available at: http://revueperiode.net/genese-dun-repas-ou-leconomie-mondiale-dans-une-boite-de-thon/.

Mattelart, A. (1992). *La Communication-monde. Histoire des idées et des stratégies*. La Découverte, Paris.

Mattelart, A. (2015). *Communication transnationale et industries de la culture. Une anthologie en trois volumes (1970–1986)*, 3. Presses des Mines, Paris.

Moullet, L. (1980). Entretien avec Luc Moullet : propos recueillis par Gérard Courant. *Cinéma 80,* 255 [Online]. Available at: http://www.gerardcourant.com/index.php?t=ecrits&e= 147#logo.

Sénécal, M. and George, É. (2018). Les méandres des discours politiques sur la création culturelle et médiatique au Canada et au Québec : avant et après Netflix. In *Création, créativité et médiations. Actes volume 2 : modèles et stratégies d'acteurs.* Société française des sciences de l'information et de la communication, Paris, 19–29.

Shafto, S. (2010). Luc Moullet's food lessons: Origins of a meal. *Gastronomica,* 10(3), 93–96.

List of Authors

France AUBIN
CRICIS
Université du Québec à
Trois-Rivières
Canada

Martin BONNARD
CRICIS
GRISQ
Université du Québec à Montréal
Canada

Dominique CARRÉ
LabSIC
Université Paris 13
Villetaneuse
France

Alexis CLOT
CESSP
Université Paris 1
France

Christelle COMBE
LPL
Aix-Marseille Université
France

Raymond CORRIVEAU
CRICIS
Université du Québec à
Trois-Rivières
Canada

Valérie CROISSANT
ÉLICO
Université Lyon 2
France

Éric GEORGE
CRICIS
Université du Québec à Montréal
Canada

Sklaerenn LE GALLO
CRICIS
Université du Québec à Montréal
Canada

Lisiane LOMAZZI
CRICIS
Université du Québec à Montréal
Canada

Ndiaga LOUM
CRICIS
PeRICOM
Université du Québec en Outaouais
Gatineau
Canada

Philippe-Antoine LUPIEN
CRICIS
Université du Québec à Montréal
Canada

Christophe MAGIS
CEMTI
Université Paris 8
Saint-Denis
France

Luiz C. MARTINO
CNPq
University of Brasilia
Brazil

Fábio Henrique PEREIRA
CNPq
University of Brasilia
Brazil

Pascal RICAUD
PRISM
Université de Tours
France

Louis-Philippe RONDEAU
NAD
Université du Québec à Chicoutimi
Saguenay
Canada

Michel SÉNÉCAL
CRICIS
Université TÉLUQ
Quebec
Canada

Annelise TOUBOUL
ÉLICO
Université Lyon 2
France

Ghada TOUIR
DCMÉT
Université du Québec en Outaouais
Gatineau
Canada

Index

S, T, V, Y

Other titles from

in

Information Systems, Web and Pervasive Computing

2019

ALBAN Daniel, EYNAUD Philippe, MALAURENT Julien, RICHET Jean-Loup, VITARI Claudio
Information Systems Management: Governance, Urbanization and Alignment

AUGEY Dominique, with the collaboration of ALCARAZ Marina
Digital Information Ecosystems: Smart Press

BATTON-HUBERT Mireille, DESJARDIN Eric, PINET François
Geographic Data Imperfection 1: From Theory to Applications

BRIQUET-DUHAZÉ Sophie, TURCOTTE Catherine
From Reading-Writing Research to Practice

BROCHARD Luigi, KAMATH Vinod, CORBALAN Julita, HOLLAND Scott, MITTELBACH Walter, OTT Michael
Energy-Efficient Computing and Data Centers

CHAMOUX Jean-Pierre
The Digital Era 2: Political Economy Revisited

COCHARD Gérard-Michel
Introduction to Stochastic Processes and Simulation

DOUAY Nicolas
Urban Planning in the Digital Age
(Intellectual Technologies Set – Volume 6)

FABRE Renaud, BENSOUSSAN Alain
The Digital Factory for Knowledge: Production and Validation of Scientific Results

GAUDIN Thierry, LACROIX Dominique, MAUREL Marie-Christine, POMEROL Jean-Charles
Life Sciences, Information Sciences

GAYARD Laurent
Darknet: Geopolitics and Uses
(Computing and Connected Society Set – Volume 2)

IAFRATE Fernando
Artificial Intelligence and Big Data: The Birth of a New Intelligence
(Advances in Information Systems Set – Volume 8)

LE DEUFF Olivier
Digital Humanities: History and Development
(Intellectual Technologies Set – Volume 4)

MANDRAN Nadine
Traceable Human Experiment Design Research: Theoretical Model and Practical Guide
(Advances in Information Systems Set – Volume 9)

PIVERT Olivier
NoSQL Data Models: Trends and Challenges

ROCHET Claude
Smart Cities: Reality or Fiction

SAUVAGNARGUES Sophie
Decision-making in Crisis Situations: Research and Innovation for Optimal Training

SEDKAOUI Soraya
Data Analytics and Big Data

SZONIECKY Samuel
Ecosystems Knowledge: Modeling and Analysis Method for Information and Communication
(Digital Tools and Uses Set – Volume 6)

2017

BOUHAÏ Nasreddine, SALEH Imad
Internet of Things: Evolutions and Innovations
(Digital Tools and Uses Set – Volume 4)

DUONG Véronique
Baidu SEO: Challenges and Intricacies of Marketing in China

LESAS Anne-Marie, MIRANDA Serge
The Art and Science of NFC Programming
(Intellectual Technologies Set – Volume 3)

LIEM André
Prospective Ergonomics
(Human-Machine Interaction Set – Volume 4)

MARSAULT Xavier
Eco-generative Design for Early Stages of Architecture
(Architecture and Computer Science Set – Volume 1)

REYES-GARCIA Everardo
The Image-Interface: Graphical Supports for Visual Information
(Digital Tools and Uses Set – Volume 3)

REYES-GARCIA Everardo, BOUHAÏ Nasreddine
Designing Interactive Hypermedia Systems
(Digital Tools and Uses Set – Volume 2)

SAÏD Karim, BAHRI KORBI Fadia
Asymmetric Alliances and Information Systems:Issues and Prospects
(Advances in Information Systems Set – Volume 7)

SZONIECKY Samuel, BOUHAÏ Nasreddine
Collective Intelligence and Digital Archives: Towards Knowledge Ecosystems
(Digital Tools and Uses Set – Volume 1)

2016

BEN CHOUIKHA Mona
Organizational Design for Knowledge Management

BERTOLO David
Interactions on Digital Tablets in the Context of 3D Geometry Learning
(Human-Machine Interaction Set – Volume 2)

BOUVARD Patricia, SUZANNE Hervé
Collective Intelligence Development in Business

EL FALLAH SEGHROUCHNI Amal, ISHIKAWA Fuyuki, HÉRAULT Laurent, TOKUDA Hideyuki
Enablers for Smart Cities

FABRE Renaud, in collaboration with MESSERSCHMIDT-MARIET Quentin, HOLVOET Margot
New Challenges for Knowledge

GAUDIELLO Ilaria, ZIBETTI Elisabetta
Learning Robotics, with Robotics, by Robotics
(Human-Machine Interaction Set – Volume 3)

HENROTIN Joseph
The Art of War in the Network Age
(Intellectual Technologies Set – Volume 1)

KITAJIMA Munéo
Memory and Action Selection in Human–Machine Interaction
(Human–Machine Interaction Set – Volume 1)

LAGRAÑA Fernando
E-mail and Behavioral Changes: Uses and Misuses of Electronic Communications

LEIGNEL Jean-Louis, UNGARO Thierry, STAAR Adrien
Digital Transformation
(Advances in Information Systems Set – Volume 6)

NOYER Jean-Max
Transformation of Collective Intelligences
(Intellectual Technologies Set – Volume 2)

VENTRE Daniel
Information Warfare – 2nd edition

VITALIS André
The Uncertain Digital Revolution
(Computing and Connected Society Set – Volume 1)

2015

ARDUIN Pierre-Emmanuel, GRUNDSTEIN Michel, ROSENTHAL-SABROUX Camille
Information and Knowledge System
(Advances in Information Systems Set – Volume 2)

BÉRANGER Jérôme
Medical Information Systems Ethics

BRONNER Gérald
Belief and Misbelief Asymmetry on the Internet

IAFRATE Fernando
From Big Data to Smart Data
(Advances in Information Systems Set – Volume 1)

KRICHEN Saoussen, BEN JOUIDA Sihem
Supply Chain Management and its Applications in Computer Science

NEGRE Elsa
Information and Recommender Systems
(Advances in Information Systems Set – Volume 4)

POMEROL Jean-Charles, EPELBOIN Yves, THOURY Claire
MOOCs

2012

BUCHER Bénédicte, LE BER Florence
Innovative Software Development in GIS

GAUSSIER Eric, YVON François
Textual Information Access

STOCKINGER Peter
Audiovisual Archives: Digital Text and Discourse Analysis

VENTRE Daniel
Cyber Conflict

2011

BANOS Arnaud, THÉVENIN Thomas
Geographical Information and Urban Transport Systems

DAUPHINÉ André
Fractal Geography

LEMBERGER Pirmin, MOREL Mederic
Managing Complexity of Information Systems

STOCKINGER Peter
Introduction to Audiovisual Archives

STOCKINGER Peter
Digital Audiovisual Archives

VENTRE Daniel
Cyberwar and Information Warfare

2010

BONNET Pierre
Enterprise Data Governance

BRUNET Roger
Sustainable Geography

CARREGA Pierre
Geographical Information and Climatology

CAUVIN Colette, ESCOBAR Francisco, SERRADJ Aziz
Thematic Cartography – 3-volume series
Thematic Cartography and Transformations – Volume 1
Cartography and the Impact of the Quantitative Revolution – Volume 2
New Approaches in Thematic Cartography – Volume 3

LANGLOIS Patrice
Simulation of Complex Systems in GIS

MATHIS Philippe
Graphs and Networks – 2nd edition

THÉRIAULT Marius, DES ROSIERS François
Modeling Urban Dynamics

2009

BONNET Pierre, DETAVERNIER Jean-Michel, VAUQUIER Dominique
Sustainable IT Architecture: the Progressive Way of Overhauling Information Systems with SOA

PAPY Fabrice
Information Science

RIVARD François, ABOU HARB Georges, MERET Philippe
The Transverse Information System

ROCHE Stéphane, CARON Claude
Organizational Facets of GIS

2008

BRUGNOT Gérard
Spatial Management of Risks

FINKE Gerd
Operations Research and Networks

Printed and bound by CPI Group (UK) Ltd, Croydon, CR0 4YY